JOE KERNAN

WITHOUT A SHADOW OF A DOUBT

Best wishes

Joe Kernan

JOE KERNAN

WITHOUT A SHADOW OF A DOUBT

Joe Kernan
with Martin Breheny

IRISH SPORTS PUBLISHING

Published by Irish Sports Publishing (ISP)
Unit 11, Tandy's Lane
Lucan, Co Dublin
Ireland
www.irishbooksandauthors.com

First published 2011

A CIP record for this book is available from the British Library

ISBN 978-0-9563598-1-0

Printed in Ireland with Print Procedure Ltd
Typesetting, Cover Design: Jessica Maile
Photographs: Front and back covers and inside, Inpho Sports Agency
and Joe Kernan's personal collection.
Additional images from Sportsfile, Sean Taafe Media, Kevin McArdle
Photography, Hugh Brady Studios, and Michael O'Neill.

To Patricia and the lads, Stephen, Aaron, Tony, Paul and Ross.
We've done it all as a team – thanks for everything.
I dedicate this book, too, to the many great players and
people in Crossmaglen and Armagh who did so much to enrich
my life in football and beyond.

Joe Kernan

contents

FOREWORDS

When Joe Kernan asked me to join the Armagh panel shortly after he took over as manager, I thought at first he was having me on. I had never been asked before and, to be honest, I hadn't thought much about it.

I was enjoying myself with Crossmaglen and I suppose I didn't see myself as a county player. Then, along comes Joe and says, "I want you to join the panel". I was surprised to get the call but when Joe Kernan asks you for something, you don't say no.

I wondered at first why he wanted me aboard and then I figured it out – it was my speed he was after! Sure what else could it be?

I'm very grateful to Joe for giving me a chance I never thought I'd get. I'd known him all my life, coming up through the ranks with Cross and then going on to win the All-Ireland club titles. They were special times and then I was lucky enough to be part of the Armagh team that won the All-Ireland in 2002.

Joe's greatest asset was the way he dealt with players and the way he explained exactly what he wanted of everyone. He is a great man for getting his plans across to you. He could get lads to do exactly as he wanted, but then we all had huge respect for him.

He knew what he wanted and he knew how to go about getting it. You wouldn't want to cross him but, as long as you were fair and honest with him, you'd get his total respect. In turn, the players respected him totally, which was why it all worked so well. He was big on loyalty to each other and the cause.

Joe was always a great man to enjoy a bit of craic but only when the work was done. Looking back at it now, it was a remarkable time for us all, something we will never forget. Big Joe was very much the man in the middle, the guy who pulled it all together.

I'm thankful to him for what he did for my career and I hope I repaid him in some small way. We had great times together with Cross and Armagh and have remained great friends to this day. Joe is a terrific football man but he's also a fine person, loyal to the last and always someone you love to meet up with.

He did an unbelievable amount of work for Crossmaglen and Armagh football, something that will always be appreciated around here.

Francie Bellew

My first encounter with Joe Kernan was back in 1992 at a hotel not far from Clones. I was part of the Armagh minor team that had just won the Ulster minor football Championship for the first time in twenty-four years and, at the post-match celebratory meal, our manager, Brother Laurence Ennis, asked Joe to address the team.

Joe had acquired legendary status in Armagh, following his playing exploits of the '70s and '80s, and you could hear a pin drop as that group of players listened. Firstly he offered words of congratulations but, more importantly, he went on to give advice on putting the Ulster victory behind us and turning our focus to winning the All-Ireland Championship.

To me, this sums up Joe's football philosophy – always aim to go as far as possible. Instead of being content with an Ulster title, Joe was always thinking about going the whole way and winning All-Irelands. This, of course, is reflected in his fantastic record with Crossmaglen and Armagh.

I was part of a good Clan na Gael side that unfortunately 'bumped into' a better Crossmaglen team who were at their peak, in the late-'90s. We had some great battles over the course of four or five years but the closest we came to beating them was a draw in 1998. You could see Joe's influence all over that team and, as much as we knew their style of play, we couldn't break it down.

Needless to say, due to the Clan-Cross rivalry, I was a bit unsure when Joe was appointed Armagh manager in the autumn of 2001. But, deep down, I knew that he was a winner and that he would do his utmost to bring us to the promised land. I needn't have worried because, in a short space of time, the sights were set on the third Sunday in September. A lifetime of dreams and ambitions were then realised on September 22, 2002 when we were crowned All-Ireland champions for the first time.

Personally, I will always be thankful and appreciative of the role that Joe Kernan played in that memorable year and subsequent years, when Armagh raised Gaelic Football to a new level that the rest of Ireland had to follow.

Diarmaid Marsden

OUR FATHER
BIG JOE

By Stephen, Aaron, Tony, Paul and Ross Kernan

One thing was certain from the start. Gaelic football was always going to play a huge part in the lives of the five lads born to Joe and Patricia Kernan.

None of us can ever remember a time when football wasn't right in the middle of everything that happened in the Kernan house. Gradually, one by one, as we came to an age when we discovered that kicking a ball was actually great fun, the game took an ever-tighter grip on us. Dad and Mum brought us everywhere. Whether it was as young spectators at games involving Crossmaglen or Armagh or later as enthusiastic kids beginning to make our own way as players, they were always with us. We really were lucky to have parents who were prepared to involve themselves so much in our sporting careers.

Dad has been through it all himself as a player so it was no great surprise that he encouraged us down a path on which he had gained so much enjoyment. He always did it in a very positive way. Negativity was clamped on – it had no part in the way he saw us developing as people or as footballers.

Despite wanting us to play football, he never forced it on us. It was as if he knew that by allowing us to develop in our own individual ways, we would come to love and appreciate the game. He rarely said much after games but he always wanted us to enjoy our football, play with pride and passion and make the special friendships which come from team sports, in particular.

Friendship and camaraderie are very important to Dad. We always knew that because we were surrounded by big GAA stars from as long as we can remember. The older two of us – Stephen and Aaron – have fond memories of Kerry greats, Ger Power and Mikey Sheehy regularly visiting our house on the Creamery Road. We also recall a young Steven O'Brien from Cork dropping into the pub to see Dad. There were days too when the whole Dublin team came in after League games and we loved to see those great men. They weren't coming to the pub just for food or drink after a game; they were as enthusiastic about seeing Dad as we were about seeing them. That was when we started to realise what it meant to have Joe Kernan as our Dad and how proud we were to say that he is our Dad.

We can still recall the gentle advice and the right word at the right time. He would always stress the importance of learning from experience, how to keep focused and how to work a way out when a game was going against you. It's something that has always stuck with us.

The thing was, of course, that our parents didn't just have five sons – it was more like 35 in any one year. The five of us were always there but there were 30 others too from the various Crossmaglen and Armagh panels over many years. As kids, you're always looking for attention and naturally we were all trying to catch our parents' eyes, trying to do something that would get their undivided attention. But with Dad in charge of various teams for so long, there were 30 others vying for attention too. From the early 1990s when Dad was helping out with Armagh until last year when he decided to leave Galway, our family outings revolved around his other 30 sons. We've never known it any other way and wouldn't have wanted it any other way.

Everything in our house changed one summer evening in 1995 when Crossmaglen – with Dad in charge – lost to Mullaghbawn in the Armagh championship. It's never nice for kids to see their father sad, upset and disappointed as Dad was after that particular game.

However, he made a promise to himself that he would achieve his personal goals and wishes for the team and, in so doing, create a legacy that would last a very long time and be of benefit to us too. At the time, it didn't seem all that clear to five young boys but in time it would reap its rewards.

A particular memory from 1996 stands out. One Sunday evening, all seven of us were returning from Mum's sister's house in Jonesborough. Cross were due to play Mullaghbawn in the county championship a few weeks later and Dad was talking about how ready our lads were and how he couldn't wait for the game when one of us (we won't name him!) piped up from the back seat: 'well don't come crying to us if you're beat.'

He slammed on the breaks and pulled in at the side of the road. Now, Dad is a very gentle and caring man but this was a step too far and everyone in the car knew it. He got quite emotional and said in a piercing voice: 'we won't be beaten; we're never going to be beaten again and if I hear you or anyone else in Crossmaglen talking about being beaten, then God help them. We'll show the country how good Crossmaglen are.'

His words hit home but not until two weeks later when Cross beat Mullaghbawn after performing in a manner that was very much in his image and likeness in terms of attitude and determination. We had seen it in the car two weeks earlier; now Cross had shown it against their great rivals. His approach to everything he did with Cross around then had a huge impact on our lives. His positive attitude was infectious. No matter the competition or the opposition, Dad's attitude was: bring it on. The bigger the better. Dad and Mum instilled a belief in us that we – and everyone else in Crossmaglen – were as good as anyone, anywhere.

He always had a great sense of ambition, too, looking from target to target all the time. When Cross won the 1996 Armagh county final, there was a huge party up in the hall. We were standing outside the dressing rooms where a massive bonfire had been lit and everyone was enjoying the night for what it was – a celebration of a county title after a ten-year gap.

Already though, Dad was looking ahead. Cross had never done all that well in the Ulster championship but Dad was convinced it would be different this time. A week before the first round against Burren of Down, Paul 'Hertz' Hearty broke his ankle on his way to work. He came up to training on crutches that night and while he was very disappointed, he had his first county medal.

Not many believed that Cross would do any better than they had before in Ulster but Dad said to Hertz that night: "We have five games to win the All-Ireland – don't worry, you will get back fit."

We thought he was nuts but he was proved right and Cross were All-

Ireland champions by the following March. Hertz was fit for the semi-finals in February but Jarlath McConville, who had done so well in his absence, held his place.

Dad's dream in 1996 had changed the way of thinking in Cross. He was never happy with what was done – there were always more peaks to be reached.

It was the same when he took over Armagh. He had an idea that to get Armagh to win an All-Ireland, he had to remove all hassle, stress and pressures from the camp so that the lads could get on with training and playing. When he said he was planning to take the squad to La Manga before the 2002 championship we thought he was mad. How could the County Board afford it? However, he had a plan and was going to make it happen. Warm weather training later turned out to be the norm for many county teams and it certainly helped Dad achieve his biggest dream of all in September 2002.

But then, he always finds a way of getting things done. And if he can't do it himself, he knows a man/woman/group who will see it through. When he gets something into his head, he won't stop until it comes to fruition. In 2002, he even managed to get a letter from Muhammad Ali, wishing the Armagh team the best of luck against Kerry in the All-Ireland, which must have been very inspiring for the players.

Like Sir Clive Woodward, who steered England to the rugby World Cup in 2003, Dad has a great talent for getting all the right people together and ensuring that they know exactly what their role is.

Whether that was with Crossmaglen, Armagh or Galway, all the backroom team were on the same message. He brought in kicking coaches for free-takers, rehab coaches for the injured, strength and conditioning coaches so that players were ready for whatever the opposition threw at them. He even had pre-hab coaches to reduce the risk of players getting injured in the first place.

His organisational skills may be very valuable in a team management situation but they can drive you mad in other ways! Sometimes there is no need for a plan, but he needs one anyway. An example of this was in two family weddings (Stephen and Aaron) over the past year. He wanted an itinerary printed for both days so that he knew what he had to do and when and where he had to do it. Sometimes, being Joe Kernan has its downsides.

Mind you, there are huge benefits to his ability to get things done. Some of us were very much the beneficiaries of that in 1992 when Armagh minors reached the All-Ireland final. Tickets were very scarce and, in fact, Dad managed to secure only one. So when he headed off to Dublin to watch the Kilmacud sevens on the Saturday, we were heart-broken as we reckoned we had absolutely no chance of getting to the final.

On Sunday morning, we had just returned from 9am Mass when the phone rang. Dad had got talking to a Croke Park steward who told him that if he could get us to the ground by 11am, he would squeeze us in. Mum didn't hesitate and within minutes we were on our way to Croke Park where we got to watch the match from the Hogan Stand, almost on the half-way line on the old concrete steps. Dad had come up trumps again.

Unfortunately, Armagh lost out to a last-minute goal. We thought we'd be heading straight home but Dad insisted on taking us to the team banquet in the Regency Hotel. He said that the team needed all the support they could get and he wanted to show how much he appreciated what they had done for Armagh, even in defeat. It was typical of how much he appreciated players and was something that would stand to him during his days as a manager.

As far as Dad is concerned, there's a right and wrong way of doing things and they must never be confused. He drummed that into us from the start, grooming us into the Cross way by allowing us to watch the lads training and also letting us see how he went about his job. From U-10 to this day, you get a hug when you're going out the door to play a championship game. He won't be at the door if it's a League game! That has been the Crossmaglen way for generations and was something he believed should be carried on.

For as long as we can remember, from Crossmaglen to Armagh to 26 Newry Street he saw his role as making life as comfortable and as rewarding as possible for his family and all who came in contact with him.

As for the five of us, we're very proud to call Joe Kernan, Dad.

CHAPTER 1
A STORY OF OUR TIMES

A wise man once said: "There's no towbar on a hearse". How right he was. I suppose we all tend to lose sight of that from time to time, but it's one of the truest sayings of all.

Nonetheless, you try to build your personal and business life with all your energies and hope everything stays solid. It wouldn't be natural if we didn't try to do the very best we can for ourselves and for our families. But there will always be ups and downs, so all we can hope for is to enjoy the good times, dig through middling times and hope the bad ones pass you by. They won't, of course, not for the whole of your life, anyway. I've had my share of hard times but, then, I've also had great times and hopefully there are more to come.

We all look back at particular years in our lives and analyse them. You could say they fall roughly into three categories: the great years, the tricky years, and the tough years you're glad are over. All you can hope for is that the first outweighs the others. For me, the year 2010 will always be, very definitely, lodged in the third category. Think of September, and you think of All-Ireland finals. All players and managers in the GAA dream of being in Croke Park in September and, while most are in charge of counties who have no real chance of joining the big-time, they all live the dream. It's what keeps everyone going.

When you're managing a county that has reasonable prospects of making serious progress in the Championship, you're in an exciting place. So, when I took over as Galway manager in September 2009, I felt that, with a bit of luck, we could be in Croke Park for the All-Ireland final a year later. Galway is that sort of county – as they showed in 1998 and 2001, when they get a run going, they grow with the challenge.

There's no point in taking on a job unless you aim to make it work, so my ambitions were at their very highest when I started working with Galway and looking ahead to the new season. Who knew what the future held for us? Maybe, September 2010 would be a memorable month for Galway and me.

It wasn't.

Some weeks earlier, I had quit Galway, having been left with no option but to resign after being told that I would have to make changes to my backroom team. I couldn't accept that interference, and left.

It was all very disappointing but it certainly wasn't the only setback I had to deal with at that time. Away from the stadia and the training grounds, I was staring at a deep and personal crisis. It had been looming for a long time but there's still something chilling about turning on the television to watch the news and seeing your face on the screen, accompanied by a report that you've been declared bankrupt. Obviously, I knew it would be announced but it was still a horrible feeling to have your business life flashed across the TV screen and on the front pages of newspapers under the headline 'BANKRUPT'.

In my case, it wasn't just me but also my wife, Patricia, and sons, Stephen and Aaron. It happened to us in early September 2010 at the end of a long battle where we tried our very best to work through the difficulties which had arisen with part of our property portfolio.

It's a lonely road but, thank God, we're a strong, close family and we'll get through it. Our tale is a familiar one in the new, chaotic Ireland, North and South. We joined the property party, buying extensively in the boom years but, like so many others, we were left holding one very large parcel of debt when the music stopped.

We did well in the good times but things changed very quickly once the property market crashed. We had a lot of property in London, in particular around Canary Wharf, which is a great location, but it was houses we bought in Northern Ireland that caused us the biggest headaches and eventually brought us to bankruptcy.

Amazingly – although in light of what has happened since, nothing should surprise anybody – the property market collapsed virtually overnight in Northern Ireland. There was a programme on TV on a Monday night where a collapse was forecast and, beginning on Tuesday morning, there was widespread panic. By the end of the week, prices were plummeting, the market was dead and we were heading for trouble.

The only thing that remained the same was the demands from the banks. Happy to lend as if there were no tomorrow during the boom years, they changed their tune in a very short space of time. Smiling faces became stern, encouraging words were replaced with lecturing tones and the image of Mr or Mrs Bank Manager as the customer's friend disappeared rapidly.

"Your debt, your problem" was very much the motto. God forbid that the possibility of bank error in speeding up the property carousel would ever be considered. I'm talking generally here, not just about our experience, but how can it all be so one-sided and how can it be right that people who took out loans to the gushing approval of banks carry all the responsibility when the mood changes?

The banks had valued all our properties prior to granting us loans but, suddenly, there was no bottom to the market so the initial valuations were way off in the new scenario. In particular, houses in Northern Ireland couldn't be sold, even at giveaway prices, so there was no question of getting rid of them and clearing the loans.

Our problems in Northern Ireland were with First Trust Bank. We tried our best to negotiate a way through the immediate problem but couldn't get anywhere. Eventually, First Trust lodged an application to have us declared bankrupt. We continued for as long as possible to try to find a workable solution which would be to the benefit of all parties, but it didn't work. We were disappointed with the bank's attitude but, obviously, it was something we couldn't change and, in the end, we filed for bankruptcy ourselves.

There isn't much to laugh at when you're hit with something as traumatic as bankruptcy, but it was comical how the banks seemed to think that I had salted away millions from my days managing Armagh. Maybe some of the guys in these banks can't differentiate between Sir Alex Ferguson and the manager of a Gaelic football team, but they definitely thought that managing Armagh had made me wealthy.

I'll say this – and the Armagh County Board will back me up – I brought more money into the county than I ever took out. Sure, I worked with sponsors and anybody else I thought could help the Armagh football project at the most exciting time in the county's history, but the money we raised wasn't going into my pocket. We had a great sponsor in Hugh Morgan of Morgan Fuels who would have done just about anything to help a cause we all held so dear.

As for the rubbish about what I was supposed to be earning in Galway, well, that's what it was – rubbish. I got expenses for travelling to Galway but it's a hell of a long way from Crossmaglen. I flew from Dublin to Galway on Aer Arann quite regularly, but there was never a week when I didn't drive to Galway. Indeed, there were weeks when I drove there and back three times. I recall one week where my diesel bill was €500. I'm not complaining – I took the Galway job because I was enthused by it – but claims that I made a fortune out of it are miles off the mark. Maybe it suited some people to say that, but it wasn't true. Nevertheless, it took me a good while to convince the banks that my football activities hadn't made me a cross between Bill Gates and Donald Trump.

I don't want to give the impression that I'm solely blaming the banks for our financial crash. We went in with our eyes open, the same as many, many others, North and South. People will say that those who went into property were greedy, but it's not that simple.

Going into property was a very natural fit for us, in that we were already in the estate agency, mortgage, letting, insurance and property businesses. I had started it all off as a small insurance business in the early-1990s. I had worked for a few insurance companies prior to that and then decided to set up on my own as a broker and things went very well. I built up a good business, developed it further over the years and, in due course, my sons Stephen and Aaron joined me. With the lads aboard, it was a chance to expand further, which we did.

I loved the idea of having a business that could provide jobs for my family, all the more since we were running it from an office attached to our house in our hometown of Crossmaglen. To me, it was all about providing security for my wife and five sons, so it seemed logical to expand the business into property at a time when it was very much the thing to do. It worked well for a few years but, unfortunately, we were in too deep when the crash came.

I'm prepared to take responsibility for what happened but, as so many others in our situation discovered, the banks don't want to know you when things start going wrong. There are tens of thousands of people all over the country who can't pay their mortgages and who can't sell their houses. For a start there's no market and, even if there were, prices have dropped so much that unfortunate people face a huge gap between what they would get in a sale and what they owe. How the hell are they supposed to bridge that?

I have no idea where all this is going to end but something has to give. It hardly makes sense for the banks to throw people out of their houses because, if they do, they will have over 100,000 properties all over Ireland and nobody to buy them. There are already tens of thousands of empty houses and that figure is increasing all the time.

What's disgusting about the crash is the way so many people, who should have seen it coming, have walked away with the huge bonuses, pay-offs and pensions while ordinary people suffer. There were very few voices warning of the trouble ahead and, those who were raising questions, found themselves drowned out by the sound of banks jangling out money in loans.

The people who were driving all this were either incompetent or they knew what was going to happen and chose to ignore the signs so that they could keep aboard the gravy train for as long as possible. So, which was it, incompetence or dishonesty? Either way, these people are a large part of the problem, yet they haven't suffered in the slightest for their part in taking the country into chaos.

The reaction to news of our bankruptcy was amazing. Apart from one newspaper and one TV station, who both went completely over the top in how they reported it, we got great support, especially from the GAA community.

I got messages of support from across all nine Ulster counties and I got plenty of support from the South too, which I really appreciated. People understood how things can go wrong and, anyway, there are very few houses in this country which aren't troubled by debt at some level.

Facing up to – and dealing with – bankruptcy is tough, but it's vital to remain positive. It's something that has to be taken on and that requires you getting the right advice from the start. There's nothing to be gained by trying to battle through it on your own when expert advice is available. So, the one thing I'd say to anyone who could be heading in that direction is this: get the right guidance and follow it.

In the current climate, the vast majority hit the bankruptcy wall through no fault of their own, so it's nothing to be ashamed of. Also, it's important to maintain self-esteem and see the future in the brightest possible light. Easier said than done I know, but you can't let it grind you down because, if you do, there's no way back.

People are resourceful and can always find a way back. That's what keeps you going. In fact, it's the only thing that can keep you going at a time when you can easily begin to wonder if the whole world is against you.

It's not. In fact, many people are going through roughly the same experience, in one form or another.

It's important that I stress that no individual or private company lost out as a result of our bankruptcy, which was important to us. The only ones involved were the banks.

As for the future, I'll take it as it comes. I now work in the drinks trade two days a week in Dublin for Donnelly Wholesale Ltd, Balbriggan and another two days here in our office in Crossmaglen. If possible, I keep Friday free for golf! Rory Donnelly, a loyal Armagh Gael, who runs Donnelly Wholesale, has been a good friend for a long time so I'm delighted to be working with him. I enjoy meeting people and, as I found all through my life, football is a great way to open doors.

The sad thing about the situation in which we found ourselves was that only a relatively small part of our business ran into trouble but, of course, when you're declared bankrupt everything gets dragged in. Our only serious problem related to the mortgages for the houses we bought in Northern Ireland. We were okay with our property portfolio in England while the estate agent, letting and financial services side of things, which Stephen, Aaron and I ran as a team, was going well. Indeed, in the middle of the recession in 2008, we also opened a residential lettings and management service which was ticking over nicely.

After we were declared bankrupt, two of our other sons, Tony and Paul, set up a new company, Joe Kernan and Sons Property Services. Stephen and Aaron are heavily involved in that and, as I said, I work in it around two days a week.

I have always been resourceful and never believed in throwing in the towel, so I'll forge on and so will all the family. Like many others, we thought we needed more but when you hit a problem like we did, you know you can do with a lot less.

It's in times like these that the GAA becomes all the more important in people's lives. The Association has always been a huge part of the Kernan way of life and will remain so. That year of 2010 might have been a bad one for us off the field but on it things were different. Football in Crossmaglen helped keep our spirits going, first when we regained the Armagh county title and then later when we won Ulster. It got better in early 2011 when Cross won the All-Ireland title for the fifth time, on St Patrick's Day.

Four of our lads, Paul, Aaron, Stephen and Tony were on the team so it was a special day for the Kernans.

It was also another brilliant occasion for Crossmaglen but, then, the importance of the GAA club in Irish life should never be underestimated, it's more crucial than ever. Going out to watch a game – and it doesn't matter what grade or what standard – takes people's minds off their problems for a while. That's badly needed in the Ireland of today. I'd like to see ticket prices lowered further for county and club games so that cost isn't an issue in preventing people from attending.

The GAA fraternity has always been good at pulling together in difficult times. We experienced it after the bankruptcy and we're very grateful for all the support we got as a family.

By the time the bankruptcy was formally announced, I had already left Galway. My departure from the Tribesmen is another reason I won't recall much of 2010 with any great fondness.

That's not to say I didn't enjoy my spell in Galway but I left with a sense of frustration that it was unfinished business. Do I regret taking the job? Absolutely not. Do I regret how it ended up? Of course.

To take things back to the beginning, it's worth pointing out that when I left Armagh after the 2007 Championship, I had no intention of taking any other managerial jobs. Armagh was my county and I wasn't keen on going elsewhere. Then, in 2009, the Galway Football Board Chairman, John Joe Holleran, phoned me and asked if I would be interested in discussing the job which had fallen vacant after Liam Sammon left. My first reaction was no way, but I agreed to meet him. A few other counties had sounded me out after I retired but I had no interest in them. However, Galway was different; my mother was from Ballinasloe so I felt an affinity with Galway that wasn't there with other counties. Also, I liked Galway football, so there was something about the challenge of taking them on that appealed to me.

John Joe sold it to me very well, explaining that since Aer Arann were their sponsors and they flew regularly between Dublin and Galway, I wouldn't have to drive from Crossmaglen all the time.

I talked it over with the family, and the lads were especially keen that I give it a go. They felt that, given my Galway connections, I would regret it if I turned down the chance. They also had great respect for Galway football and felt it was a challenge well worth taking on. Deep down, I was looking for obstacles but, all the time, there was a wee light in the background that kept drawing me back.

In the end, I agreed to take the job. I needed two local lads as selectors and was delighted to get Sean O Domhnaill and Tom Naughton. Sean had won two All-Ireland medals in 1998 and 2001 while Tom (a bit like myself!) was one of those who were unlucky not to have won an All-Ireland. I played against Tom in the '70s and '80s but didn't really know him until I joined Galway. He and Sean turned out to be excellent selectors and great to work with. We had some good times together and have become great friends as a result of it all.

Looking back at my Galway experience, a number of things strike me. For a start, we were desperately unlucky with injuries. There were times when we had ten or twelve players on the treatment table. There was never a day – from the first round of the FBD League against Sligo in January to the middle of July when we lost to Wexford in the All-Ireland qualifiers – when we could pick from a full hand. The injury to Michael Meehan, which he picked up in a League game against Kerry in March, was a severe setback and, by Championship time, we'd lost Nicky Joyce as well.

Michael, whom I had appointed captain, is a fantastic talent who would have brought so much to our attacking game in the remainder of the League and, more importantly, in the Championship. Dedicated sort that he is, he worked as hard as was humanly possible to be ready for the Championship. We brought him on for the second half of the drawn game with Sligo and started him in the replay, but he had to go off. It was deeply frustrating, at an individual level, for such a great player and person, while the impact on the team was huge.

The loss of Nicky Joyce was a blow, too. A great talent, he is someone I have a lot of time for. The famous white boots disappeared when I was there but, whatever colour he wore, he has some skill on the ball. Nicky would have made a big difference if we'd had him for the 2010 Championship. It's safe to assume that with Padraic Joyce – one of the best forwards ever to play the game – pulling the strings, Michael Meehan poaching around goal in his own inimitable way and Nicky taking on defences, our strike rate would have been considerably higher than it was. Bearing in mind that we lost to Sligo and Wexford by a point each, you can see why we were left cursing our luck.

Of course, even without Michael and Nicky we should have done better. Our form during the League was, to say the least, mixed. Brutal against Mayo in the first game, we then beat Monaghan, lost narrowly to Cork, were well beaten by Kerry, before defeating Tyrone and Dublin and losing out to Derry.

The problem was a lack of consistency. When we played well, it was very good but the bad periods could be terrible. I got a shock in the opening game against Mayo in Castlebar. I had heard so much about the famous Galway-Mayo rivalry that I was looking forward to a real battle, but it didn't happen. Mayo won easily and I was really disappointed by the lack of mental toughness Galway showed that day.

It's all very well being a skilful side but you need more than that. Afterwards, I was accused of trying to turn Galway into Armagh replicas which, of course, wasn't true. However, I did want to make them harder in certain respects. I remember a Galway man tapping me on the shoulder after the 2004 National League final in Croke Park, where Kerry had just beaten Galway by a point (3-11 to 1-16), saying, "Joe, that's how football should be played".

It was, undoubtedly, an enjoyable game to watch. However, there was very little close marking and no real intensity. Sure, there were plenty of great skills on display but they don't always win games and certainly not in the Championship.

My Galway friend seemed happy to have contributed to a game like that, even if they lost. On top of that, I presumed the Galway supporter was implying something about how Armagh played so I couldn't resist reminding him what had just happened. I turned around and countered, "Yeah, but ye lost".

The difference between Kerry and Galway that day was that Kerry could power-up the intensity and play whatever type of game was required, whereas Galway couldn't. Galway's All-Ireland winning teams of 1998 and 2001 could, but they subsequently lost that edge.

The opening League game against Mayo disappointed me terribly in that regard but things did improve. Wins over Tyrone and Dublin (we beat Dublin after making a terrible start) were encouraging but, then, something happened which caused me more concern.

In the week before the last League game against Derry, Tom Naughton remarked that he was worried about it because there was nothing at stake for Galway. We couldn't reach the final while we were free of relegation and Tom had fears that players might see it as a chance to merely go through the motions.

I couldn't understand that. It was the last game before the Championship and places were still up for grabs. Besides, we wanted to improve the consistency rate before the summer.

Tom was right. We gave a poor performance, going down tamely to Derry, who had lost their previous five games. Not only did I want Galway to sign off the League on a high, but also to put down a marker for Derry because we might be meeting them again later on. The reaction was poor and not a good sign but I felt that, once the Championship mood settled in, we'd be ready for a good run.

As it happened, we nearly fell in the first round against New York in Gaelic Park. Indeed, if it weren't for the guiding hand of Padraic Joyce, Galway might well have suffered their most embarrassing defeat in their Championship history which would have left a squad of maroon-and-white-clad players, plus one manager from Armagh, with no option but to seek political asylum in the United States: Returning home would not have been an option if New York had beaten us. We were only two points ahead with a few minutes left but, fortunately, we managed to add two more, before Cormac Bane scored a goal off a brilliant 40-metre pass from Matthew Clancy – another hugely talented player who suffered a lot of injury problems over the years which was a pity for both Matthew and Galway.

There were other little things about that trip that bothered me. A fund-raising dinner had been organised for the Friday night (the game was on Sunday) so players spent four hours on a boat going up the river. It's not what I would have wanted but it was committed to in advance, so we had to go through with it. One other aspect of the night I didn't particularly like was all the talk in the speeches about tickets for the All-Ireland final. It wasn't appropriate, especially as we still hadn't played our first game. The players behaved themselves impeccably on the night but, overall, that's not how you prepare for a Championship game, even against New York.

We had eight weeks to prepare for Sligo (how daft is it that a team can go two months between Championship games?) but we knew there was an awful lot to be done after the New York scare. Our biggest problem in Gaelic Park had been a failure to consistently get the simple things right. Joyce dug us out of a hole but we shouldn't have been in there in the first place.

Eight weeks later, we were right back in an even bigger hole at half time against Sligo, when we trailed by nine points – and in Pearse Stadium, too. We repeated the mistake of being sloppy on the basics and got punished. Still, I felt that, with the wind behind us in the second half, we had every chance of turning things around if we got some rhythm in our game.

In the end, we got out of it with a draw, after scoring 1-1 in stoppage time. I genuinely believed that the great finish would be a turning point. We had scraped out a draw so it was set up for a much better performance six days later in Markievicz Park.

We got it, too, but only in parts. We were two points up with a few minutes left but conceded three points, each of which could have been avoided. I was very disappointed with the way lads shaped up in those last few minutes. Some were inclined to leave it to others to put in the tackles and once responsibility is passed around, you're in trouble. It was much the same against Wexford a week later. Two points up late in the game and, again, we again conceded three.

Losing two games by a point in the space of a week was bitterly disappointing but these things happen and I certainly had no intention of walking away. In effect, I had six months in Galway, hardly long enough for them or me to make a definitive judgement. I would have loved to have had an injury-free year with Galway and brought in a lot of those classy U-21s who won this year's All-Ireland title.

A few weeks after the Wexford game, I met John Joe Holleran (Football Board Chairman), Seamus O'Grady (Secretary) and Milo Costello (Treasurer) for a review of where we all stood and I came away believing that everything was in place to continue for another year. I mentioned some changes that I wanted to implement for 2011 and I thought I had agreement on them.

But then I got a call from John Joe and he told me that, while they wanted me to continue, I would have to change my backroom team. I took that to mean I would have to get rid of John McCloskey as trainer and Paul Hatton as strength and conditioning coach, something I was not prepared to do. I have worked with John for years and everyone knows the regard I have for him. He had the backing of the players, too, so there was no way I was going to sacrifice a man I regarded so highly just because others had different ideas. Paul was a vital part of the set-up so, if I was to continue as manager, it would have to be my way or no way, and my way definitely included John and Paul.

Once I was prevented from appointing the people I felt would do the best job, then I had no option but to resign. I was, after all, bringing these people in for the good of Galway football.

In hindsight, perhaps some of the changes I suggested at the meeting didn't go down all that well. Maybe those suggestions caused a change of heart between the meeting and the phone call to tell me that I would have to alter my backroom team.

I was disappointed my tenure ended the way it did, but I wouldn't have a bad word said against any of the players or indeed most of the people I dealt with. I was just sorry that I couldn't take them where they were trying to go. I'm also sorry that we didn't get a chance to continue working together.

I still don't regret taking the job. If you don't try things, life would be awfully boring. I gave it a shot with Galway and it didn't work out. I'd have to say that management continues to change at an amazing rate. Even in the relatively short time I was out of the loop, between leaving Armagh and joining Galway, scrutiny levels rose considerably. So, too, did the merry-go-round where managers flit from county to county.

I took on the Galway job because I had a family connection, which is a bit different to going to a county where you have no link. Anyway, my spell with Galway lasted one season, at the end of which I had some good memories, a whole lot of disappointment and a yearning desire to continue.

Unfortunately, it wasn't to be. I still have a lot of friends in Galway and would always wish them the very best. They have some fine young talent coming through from the good minor and U-21 teams produced in recent years, so the future could be a whole lot brighter than some seem to think.

However, one thing that worries me is that, despite the unsettling effect on Galway of changing manager after just one season, they did the same thing again this year and removed Tomas O Flaharta after one season.

Why Galway keep doing this is beyond me. Players need stability and changing manager every year makes no sense, whatsoever. It's no longer my direct concern but I feel sorry for the Galway players, whom I still believe are an excellent group with the potential to be very competitive at the highest level. They aren't being given the best chance to do themselves justice. For their sake, I hope the decision-makers recognise that what happened over the last two seasons was bad for Galway football.

As for me, well, things didn't work out. But I shook hands on the way in and again on the way out which is as it should be.

Just as I closed the Galway chapter, the announcement of bankruptcy awaited me. It is no surprise, then, that 2010 won't go down as my favourite year. Instead, it was a case of good riddance and no thanks for many of the memories.

Not all of them, mind you. Our eldest son, Stephen, married his long-time girlfriend, Claire Byrne, on New Year's Eve. The reception was held in the Carrickdale Hotel, Dundalk which is owned by our good friends and loyal Armagh supporters, John and Paddy McParland. It was a splendid occasion for the two families and all our friends, a nice end to a difficult year.

Back on the pitch, Crossmaglen were back in the All-Ireland semi-final and would, of course, go on to win the title. If ever we needed a lift it was in early 2011 and, once again, the club provided it, just as it has done so often over the years.

CHAPTER 2
VIEW FROM THE BRIDGE

One wrong word here, Joe, and this could be the end. This is no game. These boys are serious. They don't give a damn about me, my family, Crossmaglen, Northern Ireland or indeed the whole of Ireland.

As far as they're concerned, this is a war zone, a strange land they know damn all about and care less. And if there's an occasional innocent casualty, well it goes with the territory.

Those were the thoughts swirling around in my head as I sat on Creggan Bridge with my legs swinging towards the water, staring at the stones and rocks far below. One little push and I'm hurtling head first to my death. It will be all over in seconds, the soldiers will speed away and I'll be found dead, probably the following morning.

Because I'm an Armagh footballer, my death will make the newspapers where it will be explained, as sensitively as possible that I was found in the river under Creggan Bridge while my car was parked up on the grass margin nearby. People will draw their own conclusions, inevitably reaching the verdict that I had committed suicide.

What else would they think? I have to say that those moments sitting on Creggan Bridge were probably the scariest of my entire life. I had no control and no way of getting out of the situation. It happened in the early 1970s as I was returning home after seeing Patricia, who was then my girlfriend.

Darkness was falling on a late summer evening and, as I approached Creggan Bridge, I saw a British Army checkpoint. Nothing unusual about that. *Here we go again. I wonder how long they'll delay me this time?*

I stopped the car and a solider approached but instead of the usual 'boot and bonnet' he ordered me to park over on the grass verge. When you're on your own on a dark road at night you do what you're told. When I got out of the car, I was surprised to be told to sit up on the bridge.

The familiar routine was to be left standing by the side of the road while the army went through the motions of searching the car. I carried nothing in my boot – other than football gear when I was training or playing a game – so that it would speed up the search but it never seemed to make any difference.

The search was as much about delaying and discommoding people as it was about security. Under the watchful gaze of the soldiers, I jumped up on the bridge, feet facing towards the road but was ordered to turn the other way.

"What's all this about?"

"Shut your mouth and do as you're told."

What really scared me was that the soldiers had told me to park the car up on the grass verge. It was as if they were leaving their options open if anything happened to me when I was up on the bridge. What happened next was probably down to how I handled the situation. If I'd said the wrong thing the tiniest push would have sent me flying off the bridge.

I don't even know if they were checking my car because I dared not turn around. I was up on the bridge for no more than four or five minutes. But it felt like five hours! I had this awful feeling that this checkpoint was different to the others. They could all be pretty menacing at times but this one was especially hostile.

"Shut your mouth and do as you're told," I was ordered. The words weren't so much spoken as spat out.

After a few minutes on the bridge, I could hear a car approaching and hoped to God it was someone I knew. It was. Local man, Barney Evans arrived on the scene and was stopped by the Army. Barney, a great man to sell cars, was one welcome sight that night! I bought him a few pints afterwards just to show how thankful I was for his good timing. When Barney arrived I was allowed to get down from the bridge. I was told get into the car, drive away and never mention what happened.

It was a shocking experience because I'm still convinced that the Army was only looking for an excuse to tip me into the river. Neither they, nor the RUC, would have anything against me personally because I kept very much to myself and based my life around work and playing football, but this was 'bandit country' and as far as most of the security forces were concerned, none of us were up to any good.

That's what happens when a place gets a reputation. South Armagh was branded 'bandit country' so, by extension, we all had to be bandits. It wasn't like that at all but perceptions can be very difficult to shake off.

Being a Gaelic footballer or hurler wasn't easy in the '70s and '80s in any part of the Six Counties. We were automatically associated with trouble by the security forces who had their own ways of making life as difficult as possible.

The most common form of harassment was the 'boot and bonnet' routine on our way to or from training or matches. You would be asked where you were going and once you mentioned Gaelic football – it was the same for hurlers – you were told to pull the bonnet, open the boot and stand on the side of the road.

It should have taken a minute or two to check the car but that wasn't the point of the exercise. No, the intention was to inconvenience and harass people. You'd be left on the side of the road for anything from ten minutes up to an hour and a half while mock searches went on, accompanied by so-called checks on radio equipment.

They wouldn't let you remain in the car while the whole charade was going on so, on wet days or nights, you were left standing in the pouring rain for as long as the bogus search went on. It would be very easy to lose the head and tell them a few home truths but it certainly wasn't in your best interests to become confrontational. That way, a half-hour wait could be multiplied by whatever length they saw fit.

I had one small experience of speaking out of turn in the early days of The Troubles. I was living with my mother in Newry Street at the time and arrived home late one wet, stormy night. I let a few shouts at the soldiers who were on patrol, reminding them that it was good enough for them to find themselves out on the streets on such a horrible night. They didn't say anything at the time but when I went out the following morning all four tyres on my car were flat.

I knew damn well that nobody from Crossmaglen was responsible, which was confirmed to me when I got a foot pump and starting working on the tyres. The soldiers across the road were laughing their heads off and pointing at me as if to make absolutely sure I knew I was being made to pay for a few stray words.

That's why it was important to keep your mouth shut when you were stopped at checkpoints. Even then, you could be held up for ages which, of course, was very frustrating when you were on your way to training or to a game.

Gerry Fagan was Armagh secretary for many years and the poor man must have been driven mad trying to sort out fixtures and re-fixtures after club games were called off because one or other – and sometimes even both – of the teams didn't make it on time.

Being stopped on our way to county training became such a regular occurrence that players got into the habit of leaving early to give ourselves extra time for what were relatively short journeys. I remember Joey Cunningham and myself being stopped on our way to training one night and, after being out on the road for quite some time, we decided to plead our case to the soldiers.

"C'mon lads, how long more? We're late for training as it is."

"Give us a break … ye know well there's nothing in the car."

The soldiers just laughed in our faces and ordered us to stay where we were. Our pleas only made things worse because they left us there for another half hour. We missed training altogether.

Players from Tyrone, Derry, Down, Antrim and Fermanagh were having exactly the same experiences. Of course, there were always boyos who would use the checkpoints as an excuse for being late for training or not turning up at all. After all, it was the perfect explanation – "Sorry about that, I was held up for an hour and a half so there was no point going on after that."

What was a manager to do? Ring up the local barracks and ask was there a checkpoint on a certain road at a certain time? Trust me, that's not how business was done in the Northern Ireland of that time.

The checkpoints were extremely annoying, especially since we knew they were being used so blatantly as a means of discommoding us but, apart from the Creggan Bridge incident, they were usually straightforward. However, there were other darker threats of which we had to be aware.

The threat from loyalist paramilitary organisations was constantly there and while, thankfully, there were very few incidents, we were always conscious of the dangers. One particular incident scared the hell out of me. I was driving out of Lurgan after training one night when a car came right up behind me. It was driving so close that I sensed something wasn't right. Instinct kicks in at a time like that and I had a feeling that whoever was in the car was up to something that didn't just involve escorting me home.

I knew it wasn't a police car so I decided that under no circumstances would I allow it to overtake me. My fear was that if I let it get ahead of me, it could block the road and I could be forced out of the car. After that, who knew what might happen?

It followed me for several miles, trying to get past at every opportunity but I held my ground. I was terrified, to be honest, but felt that my best chance was to stay ahead which I managed to do until we came closer to Crossmaglen, at which stage my pursuers veered off on another road at high speed.

I told the County Board what happened and it was decided to split up training for a while. The boys from the south of the county trained in Carrickcruppin while the rest went to Lurgan or Armagh. The County Board felt that the risks were high enough to do that and, after my experience driving out of Lurgan, I certainly wasn't going to disagree.

Of course, there was always a threat at training, especially in winter when we worked under lights. It would have been very easy for a sniper to pick off a few targets from a safe distance and then disappear into the night.

It was a tough time being a GAA man in the Six Counties, which made Armagh's advance to the All-Ireland final in 1977 such a newsworthy event. We saw ourselves as being the same as every other county and never, ever sought to play the victim card. For all that, a lot of people in the South didn't understand us.

Very few county teams from the South overnighted north of the border when they came up for National League matches. They would stay in Monaghan or Dundalk and then drive north on Sunday morning, play the game and head back across the border for their post-match meal. It was understandable, I suppose, but it did tend to create a 'them and us' situation.

Some of the brave boys who only crossed the border for a few hours would be a lot bolder when we played them down South. It was quite common to be told to "f*** off back to the black North" by opponents who didn't quite grasp the sheer stupidity of it all.

It was probably worse for Armagh than the rest because of the colour of our jerseys. It was as if, because we wore orange, we were Orangemen. Crazy, but true.

Attitudes changed over the years but the North-South divide never quite disappeared. Well, not for everybody anyway. Indeed, one of the few times as Armagh manager I lost my temper on the sideline was in a National League game against Laois in Portlaoise. A bit of a scuffle broke out near the sideline in front of the stand with players and officials becoming involved. It wasn't anything too serious and ended fairly quickly but not before one Laois man, who was part of the official party, had a right go at us.

He squared up to our selector, John Rafferty and called us orange bastards. How original! Now, on a league table of stupidity that would take some beating and, while I should have laughed at the pathetic eejit, I was infuriated. The sheer ignorance of the man. I felt like laying him out with a punch but somehow managed to restrain myself. In fairness to Liam Kearns, who was managing Laois at the time, he came to me afterwards and apologised. He didn't have to because he hadn't done or said anything wrong and could hardly be blamed for someone else's stupidity. It was an isolated incident but it showed that even in a new century there are still people who have no real grasp of the relationship between North and South.

It was an issue during most of the debate over Rule 21 (which prevented RUC and British security forces members from joining the GAA). I was never a supporter of the rule but I could well understand why many people were. It was easy enough for people in the South to support its removal but then they didn't have to live in the North where things were a lot different.

I remember having a long discussion on it with Kerry legend, Eoin

'Bomber' Liston and Niall Quinn, the former Irish striker, at a race meeting in the Curragh one year, and they were making the point that, in day-to-day terms, the rule served no real purpose but had the negative effect of giving people a stick with which to beat the GAA.

They were right in some respects but, as I pointed out to them (quite forcibly if I recall!), neither of them had ever been stopped on their way to training and made to stand on the side of the road for however long some young British soldier saw fit. Neither had they been instructed to sit on a bridge with their legs dangling over a river. In fairness, they accepted the point.

Armagh reaching the 1977 All-Ireland final did a lot to awaken people to how difficult GAA men and women in the North were finding things. We were the first Ulster county to reach the finals since the start of The Troubles so, suddenly, there was an outbreak of interest in us. For several years prior to that it was a question of watching the Ulster Championships from afar and then beating the champions in the All-Ireland semi-final. Suddenly, all that had changed and the South had to sit up and take notice.

The Southern media came to Armagh for the pre-All-Ireland build and readily admitted that they didn't even know the geography of the county. I still have a cutting from the *Irish Independent*, where the late Donal Carroll, their GAA correspondent at the time, wrote of trying to find his way to Crossmaglen to interview me.

Under a heading 'Lost on That Road to Big Joe's Place' Donal wrote that Crossmaglen was a very difficult place to find and described how he and a photographer took ages to figure out how to get there. After finding it difficult to get directions, they pulled in to the side of the road and opened up a map which drew the attentions of the British Army who gave them the 'boot and bonnet' treatment.

Donal wrote of the soldiers' politeness and their use of the word 'please'. He must have got them on a very good day, one where 'please' hadn't been locked up back in the barracks. It certainly wasn't a word I heard from them very often.

Donal, who was a lovely man and a great GAA writer, eventually found his way to our house in Crossmaglen where we had a long chat. Other GAA writers were telling similar stories about negotiating their way around Armagh. We found it all quite amusing, if a little sad. What I found most interesting was that although Crossmaglen is only sixty miles from Croke Park, it might have been in the back end of Mongolia as far as a great many people from the South were concerned.

Mind you, when Donal Carroll did get to Crossmaglen it clearly made an impression on him as he described it as "a place of considerable charm, warmth and almost embarrassing hospitality". I couldn't have put it better myself. The image of Crossmaglen as the capital of 'bandit country' in south Armagh was easily conjured up and, of course, once it acquired that reputation it was always going to be difficult to shed. Those of us who lived in Crossmaglen and surrounding areas saw it completely differently. It was home to us, a lovely part of the country where the vast majority of people just wanted to get on with their lives as best they could.

For me, and many others, life away from work (if we had any) was all about sport. It was how we expressed ourselves, how we coped with the difficulties of the world around us and how we remained a community through all the bad times.

I can't say how things would have turned out for me without Gaelic football, the Crossmaglen Rangers club and Armagh. I was never approached to join any political or paramilitary organisation, nor had I any interest in doing so, but then football occupied all my spare time. Would it have been different without the football? I simply don't know.

I knew a few people who were involved in the political struggle, but then you couldn't miss it if you lived in Crossmaglen. The effects of The Troubles were in your face all the time. We were all seen as trouble-makers just because of where we came from. In the end, we became immune to it. There were so many things that would annoy you about the way we were treated but you just couldn't let it get you down.

Probably nothing epitomised the spirit of Crossmaglen more than the long, long battle to get our beloved St Oliver Plunkett Park back from the British Army. They had requisitioned part of it as a military base in the early-

'70s, sparking off one of the longest-running rows in Irish sport.

It was a deliberately provocative thing to do as they would have known just how much the GAA pitch meant to the people of Crossmaglen. That may well be why they did it. If they had succeeded in breaking up the GAA club it would have wrecked the community, but then they would have been quite happy with that.

Of course, the British Army underestimated the spirit of the club and the people of Crossmaglen. The more the Saracens tried to disrupt club business, the greater our resolve became. There was an absolute determination not to let them get the better of us in any way.

They tried every dirty trick in the book to make life impossible for the club. Low-flying helicopters deliberately swooping over the pitch during games were quite common; if a ball were accidentally kicked into the barracks, it would either come back punctured or not at all and, as for the entrance to the ground, it was in a shocking condition.

The Saracens, tanks and trucks wrecked the surface so badly that you couldn't even walk on it without being a foot deep in mud and water. It was so bad that there were many times when we needed tractors and trailers to bring us to the pitch. Players and spectators were regularly harassed, and no allowances were made for kids. They, too, were treated badly as if it was part of a concerted effort to destroy the entire community.

There was no reason whatsoever why the Army had to use the club entrance to get to the barracks but they did it anyway. Of course, the more we complained the worse it became. For years, the army went out of their way to disrupt our club and our games but, as a community, we never let it beat us. In fact, it was used as a rallying point in a war we dared not lose.

Men like Gene Larkin and Gene Duffy were always to the forefront in the battle to end the occupation of our grounds, making sure that it was brought to the attention of everybody who mattered both in Dublin and London. Motions calling for the withdrawal of the Army from the pitch appeared on the GAA Congress agenda year after year but there was an awful lot more to the campaign than that.

The late Con Murphy, who was GAA President between 1976 and '79, took a special interest in the Crossmaglen case and did unbelievable work behind the scenes, lobbying the Irish Government who, in turn, took the case to their British counterparts. Con's interest in our problem continued long after his Presidency was over and, I have to say, he is still very warmly remembered in Crossmaglen for the work he put into trying to get the army out. He made sure that our problem was kept very much to the forefront in the South, both at GAA and Government level. A great man.

We eventually got our property back in the late-1990s in what was an emotional occasion. It had been a long and, at times, frustrating battle but it did have a plus side in that it cemented the club together in a way that probably nothing else would have.

It made us mentally harder as a town, a parish and a community and I have no doubt that it provided much of the inner strength which stood to us when we re-emerged as a major football force in the second half of the nineties. The experiences we had while the Army occupied our grounds were horrible at the time but they also showed that, however much our resolve and our patience were tested, we wouldn't buckle. What couldn't destroy us made us stronger.

CHAPTER 3
LAUNCHING THE ADVENTURE

I often wonder it if hadn't been for Michael Donnellan and Paul Clancy would I ever have got the chance to manage Armagh? Now, it might seem strange that a pair of Galway footballers could influence my career to that degree, but then life takes on so many strange patterns that nothing should surprise any of us any more.

One of my life's big turning points took place while I was sitting in the stands in Croke Park on a pleasant Saturday afternoon in July 2001.

Armagh were playing Galway in an All-Ireland qualifier and, after turning in a pig of a performance for three quarters of the way, it looked as if we were going to be beaten out of sight. Up to then, it had looked like seniors against juniors as Galway turned in one of those swashbuckling exhibitions that particular team could do so well when the mood took them.

Admittedly, it was easy for them that day. Armagh were struggling all over the place, playing like fellas who hardly knew each other let alone liked each other. They had won two of the previous three Ulster titles and were still being talked of as genuine All-Ireland contenders. They had lost to Tyrone in the Ulster quarter-final some weeks earlier but were back on track in the qualifiers after beating Down and Monaghan. Based on all the evidence, there was no reason why they should not have felt confident about pushing on into the next round of the qualifiers.

Alas, it all came apart against Galway who overwhelmed them for a long time, building up a seven-point lead in the second half. Armagh fans were completely baffled by what they were seeing. Galway were a fine team but the question was why were Armagh so flat and lethargic? Where was the pressure game they had been so good at over previous seasons? Where was the sense of togetherness they had built up?

Even when Diarmaid Marsden kicked a point to cut the lead back to six, it looked no more than a token shot against mountainous odds. It still left Armagh on a miserable six points after fifty-five minutes. You'd expect them to rack that up in twenty minutes on a good day.

And then, a strange thing happened. It was as if the Armagh lads recalled exactly who they were as footballers and men and set about delivering on it. They clicked up through the gears so rapidly that Galway couldn't respond. Armagh kicked point after point in a display which was far more in line with the form they had shown in the 1999 and 2000 seasons than anything we had seen from them up to then in 2001.

So much so that they drew level in stoppage time and were on such a powerful roll that they looked, by far, the more likely winners. You could sense that Galway were in a state of confusion. A game where they were, at one stage, heading for the easiest of wins now appeared to have veered out of their control and, as anybody who has ever been in that situation will tell you, it's very difficult to regain the initiative when the opposition have grabbed it from you and are in full flow. It really did look as if Armagh could finish the job in normal time. And, if it finished level, they would have taken a massive psychological advantage into extra-time. Yes, things had taken on an orange glow again.

The Armagh supporters were in full voice as another attack began to build from the back. Justin McNulty raced upfield but, just as he was about to deliver the ball into the attack, Michael Donnellan whizzed in and made a block. A few solos, a quick look up, a pass to Clancy and suddenly the ball was on its way towards the Railway End goal from around 45 yards range. It seemed to take an age to drop but you could tell from Clancy's raised fist, plus the reaction of both the Armagh and Galway players, that it was a point.

The winning point too. Galway 0-13 Armagh 0-12 – we were out of the Championship.

There were all sorts of recriminations afterwards when it emerged that the Armagh panel were late arriving in Croke Park over a mix-up involving a Garda escort from Na Fianna's ground in Glasnevin where they had been warming up.

The players were furious and would put their poor performance for three-quarters of the game down to that, and other niggly little issues which seemed to have cropped up in the background that year. Still, all that would have been forgotten fairly quickly if the gutsy comeback had yielded a late win.

What made things all the more frustrating for the Armagh boys was that they had to stand back for the remainder of the summer and watch Galway pick off the rest of the opposition one by one. It was as if the win over Armagh had liberated them. First Cork, then Roscommon (who had beaten them in the Connacht semi-final), then Derry and finally Meath in the All-Ireland final. From the despair of defeat by Roscommon to All-Ireland winners in a few months. That was the first season of the qualifiers, which seemed made for strong counties who had tipped over in the provinces.

Armagh beat Down and Monaghan quite comfortably in the first two rounds and appeared to have regained their balance only to be undermined by the nightmare against Galway. It's impossible to know the full extent of how pre-match problems impacted on Armagh but suffice to say that it's hard enough to win any Championship game without having to tog off on the bus on your way to the ground.

It was to be the last game in charge for the two Brians (McAlinden and Canavan), ending a term which had been very successful in Ulster and which came tantalisingly close to making a breakthrough at All-Ireland level. In 1999, Armagh had won the Ulster title for the first time in seventeen years before losing the All-Ireland semi-final to Meath.

That was the day that Oisin McConville bravely decided to play although his father, Patsy was very seriously ill. It was an impossible situation for Oisin. He – and the rest of the family – felt that playing was the right thing to do. Don't let down your team mates, your county and all that. And besides, Patsy would have wanted Oisin to play. It was typical of the McConville loyalty and spirit, but how could any player produce his best knowing that his father might have died by the time he came off the pitch? As it happened, Patsy survived until later that week. Oisin won every ball that came in but the scores just didn't come his way. It was just one of those days but the fact that he played proved how mentally strong he was.

Meath beat Armagh by four points on a day when a number of things went against us. Some of them were of our own making – particularly the dreadful shooting – but probably the decisive break came around the three-quarter mark when full-back Ger Reid was sent off by Paddy Russell for a second bookable offence. Ger was unlucky to walk and there's no doubt that his absence was crucial in shaping how the game went from there on. Armagh didn't score after that and Meath, who were brilliant at closing out games in tight finishes, tacked on the match-winning points. A few weeks later they beat Cork in the All-Ireland final leaving Armagh once again pondering on what might have been.

Same story a year later, only this time it was an even closer call in the semi-final against Kerry. It took a last-second free by Maurice Fitzgerald to earn Kerry a replay which went to extra-time. Kerry won by three points in the end and went on to beat Galway in the final, also in a replay. There was a lot of despondency around Armagh after the defeat by Kerry because there's no doubt that our boys were just as good as them in every area except when it came to putting the game away.

A year later, it was Galway's turn to beat Armagh and go on to win the All-Ireland. What the hell had the fates against Armagh? The three teams that beat us in 1999-2000-2001 went on to win the All-Ireland.

You can look at that both ways: You can convince yourself that you're just downright unlucky or else regard the near misses as a positive which can be worked on. If you can come that close to the teams that win All-Irelands what's to stop you taking the next step forward? Absolutely nothing. That would always have been very much my way of thinking. Think positive and you give yourself a chance, think negative and the world will deal you the hand it thinks you deserve.

There was a lot of frustration in Armagh after the defeat by Galway so I suppose it was inevitable that there would be a change of management. The two Brians had achieved a great deal, even if some people chose to forget that. After all, Armagh hadn't won an Ulster title between 1982 and 1999. That's a long time without a title and the fact that Down, Donegal and Derry won All-Irelands in the interim made it all the more bleak for Armagh. We retained the Ulster title in 2000, something Armagh had never done previously. This took Armagh's Ulster title tally to nine and the two

Brians had been managers for two of them. What's more, McAlinden played on the teams that won the Ulster titles in 1977, '80 and '82, while Canavan had been there in 1980 and '82. It meant that, between them, they had made important contributions to five of the nine Ulster titles Armagh had won up to then so, whatever did or didn't happen around that qualifier tie against Galway, those boys could hold their heads high. They had done a whole lot more for Armagh football than most of their critics ever did and, with a bit more luck, who knows what might have happened?

Unfortunately, it didn't work out for them at All-Ireland level and while I'm sure they made mistakes along the way, who doesn't? Sometimes you get punished for them, sometimes you don't. What if Justin McNulty had got his kick away late on against Galway? The Armagh attack were firing on all cylinders so there's every chance that one of the boys would have kicked the winner. That's how close the margin was but when it fell Galway's way the pressure grew on the two Brians.

It was no surprise when the job became vacant some time afterwards. Given the success that Crossmaglen had enjoyed I suppose I was an obvious candidate to take over and, from my perspective, it was a job I definitely wanted and a job I felt was just right for me at the time. Just as well, as I hadn't got either of the jobs I'd been in for a few years earlier.

I was interviewed for the Cavan and Louth jobs but didn't get either. Obviously, I hadn't made much of an impression! I never did find out why I was turned down but, clearly, Louth and Cavan didn't think I was up to the task. Then again, maybe the rejections were fate's way of telling me that I was trying to go in the wrong direction. Had I gone to Louth and Cavan and not made a success of it, I would probably never have been offered the Armagh job. That's the way it goes in management where all that counts are results. There's a saying that 'what's for you won't pass you' so maybe that applied to me and the Armagh job in late 2001.

Apart from several years with Cross, I also had some experience at inter-county level, working with Paddy Moriarty in the 1989 to '91 seasons. 'Paddy Mo' had inveigled me in after my playing days finished and, I must say, I enjoyed the experience and learned an awful lot. Paddy had been a great friend and colleague of mine for many years so I couldn't refuse him when he invited me aboard. As in his playing days, Paddy was very thorough in everything he did but, unfortunately, it was a period (another one) when Armagh didn't have much luck. Actually, make that any luck. We lost by a point to Tyrone in an Ulster first-round game in Omagh in 1989, by a point to Donegal in the 1990 Ulster final and to Down by two points in a first-round game in 1991. That's right – we were narrowly beaten by the eventual Ulster champions in each of those three years and, of course, Down went on to win the All-Ireland in 1991.

The 1989 clash with Tyrone in Omagh was a real tough affair. We played very well in the first half but we weren't happy with some of the treatment being dished out in particular to our forwards. Jim McConville, who would have been seen as one of our main men, took a terrible battering and tempers were running high as the teams left the pitch for half time. A bit of a fracas just outside the dressing room doors and John Lynch, as tough a player as ever wore the Tyrone jersey, took a punch to the face which left him with a black eye. I don't think he knew who actually threw the punch but we had a fair idea. And no, it definitely wasn't me!

Mind you, Tyrone had the last laugh. They were a totally different team in the second half. Kevin McCabe kicked a string of points and they eventually won by one. We got our revenge a year later back in the Athletic Grounds beating them by a point before squeezing past Down in a replay in the Ulster semi-final. However, that's where it ended as we lost the final by a point to Donegal who were a 'coming' team at the time.

We were a bit unlucky not to get a draw at least, but a '50' scored by Martin McHugh proved the crucial score. Donegal would go on to win the All-Ireland title two years later and Armagh wouldn't even get to an Ulster final for another nine years. You would never have thought Armagh and Donegal would have gone in such opposite directions after Ulster final day 1990 but then you never know what's lurking ahead in sport which is, of course, what makes it so fascinating.

Paddy Mo and I finished after the Ulster first-round defeat by Down in 1991. The game was played in Newry and if ever the ground lived up to its name as the 'marshes' it was that particular Sunday. Back then, the pitch could be heavy at the best of times back then but with torrential rain belting down from clouds so low you could nearly touch them, the game was always going to be a bit of a shambles. Actually it was worse than that, without doubt one of the messiest Championship games I ever saw.

Mickey Linden scored a penalty for Down early on but we came back to lead by two points at half time, 0-6 to 1-1. We managed just two more points while they kicked six to win a game that hardly deserved to be called an Ulster quarter-final.

If you score just 1-7 in a Championship game you don't expect to win and if you concede 0-8 you don't expect to lose but that's what happened to Down and Armagh that day. Unfortunately for us, we were on the wrong side of the low-scoring mud bath. Very few who were at that game would have thought that the pick of those the teams would have beaten Derry in the semi-final, let alone go on to win the All-Ireland, but that's exactly what happened. Down improved with every outing and ended up as All-Ireland champions.

Would Armagh have followed the same path if we'd beaten Down? Hand on heart, I don't think so. What happened over the next few years supports that view as Armagh made no impression in the Ulster Championship for a long time.

One off-pitch memory I have from 1991 was the row over the size of the logos which were allowed on jerseys. It was the first time that a sponsor's name was permitted on jerseys and I managed to get a good friend of mine, Michael Mooney to come aboard with Armagh.

Michael was always a passionate Armagh football man and was mighty proud to be the team's first official sponsor. 'Mooney Windows' was emblazoned across the jerseys for the game against Down but Michael didn't get as much value as he would have liked because the awful weather led to a smaller than usual crowd while the low standard of football meant that television highlights were cut to the very minimum that night.

Since team sponsorship was new to the GAA, there were the inevitable teething difficulties with strict regulations as to the permitted size of the company name. The GAA wanted it so small that you hardly see it; sponsors wanted it as big as they could get away with and, as a result, there were all sorts of rows and ructions. Still, embracing sponsorship was a forward step by the GAA which has since proved very lucrative for counties and, indeed, clubs.

I would never have thought, leaving Newry after the defeat by Down that evening how, eleven years on, my wife Patricia would be receiving loads of flowers from Michael Mooney in the Citywest hotel on the morning after an All-Ireland final. Wives are sometimes forgotten amid the hurly-burly that surrounds an All-Ireland but Michael was thoughtful enough to have flowers sent to Patricia on the morning after we won in 2002. It was typical of him, but then Michael was always one of the truly genuine Armagh supporters whether things were going well or badly.

Benny Tierney was the only member of the 2002 side who played in the 'marshes' in 1991 and neither he – nor I – could ever have anticipated that we'd be back together for an inspiring adventure more than a decade later.

But then, I didn't think the intervening years would take me on such a fantastic journey with Cross, one which opened up horizons that would be very beneficial to me when I eventually got the chance to manage Armagh. Paddy Mo and I should probably have stayed on at the end of the 1991 campaign. Things looked bad when we lost to Down but then they did go on to win the All-Ireland, so maybe we weren't that far off the pace.

It would be another ten years, 2002 to be exact, before I got another chance to become involved in Armagh management again. I have to say, there was no real sense of optimism around Armagh after the 2001 Championship. It was as if supporters were losing heart, suspecting that, despite all the promise of previous years, the squad just wasn't good enough to seal the deal. That was understandable to some degree but, I must say, I didn't see it that way.

I looked back over the teams that won the previous six All-Irelands and couldn't see how they were all that much superior to Armagh. Kerry, Meath and Galway had won two titles each between 1996 and 2001 and Armagh had come mighty close to all three, so the only question was, why hadn't we beaten any of them? There was certainly no shortage of effort or commitment on or off the field.

Could it be just a matter of self-belief? Did guys from Meath, Kerry and Galway have that little extra in that department? Did they think bigger? Were they that bit cuter? Did they make things happen for themselves? Did they, in some way, feel entitled to win big games and, by extension, did that help them through the pressure periods? Quite probably.

In that case, there was only one solution for Armagh: get our players answering "yes" to those questions and we might get somewhere.

Shortly after the two Brians left, I was approached by Eamonn Mackle, a fanatical Armagh supporter who was always dreaming the big dream. He had supported his county all his life with as much passion as he could muster but never saw them win anything outside Ulster. Managing Director of Freeza Meats in Newry, he was a hugely successful business man (he still is) and had been on the fund-raising committee of the Armagh County Board.

He sponsored Cross at one stage so I knew him quite well. We always got on, and were very much on the same wavelength on a lot of things. Anyway, he contacted me and put the question: "Joe, no beating around the bush, do you want this Armagh job or not?"

"What do you think? Of course I do."

"Right, leave it with me."

"Eamonn, it's not that simple. If I'm to be offered it, I'll need things done in a certain way. This has to be done right or I won't be in."

In fairness to the County Board, they were amenable to change. Having met the County Executive, I found them to be very ambitious and, once they appointed me as manager, they rowed in fully behind the big drive I was planning.

So did Eamonn Mackle. I put my cards on the table in his office in Newry. We'd need all sorts of backup. Medical, scientific, psychological, performance-developing and anything else that we thought important at any given time. That could change depending on the circumstances but I needed to know that, if I asked, I wouldn't be refused. We'd need to be allowed to structure things our way without looking over our shoulders and begging for permission all the time.

Times had changed in the GAA and we had to make sure that not only were we thinking like the big boys, we were actually ahead of them. Anything else and we were destined to stay where we had been – brave contenders who came up short. This would have to be the most sophisticated operation Armagh football had ever seen. I was thinking All-Ireland title. The days of being content with winning Ulster were over. Crossmaglen had proved what could be done so the template was there for the county team. This was the time to drive on like never before. We had the players so it was now or never.

"Eamonn, we have a right good squad here", I told him. "I've known the Cross lads since they were kids. They're special talents but they're not the only ones. If you look right across the panel, there's some talent there … great men … great footballers. They've got to be given a chance to get the very best out of themselves. Armagh owes it to them and to football in the county. We've been 'also-rans' for too bloody long. Absolutely nothing can be left to chance. If I take this job, everything has to be done like a military operation."

That's pretty much how the conversation went.

Eamonn embraced the 'all or nothing' with a level of enthusiasm which had to be seen to be believed. His office in Newry would become a major hub for Armagh football for several years. I spent a huge amount of time over there, working out logistical things with Eamonn, whose approach to everything was: If it needs to be done, it will be done. And if anybody ever queried an expense, his response would be: "Are we afraid of how much it will cost to win an All-Ireland? If we are, we might as well pack it in and let everyone else win it because they're not worrying about money. What are we at here? We have the players so let's get on with it."

Eamonn went to the County Board and informed them that I was interested. I wasn't sure how they would react because I would have had my differences with them from time to time during my days managing Cross.

Back when the National League started in October and had three or four rounds before Christmas, the County Board wanted the Cross boys to play in the League. Their view was that the county team came first which was fair enough from their standpoint but not from mine. Chasing Ulster and All-Ireland club titles had become our big project and I felt that we should be accommodated in every possible way to help make that happen. After all, it would be good for Armagh football if one of its clubs put down a marker outside the county.

As far as I was concerned, spring and summer was county time, autumn and winter was club time. It seemed a fair enough trade-off.

I'm sure there were people who thought that all I was concerned with was Cross and that I didn't give a damn about the county team. That wasn't true – far from it – but I don't think it was unreasonable to expect that the Cross players would be allowed to devote themselves fully to the Ulster club Championship in October, November and December and, indeed, up to St Patrick's Day if we were lucky enough to get to the All-Ireland final. After that the county could have them full-time.

Naturally, I wanted only the best for Cross, which was my job as manager. And, who knows, maybe winning those club All-Irelands was the crucial difference when it came to making the county breakthrough later on. I remember John Mac telling me that some of the non-Cross boys often asked him how it was that Cross could win in Croke Park and Armagh couldn't. His answer was always the same, because we went there to win, not just to compete. That's what the Cross spirit was all about. Coming second didn't register on our screens and there was no reason why it should be any different for Armagh.

I'm not saying that there was a lack of ambition on the county scene prior to my arrival but there's no doubt that it's easy to start seeing yourself in a certain way when you come from a county that hasn't won a whole lot. We needed to change that – and quickly.

The trouble was that, after losing to Galway in 2001, a lot of Armagh people were beginning to believe that the county was somehow jinxed in Croke Park. We hadn't won a Championship game there since 1977 and had lost three National League finals as well, in 1983, '85 and '94. That meant nothing to me. I'd lost several times in Croke Park as a player but could always look back and rationalise why it had happened and it certainly had nothing to do with the ground. We lost because we weren't good enough, or because we made stupid mistakes. You win if you're good enough and play well enough whether it's Croke Park, Clones, Killarney or Galway.

Still, I knew that if I got the job, one of the first areas that needed to be worked on was confidence. Doubt can be like an unwelcome guest, if it's allowed to settle in you might never get rid of it.

I was invited to meet the County Board Executive where I put on record my vision of where I saw Armagh and how I thought we should proceed as a county. In fairness to them, they bought into it straightaway. They also agreed that Eamonn would be the link between me and them. He was working with them on the financial side anyway so it seemed like a perfect fit. And it was. Eamonn is one of those boys who, if you ask him to do something, it will be done straightaway, not tomorrow, next week, next month but now – assuming of course that it's feasible and, if it's not, the next best option is pursued.

It was mighty comforting to have a man like that in my corner. His business expertise was invaluable in so many different ways and once he was working with me I had a good feeling about how things would turn out. Let's put it this way – if Armagh didn't achieve something big it certainly wouldn't be for the want of a proper back-up structure. Eamonn's approach was: Joe, you asked for this, now here it is and make sure it works.

I have to say I got on well with the County Board, too. John Moley was Chairman when I was appointed but the county convention came two months later so I didn't get to work very much with him. Joe Jordan took over in the chair from John for 2002; Paddy Og Nugent was Secretary and Peadar Murray had charge of the purse strings as Treasurer. Great guys all, whose heart and soul was in getting Armagh onto a new level. They thought big and were prepared to act on it, although I'm sure there were times they thought they had appointed a bloody lunatic as manager.

Nothing works in a county unless the manager has a very close relationship with the County Board officers. When things go well the players and managers get all the plaudits but good County Board officers are invaluable too, even if they tend to be forgotten. I was certainly lucky to have such supportive men behind me during my time as Armagh manager.

How in God's name a County Secretary does his job is beyond me but, somehow, Paddy Og always managed to remain calm and controlled even in 2002 and 2003 when the demand for All-Ireland tickets was just too crazy for words. Paddy's approach was, "If I have them, I'll give them and if I haven't, sure what can I do?" All very logical, but try telling that to people who aren't getting tickets. Like all good treasurers Peadar kept tight control of things but he always had a sense of when it was right to spend money. And if he didn't we told him, again and again if necessary.

We were lucky to have men like Gene Duffy around. Gene knew the Armagh scene inside out and back again. Not only that, but he also knew his way around the Croke Park corridors of power which was very helpful at times. He has been a great friend of mine for more years than either of us care to remember, indeed we still meet on Sunday nights for a pint and a chat in Fearon's bar in Crossmaglen along with another great Armagh supporter, Joe Taggert.

I sensed from the off that I would have a good relationship with the County Board. We were on the same wavelength so now it was a question of getting everything else in order. My first task was to appoint a trainer and selector and I didn't have to think long on either front. Having worked with John McCloskey in Cross I knew that he was one of the best trainers in the business. His knowledge of all aspects of the game, from coaching to conditioning to science, was first class so I was delighted when he agreed to join us. He was always up-to-date with the most advanced methods and never stopped looking for ways of getting an edge. That was one box I ticked off confidently.

I had played with Paul Grimley toward the latter end of my inter-county career so I had known him for a long time. He had worked with various clubs over the years and knew all the boys, especially those around Armagh city. I also wanted a selector from the north of the county but couldn't actually get anybody. I asked one or two lads but they weren't really interested, so I left it at that. No point persuading someone into a job they're not totally committed to or appointing someone just for the sake of evening up the geographical balance.

In time, the rest of the backroom team came together and they all did an outstanding job. Dr Sean Digney headed the medical side; Niall Moraghan and Alan Kelly were physios; Jackie Meehan, Julie Davis and Cathy Kelly were masseurs; Hugh Campbell and Des Jennings took charge of the psychological side; Darren O'Neill was on stats, the late Oliver Toal on video while Paddy Carolan looked after the catering side of things and Paddy 'The Bishop' McNamee was in charge of the kit. It was quite a team and, I have to say, each and every one of them played their part.

I have often been asked if I ever talked to Brian McAlinden and Brian Canavan to get their views on various players whom they had been with for several years. The answer is no. I'm not sure it would have been fair to them to start delving into things that had happened in the past. I have no doubt they would have helped me but I reckoned I would be better off making my own judgements. The most important thing was that the nucleus of a very good team was in place and it was up to me to build on that. Besides, I didn't want the players thinking I had been checking them out with the former management. This was a clean slate on all sides so it was best to keep it that way.

I knew the Cross boys well, so I set about getting an insight into the other lads whom I already knew were fine footballers, which was a good enough start for me. After that it was a matter of getting to know them as people.

One of the first decisions was the appointment of captain. Kieran McGeeney had been in the job for the previous two years, having taken over from Jarlath Burns, and from what I could see he had done exceptionally well. People might have expected me to play the Cross card and appoint John Mac who had captained us to the 1999 All-Ireland title, and, no doubt, he would have been another excellent choice.

Still, I felt that retaining Geezer was the right thing to do. I took a day off work to drive down to Dublin to talk to him face-to-face. We met for lunch in the St Stephens Green Centre, went through everything as we saw it, from both sides, and I came away convinced that I had made the correct decision in leaving the captaincy with him. I told him that I believed there was an All-Ireland in this team and that it was now a question of making sure it was delivered. Geezer being Geezer, he never had any doubt about the All-Ireland.

I'm not sure what impact it would have had on the squad if I had replaced him as captain. I'm sure he would have been just as driven but it might have impacted elsewhere. John Mac would have been an obvious choice if I had wanted to play it safe and go for somebody I knew really well, but it was important to send out a clear signal that I was thinking in Armagh terms rather than Cross terms now.

Besides, I also knew when I looked through that squad that there were leaders everywhere. Geezer and John Mac had already proven that with Armagh and Cross but we also had Enda McNulty, Paul McGrane, Diarmaid Marsden and others who each led from the front. Those boys knew what taking responsibility really meant: It wasn't something you talked about, it was something you did. And then there were the quiet men who might have said little but who did their job so efficiently. Put it all together and the mix was impressive.

I was conscious that both the panel and the general Armagh public would be keeping a close watch to see how many Cross players I included. There were some mutterings around the county that I would try to turn Armagh into a larger version of Cross which, of course, was plain daft. There's no prouder Cross man than me but my time with them was over – I was now in charge of Armagh and all it entailed. In fact, if it meant that I thought no Cross player was worthy of his place on the team, I wouldn't have hesitated to go without them and to hell with the consequences locally.

Still, that was never going to happen. John and Tony McEntee and Oisin McConville were always going to be key figures on the Armagh team, but there was another Cross boyo that I wanted – Francie Bellew hadn't been on the county panel and was beginning to look like one of those lads who would have outstanding club careers without ever quite making it onto the county scene.

Francie Bellew was still only in his mid-20s and had plenty of scope for development if I could persuade him to give it a go. In fact, I had a little plan in the back of my mind which involved both Francie and Geezer. Looking in from the outside over the previous year or two, I had begun to wonder if McGeeney was getting a little bit stale at centre-back.

Francie played centre-back for Cross so, as I looked at the options, I considered playing him at No. 6 and Geezer at No. 15 where he would have a roving brief. We always played three big men across the middle of the field with Cross – John Mac, Anthony Cunningham and Colm O'Neill – so I thought it might be a good idea to try something similar with Armagh, using Geezer as the third man with Paul McGrane and John Toal or John Mac.

I hinted at this plan when I met Geezer in Dublin and didn't exactly get a delighted reaction but I have no doubt that, had I persisted, he would have bought into it and been very effective in a roving role.

Still, before I got anywhere near trying out new formations, I had to get Francie onto the panel. There were mixed views in Armagh on whether or not he was good enough for the county team but I certainly felt he was worth a try. I knew the key part he had played in Crossmaglen's successes and was convinced there was more to him than he was given credit for outside the club. He's a quiet type of fella who keeps to himself and wouldn't have been pushing his claims for a place on the county team, either in public or in private. In fact, you wouldn't even know whether he was interested in county football, but I was damn well determined to test him out.

I knew him very well and vice-versa so, when I asked him to join the panel, I suppose he felt he had a chance of getting a decent run. He was a bit non-committal at first but, typical of him, he put his heart and soul into it once he became fully involved.

I'm not sure if the non-Cross boys rated him all that highly in the early stages but we knew all about him in Cross and understood the fine qualities he brought to the team, including a brand of honesty you don't find very often. Gradually, that got through to the whole squad and, before long, they understood exactly why I regarded him so highly.

Francie was one of those boys you couldn't annoy or you couldn't sicken. I remember bringing the Crossmaglen squad down to Bettystown beach once and telling them to go for a run to what looked like a tree away in the distance while we got the cones ready. They must have been gone three-quarters of an hour and when they came back – in considerably less good humour than when they left – I was informed that it wasn't, in fact, a tree but the base of an abandoned ship which was a hell of lot further away than it looked. I told them they were in for a lot more, and I could see a little smile break across Francie's face.

"Hey there … Francie! I'll wipe that smile off your face, I'm telling you."

We sent them off running through the sand dunes, which was about as punishing as it could get, but every time Francie passed me, he'd cock his head and give me a little smile. He was dying inside but he wouldn't let on. *Keep smiling … don't give that bastard the satisfaction of knowing I'm in pain.* Typical Francie.

I have to say that the perception of Francie – which was created by sections of the media and, by extension, held by some members of the public – was one of the most annoying things I came across during my days in charge of Armagh. There wasn't a braver, more honest player in the game but instead he was portrayed as a vicious hitman who would break an opponent in two if he got the chance. It was a horribly unfair depiction of him and I defy anybody to tell me of one sneaky punch or kick that Francie Bellew delivered in an Armagh jersey.

Yes, he was hard and tough but it was all out in the open. He gave it, he took it, he moved on. Mick Lyons once said that playing full-back was like being a member of the mafia. Kill or be killed. He was right. Mick, too, got a bad reputation which was undeserved. A case of give a dog a bad name, and all that.

That was definitely Francie's experience and he paid a heavy price for it. There were times when I felt like walking up to the referee before a game and saying, "Sure you might as well book Francie now, it will save time later".

The interesting thing is that if you talk to forwards who played against Francie, they have a much different view to the one created by the media and by referees who seemed to think that if there was a punch-up a mile away he must have caused it.

Sure, he dished out the knocks but, by God, he took them as well without ever complaining. As I said, he was as honest as they come and fearless with it. One particular instance of his fearlessness stands out. Donegal were really putting it up to us in the 2003 All-Ireland semi-final and, at one stage, looked to be about to get in for a goal. It was two against one but Francie put his body on the line, took an unmerciful bang from the two Donegal men (it was a fair challenge by the way) and went to ground as if he had been shot.

The thing was, though, he had the ball in his hands and wouldn't let go. The chance was lost for Donegal and we went on to win. Francie had to go off five minutes later but it was one of many examples of occasions where his bravery came to our rescue. So, yes, I was glad I persuaded him to join us at the end of 2001. He certainly did the state of Armagh some service.

It took him a while to settle in, mind you. While still mulling over whether to play him at centre-back and push Geezer further forward, I tried it out during the 2002 National League.

It wasn't working so I decided there and then to abandon the experiment. I went to him and said, "Francie, we'll not be doing that again. You'll be going back to the full-back line, it'll suit you better." He looked at me as if I had just told him that he was to be released from hell. "Thank God for that," he said.

Of course, he would never have complained if I had persisted with the idea. Other lads wouldn't be slow to let you know what they thought but Francie just got on with whatever was thrown at him.

He wasn't the only one to be relieved by the abandonment of the experiment. It meant that Geezer returned to centre-back where he was happiest.

If bringing Francie into the panel was a good move, convincing Benny Tierney not to leave it was equally important. Benny was coming up on thirty-three years of age at the end of 2001 and had been playing for Armagh since 1989. He had decided – unofficially at least – that it was time to pack it in after the defeat by Galway. Maybe he thought that I was planning to play the Cross card and make Paul Hearty No. 1 goalkeeper which certainly was an option. Paul had done well for Cross over previous years and, at the age of twenty-three, was very much one for the future.

In fact, he had played in the 2001 All-Ireland qualifiers so most people seemed to think that I'd automatically make him No. 1 and let Benny drift quietly into retirement. I saw it differently. This man had been around the circuit an awfully long time and knew just about everything there was to know about the art of goalkeeping. Apart from that, he was a real character, a man who made others laugh. God knows we don't have half enough of people like that in our lives so, far from seeing him as yesterday's man, I wanted him to play a big role in what we were trying to achieve.

I phoned him up, only to be told that he wasn't interested in continuing.

"Time for me to move on, Joe, especially now that there's new management in there. I'm sure you'll be having your own ideas on things," he said.

"Indeed, I will Benny. So, what time will you be home from school tomorrow? I want to talk to you properly."

I called over to his house the following day and explained why I wanted him to stay on. The bloody rogue wouldn't give me an answer immediately but he eventually agreed to give it a shot. I told him that I hadn't gone into the job just for the sake of it but to win an All-Ireland. I don't know whether or not he believed me but, in the end, he reckoned that staying on was a chance worth taking. I'm sure he didn't regret it.

Of course there were no guarantees that he would get a starting place. Hearty was a fine goalkeeper so it was a question of which of them grabbed the No. 1 slot and made it his own. Even if Benny wasn't going to be on the starting fifteen, I wanted him around the place. He was a real joker, always up to tricks and devilment that almost nobody else would get away with. He had no shame whatsoever and could drive you mad at times, but the bottom line was that he was a great man at releasing tension and pressure whenever or wherever it built up. More than that, he was an excellent goalkeeper.

Sharp in tongue and sharp in mind – that's our Benny. I was delighted when he agreed to stay on and I'm sure he was even more pleased he had returned when we won the All-Ireland. Imagine playing for Armagh since 1989, only to retire the year before we won the All-Ireland for the first time.

People used to criticise his kick-outs for not being long enough but they missed the point. Kick-outs are all about giving your outfield players the best possible chance of winning possession and Benny was very good at that. He was also first class at organising his defence and since the McNulty boys – Enda and Justin – were always likely to form two-thirds of the full-back line, it made perfect sense to have Benny aboard as part of a Mullaghbawn triumvirate.

We were extremely lucky to have two such fine goalkeepers as Benny and Paul. It was one less thing to worry about, knowing they were both so reliable. Paul suffered a serious shoulder injury in a League game in early 2002 which kept him out for almost two months, as a result Benny came back in and held onto the position for the rest of the year. He retired after winning the All-Ireland in 2002 but I was anxious to keep him on as an advisor to the goalkeepers and to be, well, just Benny.

As it happened, he stayed in our backroom team right to the end of my term in 2007. Even in his background role, he liked to act the eejit but beneath the fooling and the clowning is a very astute football brain.

Apart from getting an excellent goalkeeper and a character who would be good for the dressing room atmosphere, persuading Benny to remain was important on another front as well – it sent out a clear message that I wasn't going to automatically back the Cross lads when it came to making close calls. No, I was thinking Armagh now and while six or seven of the Cross boys were on the panel they would be treated exactly like everybody else. They knew that, too.

Of course, you would have people claiming that I leaned towards Cross players but all I can say to that is show me the evidence. Yes, I brought in Francie Bellew but I make no apologies for that. It was definitely the right thing to do.

As it happened, Francie for Ger Reid and Benny for Paul (Hearty) were the only two changes in the defence between the team that lost to Galway in 2001 and the side that beat Kerry in the All-Ireland final fourteen months later. Ger had a few injury niggles in early 2002 but battled on as best he could and got his All-Ireland medal as a sub. Like everybody else, he would have loved to be playing but, with Francie settling in so well in the full-back line with the two McNultys, Ger lost out. Still, he got his All-Ireland medal which was well-deserved after giving so much to Armagh football over the years.

By December 2001, everything was in place for the big push. The draw for the 2002 Ulster Championship had been made, handing us a clash with Tyrone (who else?) in the quarter-final. There were easier starts available but, at the same time, it concentrated our minds. Beat Tyrone and we had a right good chance of winning Ulster. Lose to Tyrone and, while the season wasn't over, it would have been an awfully long way back.

That was enough to focus the minds as we headed for the gyms and training grounds on dark winter nights.

CHAPTER 4
THE GIFT THAT KEPT GIVING

"Lads, there's a problem here. We're way behind where we should be at this stage of year. We're only playing in fits and starts, and this is Division 2! We've got Tyrone on May the nineteenth and, at this rate ... they'll eat us alive. We're only fooling ourselves if we think that winning games fairly handily down in Division 2 will be any good to us that day. Tyrone are clipping through Division 1 as if they know exactly what they're at. They're getting real tests. We're not. We've got to get something new into the mix. This is getting serious."

Early 2002 and we're going through some awful weather. Most of the first round games in the Allianz Football League were called off on the first Sunday in February due to snow, hail and rain and, while our game against Louth went ahead, it was switched from the Athletic Grounds to Carrickcruppin.

Well into the second half, I was regretting that it hadn't been called off altogether. My first big day as Armagh manager was going horribly wrong. Louth were leading by six points and looking as if they were All-Ireland champions, certainly in comparison to us. Then Stevie McDonnell popped up and scored a goal – how often had that happened over the years? – and, suddenly, we were off. We won by five points but if ever a result misrepresented the actual play this was it.

We won all but one of our games in Division 2A that spring, the exception being against Kerry where we lost by a point down in Tralee. Still, it was a good performance and, while we put up good scores on the others, the reality was that Louth, Wicklow, Leitrim, Antrim, Limerick and London weren't quite in the same class as the Tyrone team who were scorching through Division 1 and winding up for the big Ulster Championship clash in May.

The bad weather had played hell with our training schedules and, while it was the same for other counties, my sole concern was how to get around the problem so that, come Championship time, we would be ready for whatever the season threw at us.

John McCloskey, Paul Grimley and I talked about it and came up with an idea: What if we got out of the country altogether for a while? John was the physical fitness expert so I asked him how much a spell of full-time training in a warm weather atmosphere would bring us on.

"Two to three weeks," he promised.

"Right, let's do it," I said.

Of course, we then had to deal with the small matter of the cost involved. Time to talk to Eamonn Mackle, the man who believed that money should not be an impediment to Armagh winning a first All-Ireland. Eamonn went his way, I went mine and we got working on raising as much funds as we could. At this stage we still hadn't told the County Board because we wanted to have everything in place before presenting them with the news that we were planning something that had never been done before in Armagh.

The next question was, where should we go? I'd heard of the training centre in La Manga in Spain and, since I knew that part of the world fairly well, I slipped over for a few days to have a look. It was exactly what we needed.

Our last League game was over in Ruislip against London and, when we arrived back in Dublin airport, I called the lads aside and asked if they could all organise a week off work. I told them what I had in mind and they all seemed to think it was a great idea. They went away to sort out a week off as best they could.

Now we had the players onside and we had a venue, so all that remained was to break the news to the County Board which we did the following Tuesday night. When we mentioned taking the squad away for a week, the Board executive thought we had somewhere else in Ireland in mind.

"Actually, we're thinking of Spain … La Manga, to be precise."

Now, the lads on the executive wanted Armagh to win an All-Ireland as much as anybody else but they knew that taking a full squad and all the backroom team to La Manga wouldn't come cheap.

"How much is this going to cost?" they asked.

I paused for a second, before dropping out the figure as gently as I could.

"Around £30,000," I announced cheerily, trying to make it sound like I had just suggested they spend £300.

I could see the shock on their faces. In fact, they were probably thinking to themselves: "What in God's name have we done putting this lunatic in charge? £30,000 to take the squad half way around Europe when we have perfectly good facilities back home."

It was time to intervene before I was told to cop myself on.

"The good news is that this won't cost the Board much. We'll raise a lot of the money ourselves," I told them.

They didn't push me on that particular point, which was just as well because I couldn't have answered them at that stage. To the Board's great credit they backed the idea, and Eamonn and myself got working on raising as much of the £30,000 as we possibly could.

We were surprised and delighted at the response around the county. We thought business people might be sceptical about the wisdom of spending money on a venture like that but, once we explained why we were doing it and outlined the benefits it would bring, they decided to go with the roll of the dice. I will always be eternally grateful to them because the La Manga experience turned out to be worth its weight in gold.

From the day I walked into the Armagh dressing room, I wanted everything to be just right. Everybody had to be thinking the same way. We were planning on playing a team game on and off the pitch. This was Armagh United, all striving and driving in the same direction. We wanted players to create new challenges for themselves, both as individuals and as a group. Players can get a certain view of themselves through the experiences they have encountered and the manner in which others see them. It's a natural part of people's make-up.

For instance, there was a general view that one particular forward had to be handed the ball because he wasn't regarded as a natural fielder. We decided one night in training to test out that theory rather than take it at face value. We ran a catch and kick session to work out exactly where everybody stood.

It was every man for himself. Each player had to scrap for every ball, high or low, left or right. Now we knew this particular forward was a great kicker, but catching? Well, he wasn't noted for it. Hang on, maybe that perception was wrong. Bloody sure it was. He turned out to be one of the best fielders of the ball that night.

His name? Stevie McDonnell.

That's right, the man whose fielding was deemed to be substandard when, in reality, the opposite was the case. Indeed, his ability to field the ball turned into one of Armagh's most potent weapons over the following seasons and remains so to this very day.

With the La Manga project in hand, we had a Division 2 League semi-final clash with Laois to take on in Pearse Park, Longford. Laois had gone well in Division 2B under Colm Browne but we still expected to beat them. Instead, we turned in an absolute stinker, losing by four points when it could have been fourteen. This was possibly the worst performance in all my years in charge of Armagh and the fact that it came a few months into my term didn't exactly inspire confidence. This was dismal stuff.

A fairly big Armagh contingent travelled to Longford that day and left feeling there wasn't much hope for the Championship ahead. And those who weren't there wouldn't have been very impressed by the match reports in the following day's papers, some of which questioned our tactics.

"The Laois cause was helped considerably by the overly defensive tactics employed by disjointed Armagh," noted the *Irish Independent*.

No doubt about who was to blame then. Obviously the manager had got it wrong, a feeling probably shared by some Armagh supporters. And this was our last game before facing Tyrone who, at the very same time as we were spluttering incoherently against Laois, were demolishing Mayo in the Division 1 semi-final up in Enniskillen. They would do the same to Cavan in the final a few weeks later.

Boy, did we need something to pick us up after the Laois game. Luckily, we had it in the form of our week away. La Manga scored for us on a number of fronts. The facilities were excellent, the weather was nice and, despite the Laois setback, the mood among the lads was good. I wanted the week to tighten the bonds between them so that when they returned home they would feel so united that nothing could prise them apart.

There was always great rivalry between the clubs in Armagh. It had become especially intense between Crossmaglen and Mullaghbawn over the previous four or five years and one of my early concerns was that it might carry on into the county squad.

Anyway, one night in La Manga, after watching videos of Armagh against Tyrone in previous years, we were talking about the bond we'd need to withstand everything that would be thrown at us in Clones a few weeks later. Some lads, including Geezer, said a few words and then, out of the blue, John Mac stood up: "Kieran, if you need me at any time, I'm there to cover your back."

It was the way he said it that struck a chord as much as what he said. There was silence for about five seconds. It seemed like an hour and then I stepped in. "Right lads, leave it there for tonight." As the lads walked out of the room, I turned to John and Paul and said, "We have them now, boys, they're all in this together."

You would have had to be in that room to understand the mood and the atmosphere but something clicked that night that I believe was very important in moving things on in a way that had never happened before. It's difficult to explain, all these years later, but it was as if the panel had moved beyond where they had ever been before. They were heading for a new world.

We did two sessions a day for four days with one half day off. John and Paul had it down to the finest of arts so that every session was well-planned, well-focused and consequently very productive. The rest of the days were well spent, too. We all got to know each other much better as individuals and as a group. I have to pay great tribute to John and Paul for their role in making the La Manga venture so successful. They worked incredibly hard to get everything right all the time. So, too, did the medical team who worked day and night to have the lads right.

The one aim of the week was to bring a positive outlook to everything. Negatives were not entertained. It was something we locked into our psyche in La Manga and guarded with our lives as the year opened up in front of us.

We knew the reaction back home to our venture would be, at best, mixed and, at worst, downright mocking. The Armagh 'sunshine boys' and all that.

Who do they think they are? Aren't these the lads that failed against Galway last year? Aren't they the same boys who played crap against Laois a few weeks ago and now they're swanning around Spain? Bloody shapers, the lot of them.

That was why it was so important that we do everything right in La Manga. That included no alcohol under any circumstances. One of the boys sidled over to me one evening and I could tell straight away what he wanted.

"Joe, we're working mighty hard here, any chance of one night off for a few drinks?"

It was a fair question and, to be honest, a few drinks wouldn't have done them a bit of harm. Truth be told, I would have loved a few nice glasses of red wine myself. In fact, I could think of nothing nicer than going out as a group for a few drinks and a bit of fun, but I knew we couldn't do it because it might have backfired.

"There's nothing I'd prefer now than to put £1,000 on the table and let ye have a right good session," I told him. "I'd even join in myself, but we can't do it. Apart from anything else, if word got out that ye even had one bottle of beer each, imagine how that would be exaggerated back home. Before we know it, the story will be that we were on the piss every night, singing 'The Boys From The County Armagh'. No, let's keep it as it is. We're doing the right things so let's stick with them and, do you know what? If we're in trouble against Tyrone, we'll know how to get out of it when things get tight."

I have no doubt that if we'd had even one drink, word would have filtered back home and mischief would kick in. That in itself wouldn't worry me but the danger was that if stories went around that we had been drinking in La Manga it would be a boost to the opposition. That was the last thing we wanted to happen. La Manga was to be a major plus for us, not a help to the opposition.

I've had first-hand experience from my own playing days of how small rumours can take on a nasty life of their own.

I often found it hard to sleep coming up to big games. It could start on the Thursday night and run through Friday and Saturday as well. I couldn't stop thinking about the game and would often wake up in the middle of the night with all sorts of thoughts swirling around in my head.

The Saturday night before the 1980 All-Ireland semi-final against Roscommon, I rambled out for a drink to help me sleep. I drank three pints of Guinness, went home, slept well and woke up feeling great.

There wouldn't have been a word about it if we had won but we didn't and, suddenly, Joe and his pints were to blame. The team management and County Board tackled me over it. Apparently, I had downed a feed of pints, got blind drunk and had been dancing on tables. Now, anyone who knows me would understand that that wasn't my style, but when rumour meets rumour anything can happen. There's nothing like having a scapegoat tethered to the door when a team loses. Everybody else associated with Armagh's defeat by Roscommon could wipe their hands of it and instead point piously in my direction. The accusations levelled at me were pure crap but what could I do?

Truth tends to fare badly in a county that loses a big game and the manner in which we lost to Roscommon – we surrendered a big lead and ended up losing by six points – made Armagh very fertile territory for gossip.

It wasn't nice to be accused of something I hadn't done and, while I could deny it all I liked, the word was out and wasn't going to be reined in, however hard I tried. I have to say I expected more from some of the people who had a go at me but, that's life. People will believe anything they want and to hell with the facts.

We had dominated midfield throughout most of the first half but we lost Colm McKinstry to injury after half time which had a big bearing on the outcome. As for my performance, it certainly wasn't influenced by drinking three pints the night before. Okay, so it's not something I would advocate as a manager but we're talking 1980 when the approach to things was a whole lot different. The whole business rankled with me afterwards as I felt I was the only one taking the rap for losing to Roscommon. As a result, others – on and off the pitch – escaped criticism. Still, after what happened that year, I never went out on a Saturday night before a game again, right up to the end of my playing career in 1987.

Some twenty-two years later, the memory of my three pints alerted me to the dangers of allowing the lads to have a drink in La Manga. They accepted the ban but then they had bought into the whole La Manga business very enthusiastically.

As captain, Geezer was told of the plan before the others but I could see that, while he thought it was a good idea, he had some misgivings.

"You have to make sure it's a training week and nothing else," he said.

Clearly, he was concerned that it might turn into a bit of a doss and that we'd come back no better off than we when we left.

"Don't you worry about that, Kieran. A training week is exactly what it's going to be," I promised him.

From my perspective, I saw it as a glorious opportunity to do something different so that when we took to the field against Tyrone a few weeks later we'd feel we had a little edge.

John McCloskey had assured me from the start that the trip would be worth as much in four days as two or three weeks' training back home and, just as we were leaving La Manga, I asked him if it had been worth the two or three weeks he had talked about.

He smiled. "A lot more than that, Joe."

He was right. In fact, I'd say it was among the best money ever spent in Armagh. A lot had been written about it in the run-up to the Tyrone game – some positive, some neutral, some negative, some sceptical. Then there were those who were waiting to see how we fared in the Championship. If we did well, La Manga would be declared a fantastic idea, if we didn't it would be considered a waste of money. We knew what it had given us but, deep down, there was always the chance that we would be beaten. After all, we were facing the reigning National League and Ulster champions in the first round so it wasn't as if we had a handy draw.

As events transpired, we got an unexpected extra from the trip just before the Tyrone game. We were walking up the hill to the back pitch in Clones for the warm up. We met a crowd of Tyrone supporters with their red and white flags waving in front of us and they couldn't resist the chance to have some fun.

"Well, boys, ye came alright … haven't ye a grand sun tan? Won't do ye much good today, though."

I growled at them as if I was really angry but I also knew they had done us a big favour. After that little episode, the lads didn't need much winding up.

"Hear what they're saying about ye, boys? Tyrone are laughing at ye. Make sure ye take it out on them once that ball is thrown in."

La Manga. The gift that kept on giving.

CHAPTER 5
HEAVY LIFTING

Take your worst nightmare, multiply it by five and think of the feeling. Actually, don't try it, because hearts weren't meant to take such unreasonable strain.

I know what it's like because mine must have come close to seizing in Clones on the Sunday afternoon of May 19, 2002. We were deep into stoppage time in the first round Ulster Championship quarter-final against Tyrone with the sides level and looking as if they had booked in for a replay a week later.

Then, Tyrone launched one final attack and, suddenly, the ball was in the hands of one very dangerous man. Now, if there was one man you didn't want to see getting possession at any time, let alone in the closing seconds of a drawn Championship game, it was Peter Canavan.

People talk of genius and of true greatness, terms that can sometimes become attached to a player without him actually deserving it but, in Canavan's case, they very definitely applied. This guy was the real deal, a wonderful talent who did more for his county than will ever be fully realised. I'll tell you this, no one deserved an All-Ireland medal more than him for all that he had done for Tyrone and Gaelic football.

Not that I was harbouring such generous thoughts in the closing minutes of the 2003 All-Ireland final when Tyrone were beating Armagh. Still, he too had had his disappointing days – indeed, a great many of them – so he was entitled to a change in fortunes. It was a pity, though, that the biggest ones came against us in 2003 and 2005.

The strange thing is that his big chance might have come a year earlier if he'd nailed a stoppage time chance against us in that Ulster quarter-final in '02. Instead, he passed the ball to Richard Thornton, who had earlier come on as a sub, and his shot for what would have been the winning point flew wide. I often wondered why Canavan didn't have a go himself. I can only figure that he reckoned by passing to Thornton, who was in a better position, it was a guaranteed point. It goes to show – there's no such thing as a guarantee in Championship football.

It was my first Championship game as Armagh manager so you can imagine the relief I felt. Had we lost, I would have been ridiculed everywhere, including back home in Armagh. What's more, I don't think we would have done well in the qualifiers. We would have been in the first round and I suspect that after investing so much energy and effort in the Tyrone game, we might have been totally flat.

It really was all or nothing for us that year. We had built everything on the certainty of what we were doing. We had tightened the squad as a group, tweaked the line-up and the overall approach and hit the Championship in straight-line mode. Had we lost to Tyrone, it would have seriously dented everything. Yes, we would have repaired it as best we could but just as a crashed car can be made to look as good as new, it's still a crashed car. We wanted to win so badly in 2002 that if we had tipped over at the very first fence, it would have been mighty hard to pick ourselves up. We would have drawn Wexford in the first round of the qualifiers and, while Tyrone just about survived it down in Wexford Park, I'm not at all sure we would have. As I say, it was all or nothing that summer.

The jibes from the Tyrone supporters about sun tans on the way into the game hardened the resolve but, deep down, we knew what would have followed had we lost. All the more so, since we had taken a three-point lead into stoppage time only to be pegged back by a goal from Sean Cavanagh.

The general view in Ulster – and beyond – after the drawn game was that the psychological edge rested with Tyrone for the replay. It was they who had rescued the day before coming so close to actually winning it and they were, of course, the form team of the year up to then.

They were the defending Ulster champions, had won the Division 1 League title for the first time and looked very much like a side on the up, whereas there were still doubts about whether Armagh could shake off the disappointments of previous seasons. Tyrone were favourites again in the replay but all week I felt that we would gain more from the game than they did. We had been in Division 2 of the League where we weren't getting the same degree of competitiveness as Tyrone were against the big boys in Division One. Now, with a real test behind us, we were ready to drive on.

Of course, it was frustrating to have conceded a late goal and be forced into a replay but it was a whole lot better than waiting for the qualifier draw. My good friend, Martin McHugh, described the replay as the second best game he had ever seen – that honour went to the 1994 Derry-Down clash – but he reckoned the Armagh-Tyrone game of 2002 came very close to matching it. To be honest, I haven't a clue whether he's right or wrong. When you're in the middle of something as tumultuous as that, it's all about the next ball, the next chance, the next score and the next scare. You don't give a damn if it's a 0-2 to 0-1 result as long as you're on the 0-2 side.

Canavan missed the replay through injury which should have been a big plus for us but the other Tyrone forwards – Stephen O'Neill in particular – shared out the responsibility and actually scored more often than we did. The difference was that we got two goals from John Mac and Barry Duffy and won by three points, 2-13 to 0-16.

It was level heading into the final ten minutes but the goal by Barry, who had come on for Ronan Clarke, settled it in our favour.

We were on our way.

There's no doubt that surviving those two games against Tyrone were the making of us. They were by far the toughest opponents any team in the country had to face in the first round and, in fairness to them, we weren't exactly the draw they would have wanted either. Whoever won that game were always going to be serious All-Ireland contenders.

It was the first instalment in a rivalry that would move to a new level over the next few years. We had six Championship clashes with Tyrone during my term as manager and it couldn't have been any closer with two wins each and two draws. Remarkably, there was only one point between us in the aggregate totals from those six games. We scored 6-67 (85pts) while they scored 2-78 (84pts). I wonder if any rivalry ever produced such an even balance in six games played over four seasons? It showed just how even the sides were in that period.

We probably brought the best out in each other but, on the other hand, we were probably a bit unlucky that the two counties had their best ever teams at exactly the same time. Otherwise, we would both have won more. Tyrone would always feel that if they had beaten us in 2002, they would have won the All-Ireland while we're equally convinced that, were it not for Tyrone, we would have won the 2003 and 2005 All-Irelands.

Anyway, it was first blood to Armagh in 2002 when we won the replay. The danger was that having spent so long building up for the Tyrone game and then having an all-out war with them for one hundred and forty minutes, we might have been vulnerable against Fermanagh in the semi-final. Fermanagh were an improving side at the time and hit poor Monaghan for 4-13 in the first round on the famous day that Rory Gallagher scored 3-9.

In a strange sort of way, he scored too much. He was the pin-up boy in the media before our game which suited us down to the ground. We put Enda McNulty on him, knowing well it was exactly the sort of challenge Enda would relish. He did more than that – Gallagher didn't score from play and we racked up the points to win comfortably.

McNulty was the ideal man for that sort of challenge: There was no better man-marker in the game and, the bigger the reputation his opponent had, the more he liked it.

Donegal were waiting for us in the final and, having beaten Down and Derry, had built up a confidence base which we knew we would have to attack as early as possible. The thing about Donegal teams is that if they get their game going and are confident in themselves, they play with a real swagger. You've got to smother them as early as you can. Let them settle into a rhythm and they'll throw the ball around and get you chasing them. That's the sort of game they love. We couldn't let that happen.

Two minutes into the game and we were a goal up. I'd love to be able to say that it was the result of a smart pre-planned move which was perfectly executed, but it wasn't. It was, in fact, down to an error by Donegal goalkeeper, Tony Blake, who seemed to get his feet wrong as a ball bounced in the square off a Diarmaid Marsden delivery. Blake only succeeded in batting the ball out and John McEntee pounced to knock it to the net.

It settled us into an early rhythm and, while Donegal came back to draw level in the first quarter, I was happy with how our overall game was shaping. In the end, we won by 1-14 to 1-10, having had to survive a scare around the hour mark when a Donegal goal pared our lead back to two points. We reacted well and had more than enough mental strength to steady things and win the last ten minutes.

Winning a provincial title is always special, irrespective of how many times you've done it. I would suggest that winning the Ulster title is the most special of all because it's the hardest to win, certainly in a year when your first game is against the reigning champions and the newly-crowned National League champions. It may have been Armagh's third Ulster title win in four years but it was still very important to savour it for what it was. After all, Armagh had only won it seven times prior to 1999 so it wasn't as if we were overly familiar with the Anglo-Celt Cup.

For all that, it was no more than a staging post. I hadn't gone in as manager just to win an Ulster title; the squad certainly weren't content with it and the mood around the county was one of expectation. In many ways, that was good. The days when Armagh people went to Croke Park hoping for the best but fearing the worst were coming to an end. Cross had shown what could be done at All-Ireland level and, with the right approach, there was no obvious reason why Armagh couldn't expand on it. Still, we were now leaving the Ulster scene and heading into territory which had proven non-negotiable over previous seasons.

We had jumped three fences but were facing three more if we were to go where no other Armagh team had gone. I would never have been the biggest fan of the 'back door' and I certainly wasn't in 2002 as it presented us with an extra game that had only been added to the circuit a year earlier.

Under the old system, we would have been straight in against Dublin in the All-Ireland semi-final but now we had to deal with Sligo, opposition with whom we weren't at all familiar. In fact, we had never played them in the Championship and wouldn't have come across them all that often in the National League either. It was later claimed that we took them for granted, which was absolute rubbish. They had beaten Tyrone in the qualifiers, having earlier launched a massive revival effort which came mighty close to reeling in Galway in the Connacht final. We would have been pretty stupid indeed to take for granted a team that had beaten the National League champions and ran the reigning All-Ireland champions very close.

Sligo have a history of producing teams that play with no fear. Even when they weren't playing consistently well, they could always throw in a really good performance. It had been their pattern for years.

I now know all about Sligo from my experiences against them during my one year with Galway in 2010 and, even back in 2002, I had a good idea that they would be very tricky quarter-final opponents for Armagh. Actually, they were a lot more than that.

To this day, I can see our All-Ireland ambitions about to evaporate into the sky over Croke Park as Dara McGarty bore down on our goal in the closing seconds. It was Tyrone all over again only, this time, we were a point ahead whereas we'd been level when Richard Thornton had kicked wide in Clones a few months earlier.

Sligo, who had a man sent off, had pared back a six-point lead and McGarty was now in the ideal position to finish it off with a goal. It seemed like an age as he came closer and closer to goal. Using all his cunning and experience, Benny Tierney stood his ground as if trying to coax McGarty into having a shot for goal. I'm sure McGarty thought about it but, just when it looked as if he was ready to pull the trigger, he decided to play the percentage game and punched the ball over the bar for the equaliser. It was an understandable decision at the time, but I often wonder does he regret not having gone for glory? Thank God he didn't because a goal at that stage would certainly have changed the course of Armagh history.

His point was the last score of the game. I don't even want to think what would have happened if he had gone for a goal but, of course, Benny has always insisted he would have saved it – "Course, I would. Isn't that what I do?"

In fairness to Benny he had read the situation well and, by holding his ground, he probably coaxed McGarty to take the match-saving certainty rather than gamble on shooting for a goal. That's what he'd have you believe anyway!

More relief, but it quickly gave way to frustration. We had the match secured at one stage in the second half but instead of pressing on and seeing it out comfortably, we had become edgy and defensive. By doing that, we invited Sligo on to us and they gladly accepted the offer and could so easily have won. I kept the lads in the dressing room for a long time afterwards. We all knew that what had happened was the direct opposite to everything we'd been working on all year. We would have to go back for a second go at Sligo.

Was the Croke Park syndrome coming back to bite us again? I refused to accept that because I never believed in it in the first place. Players, not grounds, win and lose games. No, this was all down to our own failings. Full credit to Sligo, of course, but when you're in control of a game against fourteen-man opposition, there's no excuse for tossing away the advantage and ending up relying on a lucky break at the end.

We wanted the replay in Croke Park but, for some strange reason, it ended up in Navan, which seemed a very strange venue for an Armagh-Sligo clash. Once again, we opened up a big lead – this time all the way to seven points – and, once again, Sligo came back at us.

And how. They cut the lead right back to two points and the big talking point came deep into injury time when Sligo felt they should have been awarded a penalty. McGarty slipped the ball to Sean Davey who was surrounded by our defenders in the square.

Was he fouled? Of course not! It's just that we were good at smothering opposition in that type of situation. Seriously though, I really didn't think it was a penalty but I would say that wouldn't I? Sligo were adamant that it was. They were furious with referee Seamus McCormack of Meath but, in the end, his was the only opinion that counted. I've watched the incident over and over again and I genuinely believe that our backs didn't concede a foul. We had worked on that type of defensive block and while some referees will give a free when a player is surrounded it's very often not the right decision.

In fairness to McCormack, it was a desperately close call but, as with Thornton and McGarty chances in the first Tyrone and Sligo games, the break went our way. Maybe it was destined to be our year after all. Those crucial breaks seemed to treat Armagh as a no-go area in 2000 and 2001 so maybe it was payback time. If so, we were delighted to cash in.

Despite losing a big lead, there were several aspects of our play against Sligo that we could be very happy with, especially in the replay. Paul McGrane made some brilliant catches around midfield, Steven McDonnell kicked five points from play, Ronan Clarke scored 1-2 from play while Oisin was on fire from play and frees.

We won by 1-16 to 0-17.

And yet, we had once again fallen into our old habits and allowed the opposition to not only come back at us but to damn near win the game. No question, it was a concern. If we kept that up, there was no way we would survive much longer because we were moving up in class all the time.

Tommy Lyons was in the stand in Pairc Tailteann making notes for the semi-final and I'm sure he was one happy man as he headed home that evening. Dublin had demolished Donegal in their quarter-final replay the previous day and suddenly the whole city began to dream of the All-Ireland.

Dublin had ended a long dry spell without a Leinster title and looked very much like a team with a bright future. As ever, they were surrounded by a level of hype that only Dublin can generate. Lyons was in his first season in charge and had added to the drama and excitement with his colourful personality. The new Hogan Stand had opened that year so Croke Park was now a totally different place to what it had been in previous times.

There was a time when it was felt that Dublin had an advantage playing in Croke Park but those days were gone. The old Croke Park used to be Dublin's home ground for League games so there was a sense that it was very much their personal property. They liked to give that impression, too, as Tyrone discovered in 1984 when they ran down to the Hill 16 end for the warm-up. When Dublin came out they got in among the Tyrone players, much to the amusement of the crowd. The trouble for Tyrone was that, while they made a stand before the game, it seemed to impact on their concentration and they ended up well beaten.

That's why it's important to keep things in perspective and not get drawn into anything that might prove a distraction. Inevitably, there was talk in the media beforehand about Armagh's poor record in Croke Park. We had been beaten there in 1999, 2000 and again in 2001 and we didn't exactly electrify the place against Sligo in the 2002 quarter-final either. It had nothing to do with Croke Park but the danger was if players were reminded of previous failures there it wouldn't help the cause.

Dublin were installed as favourites which suited us perfectly as it turned the pressure on them in a way they hadn't experienced before. They had built up so much momentum that summer that a lot of shrewd football people believed they were the real deal while we were regarded as being patchy and inconsistent.

That was understandable but we still managed to survive all the close calls and, while others doubted our capacity to survive the sort of heat Dublin would produce, I had no fears whatsoever about the mental strength of the squad to cope with whatever was thrown at them. Besides, how good were Dublin? What had they done to merit the label of hot favourites?

One way or the other, it would be a defining day for Armagh. The question was, could we survive Dublin's momentum when they turned on full power? The answer was yes. Paddy McKeever's goal early in the second half put us three points clear but, almost immediately, Ciaran Whelan sent a thundering shot to the net in front of Hill 16. It was the sort of inspiring score that can really lift a team and, when Dublin pulled two points ahead just past the hour mark, they looked favourites to win.

It was a position we'd been in before that season and, to be honest, I think the Tyrone and Sligo experiences stood to us. Points by Clarke and John Mac, and we were back level. Oisin put us ahead in the sixty-seventh minute but, with stoppage time, there were still five minutes to go. The tension was absolutely incredible in those closing minutes as both sides threw themselves into the contest with as much courage as they could possibly muster. Both had chances but didn't take them.

And then, deep in stoppage time, Enda McNulty was penalised – harshly in my opinion – by referee, Michael Collins. It was a free in to Dublin to be taken by Ray Cosgrove who had been in remarkable shooting form all summer. In fact, he was one of the summer sensations that year, playing with a confidence and a swagger that created the impression that he simply couldn't miss. He had already kicked six points against us so you certainly wouldn't have backed against him on this one either.

However, it was the dying seconds of an All-Ireland semi-final so the pressure was really on him. I ran out to Paul McGrane and told him to run alongside Cosgrove in his run-up to the kick. It doesn't matter whether you're playing darts or taking a free, there's always a risk you'll be distracted if you catch something out of the corner of your eye.

Cosgrove's kick looked to be headed a few yards wide but he had put a good curl on it as it sailed towards goal. Ever so gradually it began to draw around and, in those split seconds that seemed to go on forever, it hung in front of a silent Hill 16.

Then, thud!

It hit the post and bounced back out.

Still the danger persisted, but Justy McNulty jumped highest and batted the ball down to Francie Bellew who passed to John Mac. Final whistle.

All over!

Armagh were back in the All-Ireland final for the first time since 1977. Truly, a remarkable moment. I suppose I had been resigned to facing a replay when Cosgrove faced up to that free, but now it wouldn't be necessary. We had gone further than any Armagh team for twenty-five years.

My wife, Patricia, would always say that there was a greater sense of relief and emotion after winning that game than there was at the final and, in a sense, she's right. Reaching a final is such a big thing while losing a semi-final is a horrible feeling, all the more so when it's a tight finish. The Armagh boys knew what it was like from 1999 and 2000, and to lose a third one would have been absolutely devastating.

Instead, we had won in the most dramatic circumstances imaginable. It had been one hell of a three months since we began the crusade with the trip to La Manga. We had survived two replays and had now won an All-Ireland semi-final by a single point.

We had enjoyed our fair share of luck against Tyrone in the drawn games, against Sligo in both games and against Dublin, but there was a lot more to it than that. There was something about the squad ever since we had been in

La Manga that convinced me they were ready for anything.

The winning mentality that Crossmaglen had built up in the three All-Ireland wins was now buried deep in the county psyche. Question was, could it take us to where no other Armagh team had been?

Almost inevitably, Kerry awaited us in the final, having rebuilt their season through the qualifiers after losing the Munster semi-final to Cork. They were a completely different side through the back door, easily beating Wicklow, Fermanagh, Kildare, Galway and Cork to present themselves for All-Ireland duty as the hottest of favourites. The quarter-final win over Galway was especially significant. Galway were the reigning All-Ireland champions and gave themselves every chance by scoring an early goal, but Kerry took them apart from there on. They were men on a mission after what had happened to them in 2001 when Meath humiliated them in the All-Ireland semi-final by fifteen points.

Now, they were getting ready for redemption.

Losing to Armagh for the first time in the Championship was not an option, as far as Kerry were concerned. They always come to Croke Park to win finals, not to participate in them. Funny enough, that's exactly what I was thinking, too. Only it was Armagh, not Kerry that I had in mind. It was time for the final push.

CHAPTER 6
DELIVERANCE DAY

They were the longest few seconds of my entire life. The din from the Armagh supporters was setting up some nice business for ear specialists somewhere down the line but, despite the noise, the raw emotion and the colour, I felt as if I was in an isolated world shared only with Oisin McConville and Declan O'Keeffe.

Having completed a one-two with Paul McGrane down to my left heading towards the Railway End in Croke Park, Oisin is bearing down on the Kerry goal. Oisin v O'Keeffe. For the second time this afternoon, it's down to them. Nobody else counts.

It was the same in the first half when Oisin faced up to the Kerry goalkeeper from the penalty spot. O'Keeffe won that head-to-head, diverting Oisin's kick away for a save that many thought would decide the 2002 All-Ireland final. That happened just before half time and now, nineteen minutes into the second-half, the same pair are eye-balling each other again.

If Oisin wins the duel, I'm convinced we'll win the All-Ireland; if O'Keeffe wins it's probably Kerry's day.

They are four points up so, while we're back playing well, we need to make a real break. Basically, we need a goal. And now we have the chance. There's still a lot of work to be done but we have the right man on the case. It feels like an absolute eternity as Oisin strides forward, priming himself for possibly the most important kick of his career.

There's no one I'd want more in that position right now. I've known him since he was a kid and if there's one thing he doesn't lack it's self-confidence. Ever since he pulled on his first pair of football boots, Oisin believed he was the best. Cool, cocky, composed. Maybe even a touch arrogant. It's what makes good finishers in any sport the special breed they are.

Oisin, we need you now like never before.

Although he missed his penalty in the first half (or more accurately, O'Keeffe saved it) anybody who thought he might take the safe option second time around and punch the ball over the bar doesn't know Oisin.

No, he'll go for it alright.

A few more steps. He lets fly.

A whizzing drive beats O'Keeffe near the post and the ball is nestling in the Kerry net.

We're back in business. The day swings our way.

It was the first time that an Armagh player had scored a goal in an All-Ireland senior final since a certain J. Kernan whacked home two in the second half of the 1977 final against Dublin, but things were very different back then. We were chasing Dublin from a distance and, whatever we did, they did more: We got three goals, they got five; if we got five, they'd get seven. It was that sort of day. Dublin's day.

My goals were consolation efforts, pleasant at the time but never going to make any real difference to the outcome, whereas Oisin's strike was a game-changer. I glanced up at the scoreboard and then down at my stopwatch.

Kerry 0-14 Armagh 1-10; fifty-four minutes gone, sixteen to go, and we're getting stronger.

We're back in this game in a big way. The dream is on.

Suddenly, there was an amazing sense of energy around the place, a feeling that something special was about to unfold. Paidi O Se was on the sideline, gesturing wildly as he tried to connect with his players. You could see the concern on his face. You could sense, too, that the Kerry players were worried. They weren't reading from their own script any more. For the first time, there was a doubt in their minds. We had out-scored them by 1-4 to 0-3 since the thirty-second minute and also missed a penalty. We were expanding all the time and they weren't responding. This was different to anything Armagh had ever experienced before. We knew it and, equally importantly, Kerry knew it.

It wasn't what they – or most of the country – expected but it was happening right there in front of 79,500 spectators. Most people usually favour the underdog so we would have had the support of most other counties in our quest for a first All-Ireland. Still, the general view was that when the game was there to be settled, we'd come up short.

What was it my good friend, Colm O'Rourke wrote in the *Sunday Independent*? "In sport, like everything else, the cream always rises to the top. In the process, weakness is exposed, the fittest survive and class wins out. In simple terms, my belief is that Kerry have the better players in terms of pace and skill. So it's Kerry to win."

No complaints with his assessment, it was based on what he had seen up to then, but we believed the past was a different world and there was a lot more to come from our team.

Pat Spillane described the clash as Manchester United v Wimbledon: "The aristocrats against the dogged". Guess who he thought were the aristocrats? Somehow, I don't think they were wearing orange.

Wherever you looked, the view was that Kerry would be too slick for us and that their tradition of winning All-Irelands would eventually prevail. It was certainly the view in Kerry if the anonymous letter I received the week before the final was any indication.

I had received dozens of 'good luck' cards after we beat Dublin in the semi-final, which was very heartening. Armagh people all over the world were touched by the emotion which came with being back in the All-Ireland final after twenty-five years and were keen to let the players know how much they appreciated and supported them, even if they couldn't be in Croke Park for the final.

I loved opening the letters and cards because it kept reinforcing the importance to Armagh people everywhere of what we were trying to achieve as a group on behalf of our county. As usual though, somebody tried to spoil it. At first, I didn't notice the Kerry postmark on one particular letter whose writer, shall we say, wasn't in any mood to share our joyous view of where we were. It read:

Dear Joe,

   Just a note to inform you not to be too hard on your boys during training because no matter what effort you put in, it will all be in vain because our

*lads are in top form. I reckon that some of our subs alone would beat ye
hands down. The speed and accurate kicking of our boys will leave Armagh
reeling, looking after the ball, it will be going so fast. Nothing less than a
cricket score, another All-Ireland for Kerry, doom and gloom for Armagh.*

So long.

Rathmore,

Co. Kerry.

The sentiments expressed by 'Rathmore' were very much the exception
as we got lots of support messages from non-Armagh people who wanted us
to win. I don't suppose they were being anti-Kerry but, hey, this was David
against Goliath. After all, Kerry had thirty-two All-Ireland titles and poor,
old Armagh had none. Well, not just yet anyway.

That presented us with our first challenge. All-Ireland finals were nothing
new to Kerry but they were to us, so it was important that we handled it right
because otherwise we would be beaten before we even arrived in Croke Park.
I recall reading Mick O'Dwyer's account of Kildare's attempt to win the 1998
All-Ireland final and one of the points he made was that, after beating Kerry
in the semi-final, he would have loved to take the team out of the country to
some quiet destination where they could prepare in peace and return on the
day before the game.

Instead, they got caught up in the most unbelievable hype while opponents,
Galway, who, as a county, were far more used to playing in All-Ireland
finals, worked away quietly. John O'Mahony must have been delighted to
see the spotlight shine in Kildare's direction because not only was Kildare
a madhouse, they were also raging hot favourites. If the hype in Kildare in
1998 was unreal, what happened in Armagh four years later took things to a
new level.

I remember walking down the street in Cross one day and spotting a duck
painted in gaudy orange. What's more, it seemed quite happy! I half expected
it to open its beak and quack out a raucous version of the 'The Boys From
The County Armagh'.

Everywhere you went all over the county, it was the same. Sheep, cows, goats, houses, offices, cars – you name it, they were painted orange. It was as if a battalion of brush-wielding maniacs had moved in overnight after the semi-final and set about turning the whole of Armagh into an orange bowl.

It was great to see and even better to be part of because, at long last, the people of Armagh had something to savour and enjoy. God knows, we knew disappointment on the football fields and we knew upheaval and unrest during The Troubles but, at long last, we had something to feel really good about. Nobody under the age of thirty had any memories of our previous appearance in an All-Ireland final and, since the one prior to that was in 1953 – the year before I was born – it gives some idea of how rare and precious the big days were in Armagh.

It was all very exciting but it also presented us with a real test. Handle it right and we had a good chance of winning a first All-Ireland, get it wrong and we'd be forever left wondering. It wasn't easy for the players who had suddenly become celebrity figures. Tributes were being posted to them at every crossroads, poems and songs were being written and, wherever you turned, there was a sense that Armagh was alive and alight to a whole new world.

We worked with psychologists, Hugh Campbell and Des Jennings, in an effort to keep emotions under check and to recall, at all times, why we were feeling the way we were: Far from holding us back, this would take us to the next level. The key was to remember that being in the final was only part of the process. We were there not just to compete and enjoy the big day, but to win. Otherwise, it would have counted for nothing. I knew that from 1977.

This 2002 squad had a large residue of hurt from what had happened to them over the previous few years. Central to that was the memory of the two close calls against Kerry in the 2000 All-Ireland semi-final draw and replay. Essentially, our team was much the same as that which had lost to Meath, Kerry and Galway over the previous three years so they knew all about pain, misery, rejection and dejection.

Now, they had a chance of redemption but, in order to achieve it, it was crucial to get everything right in the build-up to the final. We were lucky that we had a very sensible bunch of lads who were able to separate the hype from the reality in their own minds. Just as well, because otherwise their heads would have been all over the place.

Press night was a typical example. We doubled it up with a meet-the-fans night and it turned into complete madness. Not only did every journalist in the country turn up but half of Armagh were there, too. Again, it gave the players a sense of just how important the whole thing was. Of course the danger was that, if not handled properly, it would drain them.

I knew that wouldn't be an issue for Kerry who were better used to preparing for All-Ireland finals. However, there was a positive in it for us if we could harness the energy and goodwill which the occasion had engendered among Armagh people. Also, the way we had beaten Dublin in the tightest of finishes had, I felt, provided the finishing touch. You can preach all you like about self-belief but, in the end, it's either there or it's not and it was certainly there against Dublin when we needed it most.

We had finished poorly against Sligo in both quarter-final games, sparking suggestions that we couldn't see things through to the finish and that, ultimately, we would be caught out because of it. The Dublin game changed that perception, or at least it should have. We had taken their best hits and still won, something that might not have happened in the past.

Still, we knew that Kerry would be different to Dublin. Kerry always regard All-Ireland finals as their stage, the occasion when their pedigree as the most successful football county in GAA history is used as a weapon to reinforce their own confidence and undermine the opposition.

'Rathmore' wasn't speaking for the whole of Kerry in that disparaging little note which was sent to me but I have no doubt that, deep down, the Kingdom view was that reputation – theirs as proven winners, ours as a county still waiting for a first All-Ireland – would be a factor on All-Ireland final day.

To be honest, it looked at times in the first half as if Kerry's perception might be right. We had done everything right in the build-up to the final, including travelling to Dublin the day before the game. Armagh is close enough to Dublin to travel on match morning but I didn't want the players hanging around at home on Saturday. The chances were that every house would have had fifty to one hundred well-wishers dropping in and, while done with the best of intentions, it would have been a nightmare for the players.

That was one thing we were determined to avoid. We wanted the players feeling fresher than ever by 3.30pm on Sunday. We wanted them feeling so good about themselves that by the time referee, John Bannon, was throwing in the ball, they would be primed and ready for anything. I think we succeeded, too, yet our first-half performance was poorer than it should have been.

It may have been an over-respect issue. We had talked at length about how dangerous it would be to stand off Kerry. They had run up some very big scores in the qualifiers and then hit Galway for 2-17 and Cork for 3-19 in the All-Ireland quarter-final and semi-final, so we didn't need any reminding about the threat their attack posed. Give them space and they'll destroy you. We would have to be a whole lot more secure in defence than either Galway or Cork had been.

The strange thing was that, while we might have expected to be a bit tentative in the opening period, we did well enough until the second quarter. We headed into it leading by a point and came out of it at half time trailing by four points, having been out-scored 0-7 to 0-2. Kerry completely outshone us in that period. They were getting their passes away quickly and accurately, they seemed sharper to the breaking ball and built up a rhythm which we couldn't match. And, on top of that, we missed a penalty. Those who fancied Kerry to be too smart for us would have thought their views fully vindicated.

And yet, there were little things that showed we still had the right attitude. Enda McNulty won one ball by his finger tips which, if it had beaten him, would have almost certainly resulted in a goal as Colm Cooper was lurking just behind him. The thing was though, Enda read it right, won the ball and averted the danger. He was still attacking the ball, rather than hanging in behind his man and playing the percentage game. It's the only way to play Kerry.

Much has been made about speeches and throwing a plaque against the wall at half time but, in the end, it came down to whether the players were good enough to turn things around in the second half. Diarmaid Marsden had scored the final point of the first half to cut the margin to just four points (0-11 to 0-7), which was very important.

From a psychological viewpoint, there's a world of difference between a four-point margin compared to say, six or seven. I always thought that Marsden's point just before the break was crucial as it meant we finished the half strongly which was something we always tried to do. Effectively, we had finished on a high rather than a low. The heads hadn't dropped but then much of our work all year had focused on that aspect of our game.

It was, as we always stressed, another crucial inch in getting us to where we were trying to go. An inch here, an inch there – they all add up in the end. We had taken our cue from the movie, 'Any Given Sunday' and the famous address by Tony D'Amato, coach to the Sharks, an American football team.

Even if you knew nothing about sport, this would inspire you. We used to play it on the team coach, timing it to end just as we arrived in the car park. To this day, it puts the hair standing on the back of my head when I listen to Al Pacino's famous delivery.

It lasted three minutes, with the closing lines as follows:

"Now, I can't make you do it.

"You gotta look at the guy next to you, look into his eyes.

"Now I think you're gonna see a guy who will go that inch with you … you're gonna see a guy who will sacrifice himself for this team … because he knows that when it comes down to it … you're gonna do the same for him.

"That's a team, gentlemen … and either we heal now, as a team … or we will die as individuals.

"That's football guys.

"That's all it is. Now, what are you gonna do?"

We tried everything we could to give us a little edge all the time. At half time in the semi-final against Dublin, I produced my All-Ireland jersey from the 1977 All-Ireland final. I had almost swapped it with Brian Mullins at the end of that game but thought better of it. It was his fourth final so he had plenty of jerseys, but I wanted to hold onto mine. I didn't think it would be the only one I'd get but I held onto it all the same.

It came in handy against Dublin in 2002. I was able to show it to the lads and tell them that's what they were playing for. You can't win a final until you're in it so the first priority was to get there.

We tried other little gimmicks too.

In the run-up to the final, our psychologists, Hugh and Des came up with the idea of getting a letter from Muhammad Ali, wishing the squad the best of luck. They contacted Ali's people and, sure enough, the letter arrived, which we then photocopied. Early on the morning of the game, we shoved a copy under the players' bedroom doors so that when they got up they were greeted with a letter from Muhammad Ali, no less. It was something else for them to talk about and ease the tension.

Having shown my 1977 All-Ireland final jersey to the lads at half time in the semi-final, I had to come up with something different for the final. I talked it over with Eamonn Mackle and we came up with a plan. I had received a plaque after the 1977 final and while it was a nice memento of the occasion, it still represented defeat. Eamonn had bought an All-Ireland medal at an auction somewhere so we brought along both the plaque and the medal.

I showed them the plaque. I talked of having it for twenty-five years.

I said I didn't want them looking back in twenty-five years time with nothing to show for playing in the All-Ireland final except a loser's plaque. I hurled the plaque against the wall and pulled out the All-Ireland medal that Eamonn had acquired.

"Boys, this is what you want and it's there for you. Just go out and make sure you each have one at the end of the game."

After putting so much into the whole year, we were heading for the final push. By the time we were all back in the dressing room again, we would either be All-Ireland champions or dejected losers. I knew how the latter felt and I certainly didn't want those players to experience it. Only they could ensure that they didn't. They were about to head out for thirty-five minutes of action which would define their careers.

I felt that if we could get the first point of the second half it might just steady things. It wouldn't put a major doubt in Kerry's minds but it would ensure that we keep on believing in our ability to get the job done. It would also keep us in position for a big drive later on.

We had a few early scares but Mike Frank Russell missed two good chances before Marsden popped up to kick a precious point. Our game improved from there on, but we were still four points behind until Oisin hit what was probably the most important goal in Armagh history. What happened from there on was truly remarkable. The intensity was unbelievable as, ever so gradually, we began to squeeze the resistance out of Kerry. It's never an easy thing to do – and certainly not in an All-Ireland final – but, inch by inch, move by move, tackle by tackle, the lads managed it. They were playing Kerry as equals, not as hopeful contenders against the masters. They believed their time had come, because it had.

The equalising point typified the new Armagh.

Geezer delivered the ball to Ronan Clarke who turned Seamus Moynihan inside out before scoring. It was some sight. Moynihan, Footballer of the Year in 2000 and one of the best defenders of his generation, yet here he was being beaten by a nineteen-year-old in his first season.

Ronan took his big chance to make a name for himself after Tony Mac got injured in the first game against Tyrone and turned into the find of the season. His youthfulness probably helped him in the All-Ireland final because he had no fear of anybody or anything. He scored three superb points which was some achievement against Moynihan. His third point brought us level with eleven minutes to go and, although nobody knew it at the time, there would be only one more point in the game.

It came our way in the sixty-second minute when Stevie McDonnell angled a delightful kick over the bar. The delivery from Aidan O'Rourke to Stevie was the pass of the Championship. It was beautifully weighted away from the defender and Stevie did the rest.

We're ahead! It's there for us!

The door was open to Armagh for the first time in history. Could we go through it?

It was at this stage that the gruelling work we had put in all year took on huge significance. It left us feeling we could cope with anything. We battled for everything in the air, on the ground or wherever else it was necessary. This was open warfare with both sides deploying their full range of artillery. I remember one incident near the end where the ball was bouncing between several players, almost ping-pong style. It hit a hand here, an elbow there, a shoulder somewhere else as several players tried to grab it but, in the end,

Paul McGrane won it. I turned to the boys behind me on the sideline and said: "We have it."

There was something about that moment that captured the Armagh mood. You could sense it in the Kerry players that they hadn't expected this. And how could they have, especially after going so well in the first half? They should have been much further ahead at half time but, even though they weren't, they would have expected to build on their earlier superiority. It's what Kerry believe they can do in finals. Now, they were trailing by a point and facing a force never before experienced against Armagh.

For all that, they came mighty close to grabbing the equaliser. Just as I can so vividly recall Oisin bearing down on Declan O'Keeffe before scoring our goal, I can still see Eoin Brosnan galloping into a shooting position at the Canal End.

Jesus Christ, lads, where are ye, how has he got so much space? What's happened?

Brosnan wound himself up for what looked certain to be the levelling point. The kick seemed to be on its way between the posts but then, as if blown by the collective breath of every Armagh person in Croke Park – and indeed all over the world – the ball veered wide.

There was still well over two minutes' stoppage time to go but that was to prove Kerry's last big chance. The referee played three minutes and sixteen seconds added time, which appeared to me to be more like an hour. I was screaming at John Bannon to blow it up but he had to play to his watch, even if it did seem to be ticking unbelievably slowly.

Jesus Christ, John … has it stopped altogether?

Then, Justy McNulty attacked the ball, broke it to Tony Mac who passed to Geezer. At last, the final whistle.

The game was over.

I'm sure Justy thought back to the previous year when he had his kick blocked down against Galway when it looked as if Armagh would win that crucial qualifier game. Of course his character was never in doubt and he still had the courage to make that vital touch late in the All-Ireland final when a lesser man might have held back. Not Justy. That's the way he was. Brave and honest all the time.

Armagh were All-Ireland champions for the first time. Deliverance day had arrived. For a few seconds, I felt as if I was on my own, surrounded solely by a serene ocean of relief but, of course, it didn't last long. Suddenly, the hordes arrived in an orange torrent to begin the celebrations that would go on for months.

It's amazing the emotions you experience in a situation like that. It was the most precious moment of my sporting life, yet I couldn't resist telling one particular Armagh fan what I thought of him when he came bounding over to me with out-stretched arms, face beaming in delight. He was full of the joys of the day but I knew that he had spent all year ridiculing Francie Bellew and bad-mouthing me for playing him. He contended that Francie was an ordinary club player and I was playing him only because he was from Crossmaglen. Now that we'd won the All-Ireland, we were all great guys but I knew damn well that if we'd lost he would have been the first man to blame me. Francie would have got a lash, too. I have no time for that sort of person and I let him know in no uncertain terms, even as the bedlam went off all around us. The Armagh fan was a bit taken aback, but I didn't give a damn. I knew what he'd been saying all year, so I wanted nothing to do with him or his hollow congratulations.

It seems strange that I should have been thinking this way at such a special time but I hate hypocrisy. Anyway, it was all over in a second and I got down to the real business of enjoying the wonderful moments. I knew what it was like to stand in Croke Park as a player and watch the opposition take Sam Maguire so now I was trying to take in the incredible sense of satisfaction felt by every Armagh person, at home and abroad. We'd been through a lot over the years but that didn't matter any more.

What made our success all the sweeter was that we'd beaten Kerry and Dublin – the big two in All-Ireland terms – in the semi-final and final. There could be no question marks against our right to be All-Ireland champions. It should never arise anyway because the team that wins the All-Ireland is the team that deserves it but, quite often, you'll hear jibes about how a team won the All-Ireland without playing X or Y.

I didn't hear from 'Rathmore' again – I wonder why? – but I'd have to say that everybody from Kerry that I did come across was very gracious in defeat.

It was the same with the Dubs when we beat them in the semi-final, in fact some of their supporters clapped us down the road as we headed for home which was a nice gesture.

What happens after an All-Ireland final becomes a bit of a blur for the winners – well, it did for us anyway – but it's no less special for that. It got so crazy on the pitch that I climbed up the steps of the Hogan Stand just to savour the moment and watch the sea of orange swaying in front of us. The players came up the steps, one by one, and I suppose it was then that I fully realised what we had all achieved together.

I had played my part but the success was all about the players. These were the lads who people claimed wouldn't quite make it in the end, the lads who had endured the disappointment of losing their first All-Ireland semi-final in 1999, the misery of being edged out by Kerry in extra-time a year later and the sheer horror of completing a Croke Park losing hat trick against Galway just fourteen months earlier.

Finally, it had all come right in the most dramatic circumstances imaginable. We had not only won the All-Ireland but laid to rest the Croke Park bogey once and for all. One-point wins over Dublin and Kerry – not many Armagh people ever thought they would see it happen.

Those who were lucky enough to be in Croke Park that day certainly enjoyed it and, as I would learn over the coming weeks and months, Armagh people all over the world were united in a common bond that spanned international boundaries and date lines.

Back in Croke Park, it was just sheer madness. Patricia and all our sons, except Paul, managed to get down the tunnel and into the relative safety of the dressing room area. We have a lovely picture of Patricia, Tony, Stephen, Ross, Aaron and me with the Sam Maguire Cup in the tunnel, but there's no Paul. The lads got separated in the throngs during the presentation but four of them managed to nudge through the Garda cordon. They told them they were my sons and, in fairness, the Gardai let them through but, by the time Paul arrived, they were getting a bit suspicious – Another Kernan? How many sons has Joe Kernan got?

Paul couldn't convince them of who he was so he was stuck on the outside for a while. Luckily, Benny Tierney went out to meet somebody and managed to bring Paul in but, I'm afraid, he's not in the picture.

The next thirty-six hours really were mayhem. Sunday night in the Citywest Hotel ... the atmosphere ... the craic ... the sheer sense that God was in his heaven toasting Armagh's success. The homecoming on the Monday night was everything it could be and a whole lot more.

One funny incident from the return home was that we left Citywest without Paddy McKeever. We couldn't find Paddy anywhere and, wherever he was, he probably thought we wouldn't go without him. In the end, we had to leave him behind and head for the Carrickdale Hotel but, when we arrived, there was Paddy – he'd taken a taxi and got there before the rest of us. I don't know whether he billed the County Board for it but, if he did, I hope they paid up. It's not every day you win an All-Ireland title.

It wouldn't be the last time that we left without a player. After the 2005 Ulster final replay win over Tyrone in Croke Park, we pulled out without our Aaron. I had a rule that if the bus was supposed to leave at a certain time then it left, so it was up to everybody to be there on time. For some reason, Aaron got delayed in the players' lounge and, since mobile phone reception is unreliable in parts of Croke Park, we left without him. He made contact with his uncle, Gerard Morgan, who brought him home. Aaron wasn't best pleased but rules are rules whether or not you're the manager's son.

If we could leave without Paddy McKeever after the 2002 All-Ireland final, we'd leave without anyone. Paddy saw the funny side of it, eventually, but then Monday, September 23, 2002 was a special day for Armagh people, one which wasn't going to be ruined by anything. I suppose, for me, the highlight was coming back home to Crossmaglen, my town, my home, the place I had lived all my life. Only, now, we had a special guest in our midst in the form of Sam Maguire.

Who would have thought, all those years ago when Armagh football seemed to be at nothing, that the great day would come? Now, in the space of five years, Crossmaglen had won three All-Ireland club titles and Armagh were All-Ireland champions. It really was as good as it gets.

The next few months passed in a mad whirl of celebrations, functions, travelling, presentations and award ceremonies. This was all new to Armagh so everybody wanted a piece of the action. It was very enjoyable but it was exhausting, too. We could have been out every day and night of the week if we had accepted even half of the invitations that arrived from inside and outside Armagh.

One of the most special days that I still treasure was when Gene Duffy and I took the Sam Maguire Cup to Daisy Hill hospital in Newry. Gene organised it and, to be honest, neither of us knew what lay ahead. We thought it would be a matter of bringing in the cup for half an hour or so but, instead, it turned into a four-hour session.

The normal routine of the hospital was totally disrupted by the arrival of Sam. All ages from the oldest down to very young children turned our visit into a splendid occasion which, personally, I found very fulfilling. Catholic, Protestant ... they all joined in and it didn't matter a damn whether or not you were from Armagh – this was a chance to share in the joy of a big success and the patients and staff of Daisy Hill certainly did that in style.

It was a day of laughter and tears as people let their emotions flow. There was something incredibly warm about it and I remember turning to Gene as we left the hospital, saying, "Wasn't that really something?"

Once the county Championships were completed, most of the players could relax and enjoy the celebrations but Crossmaglen had, once again, won the Armagh title so it was straight into an Ulster campaign. Their quarter-final clash with Errigal Ciaran of Tyrone turned into a marathon three-game affair with Errigal winning the second replay by three points. It was always going to be tough on the Cross boys who had been on the Armagh squad, but it showed just how dogged they were that they still came so close to beating Errigal, especially in the first two games. In the end, they lost out and while Cross would always be disappointed not to keep the club run going, I'm sure there was a sense of relief, too, among some of the lads. After all, it had been some year.

It was difficult to keep track of Sam Maguire in the weeks that followed the All-Ireland but there was one night that I had him booked in as a special guest. His only commitment on New Year's Eve was to be in the Kernan house to ring in the New Year.

Myself in the 1977 All-Ireland final. It was heartbreaking to lose to Dublin, but we could have no complaints. The Armagh team, back row, left to right, Peter Trainor, Sean Devlin, Larry Kearns, Brian McAlinden, Tom McCreesh, Colm McKinstry, Kevin Rafferty, front row, left to right, Noel Marley, Denis Stevenson, Joe Kernan, Jimmy Smyth, Paddy Moriarty, Jim McKerr, John Donnelly, Peter Loughran. All-Ireland GAA Senior Football Championship Final, Dublin v Armagh, Croke Park, Dublin.

The 1979 Ulster Railway Cup team. There were seven Armagh players in the team including Sean Devlin, Paddy Moriarty, Denis Stevenson, Peter Loughran (RIP), Jimmy Smyth and Brian McAlinden. I'm third from the left in the front row.

My parents, Joe and Joan Kernan.

A family photo with (l – r) me, my sister Annette, Mum, my late brother Raymond, my brother Patrick and my sister Olivia.

Trying times. A British Army helicopter hovers over Crossmaglen Rangers' pitch during the occupation which lasted for many years. It was a tough time for everyone but out of that adversity was born a determination which served Cross well on the pitch.

In 1975, I was lucky enough to be captain of the Crossmaglen Rangers team which won the Armagh Senior County Championship. On the left is Larry Kearns getting the Man of the Match award – on the right is my 'tache!

The lads were always great man-markers. (L-r) Tony, me, Paul, Aaron, with Stephen at the bottom.

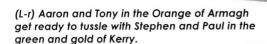

(L-r) Aaron and Tony in the Orange of Armagh get ready to tussle with Stephen and Paul in the green and gold of Kerry.

(L-r) Aaron holds the ball while Tony sits on Ger Power's knee and Stephen wears a Kerry jersey Ger brought for the lads. Anytime Kerry played against a Northern team, Ger would always come and visit our house.

In 1995, after the ROI v England International was abandoned following rioting by some English fans, we met Vinnie Jones in a Dublin hotel. Vinnie did his best to repair relations between the two countries by spending all evening with us, and insisted on paying for our dinner.

Sibling rivalry! Aaron and Stephen battle it out despite not even having a ball!

Stephen shows me how it's done in the run-up to the 1985 National League final against Monaghan.

Myself, Crossmaglen captain Benny Cassidy and Arthur McAvoy with Brian and Declan Smyth. Brian was a very special Cross supporter who has sadly since passed away.

The 1984 All Star team which was managed by Dublin's Jimmy Gray. I'm fifth from the left in the back row.

Playing on a star-studded Cavan team against Tyrone in the New York Championship in 1985. Also aboard were Paidi O Se, Mike Sheehy, John L. McElligott, Ger O'Keeffe, Ger Power, John Egan (all Kerry), Michael Dempsey (Laois) and Gerry Carroll (Offaly).

Big Apple but a small world. I share a laugh with Michael Dempsey (Laois) after the Cavan v Tyrone game in 1985. Michael is now doing a great job as one of Brian Cody's right-hand men in Kilkenny.

Start them young.
Stephen and Aaron
keep me company in
the pre-match parade
for the 1986 county
final. Jim McConville
is behind me and our
third team mascot,
Oisin McConville, is
behind him.

Heartbreak.
My last game
with Armagh
ended in defeat
against Derry in
the 1987 Ulster
final. Aaron and
Stephen share the
disappointment.

Getting kitted out for the 1977 All-
Ireland final against Dublin. (L-r)
Gerry Fagan (County Secretary),
Paddy Moriarty (team-mate), myself,
John O'Reilly (County Chairman),
Jimmy Smyth (team captain) and Joe
Canning (County Treasurer).

A major celebration dinner at the Carrickdale Hotel, featuring the Crossmaglen team that won the 1999 All-Ireland title.

With old friends and good judges. I celebrate with Ollie McEntee and Donal McKenna at a presentation occasion following Crossmaglen's first All-Ireland win in 1997.

Helping the Cross lads in 1997 – what a year!

I hear ye! Myself and Ross after Cross won the 1997 All-Ireland club final.

The team that beat Na Fianna to win the 2000 Club title.

Patricia and I celebrate the 2000 club win.

Patricia and myself with Denis Law at the 2000 Belfast Telegraph Awards in the Europa Hotel, Belfast.

Three heads are better than one. I take advice from 'Banty' (Seamus McEnaney) and former Derry great, Tony Scullion, while managing Ulster in the 2009 Interprovincial final in Ruislip.

The 2007 and 2011 Crossmaglen teams which won the All-Ireland Senior Club titles.

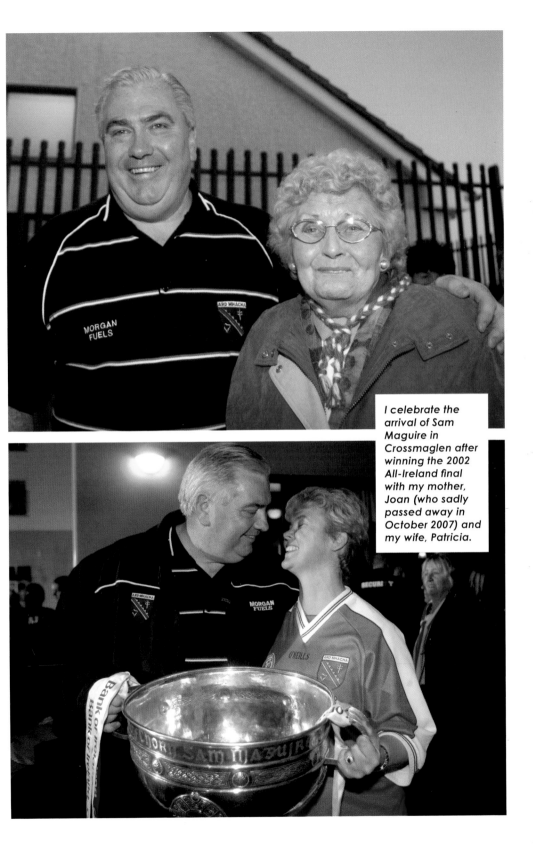

I celebrate the arrival of Sam Maguire in Crossmaglen after winning the 2002 All-Ireland final with my mother, Joan (who sadly passed away in October 2007) and my wife, Patricia.

I'm flanked by Stephen and Aaron after Armagh beat Donegal in the 2004 Ulster final. It was a special occasion as the game was played in Croke Park.

What goes up… After the euphoria of winning Ulster in 2004, we were dumped out of that year's All-Ireland quarter-final by Fermanagh and I had to console my son, Ross, who was learning a tough lesson about the downs of football.

Stephen, Aaron and their club and county team-mate, Michael McNamee, raise the All-Ireland U-21 trophy in 2004.

The lads with the rest of the 2004 All-Ireland winning Armagh U-21 team.

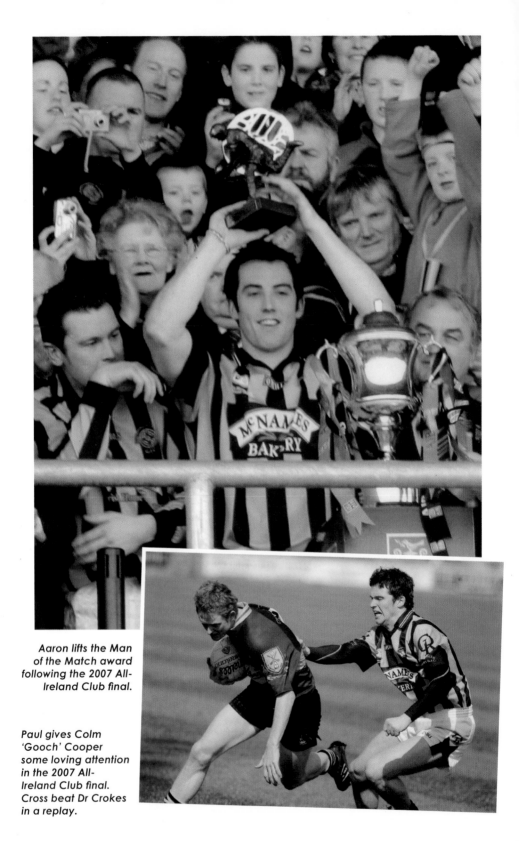

Aaron lifts the Man of the Match award following the 2007 All-Ireland Club final.

Paul gives Colm 'Gooch' Cooper some loving attention in the 2007 All-Ireland Club final. Cross beat Dr Crokes in a replay.

I had the All-Ireland runners-up plaque but my great pal, Eamonn Mackle, produced an All-Ireland medal to show the lads at half time in the 2002 final.

Celebrating with Sam and my life-long friends and former team-mates, Thomas and Benny Cassidy.

There's no better way to round off the week than talking football over a Sunday night pint with Joe Teggart and Gene Duffy in John Fearon's pub in Crossmaglen.

Staunch Orangemen! Paddy and John McParland who run the Canal Court and Carrickdale Hotels and who have been huge supporters of the 'Armagh Project'.

Myself and Patricia enjoy a meal during a break to New York with my friend and lifetime Crossmaglen Rangers supporter, Kevin Keegan, and his wife, Jerry.

The lads with their partners – two have already signed, so just three more to go! (L-r) Claire, Stephen, Maebh, Paul, Aaron with the latest Mrs Kernan, Marianne, Patricia, myself, Tony, Sinead and Ross and Emma.

Four of the lads pose at Aaron's wedding in Clare on September 10, 2011. (L-r) Aaron, Tony, Paul and Stephen.

My cousin and International showjumper James Kernan in the Rangers' hall with Tony, Stephen, Aaron and Paul after the 2011 All-Ireland Club Final.

Four of the best. Stephen, Paul, Aaron and Tony with the Armagh, Ulster and All-Ireland trophies, all won between October 2010 and March 2011. Between myself (as player and manager) and the four lads, we'd been involved with Crossmaglen teams which won 37 Armagh Senior titles, 21 Ulster titles and 11 All-Ireland titles up to October 1, 2011.

It was a wonderful occasion. All of Patricia's family were there and we had all our friends and neighbours, too, plus the crowd from Fearon's bar. Truly a night to remember and all in the company of Sam Maguire.

I wanted the Cup with me that night to end 2002 on the highest note possible and to look forward to the start of 2003. By New Year's Day, we were talking about having won the All-Ireland title "last year". Already, there was a new challenge on the wind. It was one I believed we were ready for because the squad were still relatively young and, having finally made the All-Ireland breakthrough, they would have a new sense of wellbeing and confidence which had to be of considerable benefit. Yes, there were lots of challengers out there but none that we felt we couldn't handle if we avoided injury and built on the momentum of the remarkable year we had just lived through.

It still angers me when I think about it.

A man puts his heart and soul into being the best he can, strives to the very limit to achieve his target, yet has his world turned upside down in circumstances over which he has absolutely no control.

I've seen a lot on the football fields of Crossmaglen, Armagh, Ulster and beyond in over forty years involved at a high level and I have to say that nothing ever annoyed or frustrated me more than what happened to Diarmaid Marsden in the 2003 All-Ireland final. I'll say it straight – his dismissal fifteen minutes from the end of the game against Tyrone cost Armagh the title.

I haven't a doubt in the world that if Diarmaid had been there over that crucial finishing stretch, Armagh would have won the two-in-a-row. Now, if he had done something that warranted a dismissal we could live with it.

Do the crime, do the time and all that.

In this case, there was no crime but plenty of time. Well, certainly enough to sway what, unsurprisingly, had been a tight, tense game where inches were always going to be crucial. Instead of having Diarmaid's intelligent presence menacing the Tyrone defence on the run-in, we were down to fourteen men after he had been sent off by referee, Brian White of Wexford.

It happened like this.

Tyrone wing-back Philip Jordan ran at Diarmaid who instinctively put up his arm in self defence. Jordan went down as if he'd been hit by a crowbar, the Tyrone crowd starting baying for Armagh blood and suddenly Diarmaid was in the referee's firing line.

If White saw the incident clearly, I have no idea how he could have sent Diarmaid off on a straight red card, which implied he had been guilty of striking. Was the ref serious? A guy is running straight at you and you're supposed to stand there with your hands down by your sides and take what's coming? Would Brian White do that if somebody ran at him? I don't think so. Our view was that Jordan was the aggressor and Diarmaid was merely defending himself which is one of the most basic human instincts.

If White saw the incident clearly, sending off Diarmaid was a strange decision and if he was in any way unable to see how could he wave red? Diarmaid's cause wasn't helped by Jordan's lengthy spell getting treatment. Funnily enough, Jordan seemed fine for the rest of the game so there couldn't have been that much damage done, and, even if there was, Jordan would have to answer the question – why did he run straight at Diarmaid in the first place?

I have to say, too, that I was disgusted by the actions of at least one Tyrone player who mockingly clapped Diarmaid off the pitch. There's an honour among players – or at least there should be – and to see a man gloating at an opponent's bad luck in an All-Ireland final is something I could never understand. It's not the GAA where I was brought up or one I ever want to be part of. Those Tyrone players who were close to the incident knew full well that Diarmaid should not have been sent off.

The strange thing was that Diarmaid might not have been on the pitch at all at that stage. He had to come off with a head injury in the first half and had only returned five or six minutes before being sent off. The man was distraught afterwards. He knew he had done nothing wrong but now had to live with being sent off in an All-Ireland final on a day when his side lost by a single score.

In playing terms, it meant he would miss the first game of the 2004 Ulster Championship but, in real terms, it had placed a black mark against his name which had to be challenged, even if it might have looked look like no big deal to outsiders. The All-Ireland was over, Tyrone had won and while Diarmaid would miss one game in the 2004 Championship it was months away.

Back in Armagh, we viewed things very differently. We were furious that he had been wronged. Meanwhile, Diarmaid was conscious of the fact that, among other things, his little girl, Lara, who was too young to understand at the time, might ask him in years to come why was he sent off in an All-Ireland final. He could explain as much as he wanted that it was an injustice but the record books would show otherwise unless he had his name cleared.

I was surprised we had to go down that route. If Brian White had taken a look at the video afterwards he would surely have seen the incident in a different light. Brian was one of the most experienced referees in the business at the time and was well used to big occasions, including All-Ireland finals, having officiated at Kerry v Mayo in 1997 and Galway v Kerry in 2000.

He didn't change his view of the incident between the end of the game and writing his report but, even then, you would have thought that the Games Administration Committee might have decided in favour of Diarmaid on the basis of video evidence. But, no, he was suspended and we had no option but to set about having it overturned. The final port of call in that frustrating process was Central Council and, to their credit, they acknowledged that an injustice had been done. The suspension was struck out and while it was of no value to us or Diarmaid in footballing terms, it at least cleared a good man's name which was very important to everybody.

So, how can I be so convinced that we would have beaten Tyrone if Diarmaid had still been on-board? Check back on the 2002 All-Ireland semi-final against Dublin, when did we perform best? Over the final fifteen minutes. The 2002 All-Ireland final against Kerry? Same story. The All-Ireland qualifier against Dublin just over two months before the 2003 final? The All-Ireland semi-final against Donegal? Again, we finished very strongly every time. By now, it had become one of our trump cards.

We had been accused, understandably, of having problems seeing games through to the end after two close calls in the 2002 All-Ireland quarter-finals against Sligo but it was something we had sorted out. By September 2003, we felt we could out-grind anybody over the final ten to fifteen minutes.

For all their resolve and resilience, that included Tyrone.

Mickey Harte has acknowledged that they recognised our ability to finish games very strongly and were determined to match us. The thing is, though, when it came down to that final heave, they had fifteen men pushing together whereas we, through no fault of our own, had only fourteen. That's one hell of a difference in a game which was played with an incredible intensity from start to finish.

In the end, a mere total of twelve points won it, which shows how hard it was to create openings on that particular day. Only once in the previous twenty years (Cork 0-11 Meath 0-9 in 1990) had such a low score been enough to win an All-Ireland final. But then, it was always going to be that way because, by September 2003, there wasn't much that Armagh and Tyrone didn't know about each other. It was the fifth time – including one replay – the counties had met since 2000 and, while both had changed managers along the way, many of the players had been involved in all the games.

We started slowly in the final and were four points down after sixteen minutes, and three behind at half time. We hadn't converted enough of our chances into scores and much the same pattern continued in the third quarter when we again fell four points behind.

We pared it back to three and then Diarmaid marked his return to the fray with an excellent point. Tyrone went three up at the three-quarter mark but I still felt quite confident that we would raise our game on the home stretch and wear them down. We were good at that and, besides, we knew we could do it after our experience against Kerry the year before. We were ready to drive on but Diarmaid's dismissal changed everything.

Psychologically, it was a huge lift for Tyrone to see him on his way to the bench. He had been our third highest scorer in that year's Championship, behind Stevie McDonnell and Oisin McConville, and would have been a key presence in that mad scramble to the finishing line.

Instead, he was a forlorn figure on the bench. Everyone still talks of Conor Gormley's brilliant block on Stevie McDonnell as he let fly for what would have been the equalising goal late on and, while there's no doubt it was crucial, I still hold it was not as important as Diarmaid's dismissal. Fair play to Gormley, it was brilliant play and he was rewarded for it. Unfortunately for us, good play had nothing to do with the circumstances which handed Tyrone such an important advantage when Diarmaid was sent off. Neither, it must be said, had fair play.

Don't get me wrong, I didn't in any way begrudge Tyrone their success. If we weren't to win the All-Ireland, it was great to see Sam Maguire coming to another Ulster county, especially one which, like ourselves, had waited so long to make the breakthrough. What made it hard for us to stomach was that we hadn't been given a fair chance to slug it out with Tyrone to decide who was better on the day.

Of course, there are many who would say we were lucky to be in the final at all. This was only the third season the 'back door' was open and we availed of it to revive our Championship season after being beaten by Monaghan in the preliminary round in Ulster. I would have had mixed views on the introduction of the qualifiers in 2001 but I was damn glad of them on that May evening two years later when Monaghan beat us.

We were badly hampered by injuries at the time and started without Kieran McGeeney, Enda McNulty, Ronan Clarke and Oisin McConville of our All-Ireland winning side and, while the latter two came on, they weren't anywhere near at full power. It meant disruptions in four of the five outfield lines and, while we prided ourselves in having a strong squad as well as a strong team, that was still a serious hit.

We hadn't been able to get any decent rhythm going all day and Monaghan exploited that with great efficiency. Colm Coyle was in charge of them at the time and had them really fired up for the game, which was to be expected. After all, Colm knew a thing or two about local wars after the many Meath-Dublin battles he had been involved in as a player. Monaghan had known the draw for months and would have relished every training session that took them closer to a clash with the All-Ireland champions. Even when they had a man sent off early in the second half, it made no great difference to the flow of the game. It was that sort of day. Monaghan were switched on to its demands while we weren't. In those circumstances an extra man wasn't going to make any difference. We lost 0-13 to 0-9 and couldn't have had a single complaint. Monaghan wanted it more than we did proving, once again, that desire has a huge influence on any game.

Injuries apart, our form had dipped in the second half of the 2003 League which was probably to be expected. We had all been on a hectic round of functions, celebrations, holidays and All Star trips up until January and, while we couldn't wait to get back on the field, there were probably always going to be consequences, somewhere along the way.

The effects tend not be apparent early in the League because All-Ireland champions almost always begin the new season with a swagger. We had an added incentive to start well because the GAA decided to launch the League with an Armagh-Dublin clash in Croke Park. It was a great idea. We wanted to get back to Croke Park to re-live the great days of the previous year and maybe even to show off a bit, while Dublin were mad keen to sink us. Deep down, they felt that they – not we – should have been All-Ireland champions.

The game was played on a bitterly cold Sunday in early February but still attracted 55,000 people. The atmosphere was more like a big Championship game than a League opener and, I have to say, we really enjoyed it, not least because we gave an exhibition. There's something about playing Dublin in Croke Park that really gets the adrenaline flowing. A huge crowd is always guaranteed and, with it, a special atmosphere. Tommy Lyons, who was managing them at the time, had the knack of hyping things up and, with memories of the All-Ireland semi-final clash still fresh in everybody's mind, even neutrals turned out that day.

We won by 1-15 to 0-7, having completely dominated the second half. Tony McEntee was outstanding, turning in one of those remarkable performances that he did so often. I often felt guilty about how we used poor old Tony to fill in wherever a gap appeared but he was so versatile, we could have played him anywhere from No. 2 to No. 15. Very few players can do that. He had an uncanny capacity to win balls that others wouldn't and to get his body in the way of opponents at exactly the right moment.

He controlled Croke Park in that League game against Dublin which was great to see because, despite winning an All-Ireland medal, the 2002 Championship had been a bit of a disappointment for him. He missed most of it after breaking his ankle in the first round against Tyrone and, although he came on in the final, it was frustrating for him not to have been more actively involved in that great odyssey.

I always thought it a great shame that neither of the McEntee brothers won All Star awards. Tony deserved one for his versatility alone and how John went through all those years without being selected is beyond me. In my view, John should definitely have been the All Star centre-forward in 2002. Instead, it went to Sligo's Eamonn O'Hara, a great player and an outstanding servant to his county, but in 2002 he played mostly as a midfielder, yet got the All Star at centre-forward. That might have been okay had there been no outstanding candidate for centre-forward but there most definitely was. John McEntee scored 2-9 from play in the Championship as well as being consistently good in other aspects but still missed out on an All Star award.

It was suggested afterwards that the reason he wasn't selected was because he had to go off injured in the first half of the All-Ireland final so, naturally, he hadn't made as much of an impact as would normally have been the case. The point was that he had done more than enough to win the All Star in the run up to the final but that was obviously forgotten. Besides, O'Hara didn't play in either the semi-final or final. Good luck to the Sligo man, it was great for him to win an award but he was a candidate for midfield that year, not centre-forward.

However, with midfield going to Paul McGrane and Darragh O Se, O'Hara was moved into attack and John lost out. There were other years, too, when I felt John was hard done by in the All Star selections. I know every manager will look favourably at his own players but I would still argue that John McEntee should not have ended his career without an All Star.

We started 2003 in excellent form but didn't maintain it. Our early momentum saw us take full League points against Dublin, Cork, Donegal and Roscommon but then we lost to Tyrone, Galway and Kerry. It turned out to be one of those years when eight points was enough to qualify for the National League semi-finals (we beat off Cork and Kerry on scoring difference) where we met Laois, who were on their revival kick under Mick O'Dwyer. They beat us, too, leaving us going into the Championship off four successive defeats, which wasn't exactly how we had planned it. I was unhappy with the way our performance levels had dropped but, at the same time, wasn't unduly perturbed at being eliminated from the League because, had we qualified for the final, it would have been on the Sunday before our Ulster Championship clash with Monaghan.

That was bizarre planning by the GAA and thankfully doesn't happen any more but, in 2003, the final was fixed for May 4 and we were due to play Monaghan on May 11. Luckily, it didn't make any difference in the end because we lost to Monaghan anyway.

I put on the bravest possible face for the media afterwards but, inside, I was burning up. We were still in the Championship but things had changed dramatically. That aura of invincibility which we had hard-wired into every thought process over the previous fifteen months was gone. From now on, every opposition would view us differently. The respect which being All-Ireland champions brings wouldn't be there any more. They'd see us as being vulnerable, especially after losing to a Monaghan team that hadn't done anything especially noteworthy in Division 2 that year.

Normally, we'd slip quietly down the hill from St Tiernach's Park and away to the left out of Clones but this time I told the bus driver to take us straight down through the town. It was the last thing any of us really wanted but it had to be done. The Monaghan fans were lining the streets, glasses in hand as they celebrated their biggest win for years. Watching the Armagh bus inching down the road was the perfect way to finish off what had been a smashing day for the blue and white.

Deep down, they knew that we would probably go much further in the Championship – which was the case as Monaghan lost to Down next time out in Ulster and to Meath in the qualifiers – but that didn't matter as they thumped the side of our bus on that particular May evening.

We were only inches apart but the difference between us couldn't have been greater. Their joy, our pain. I wanted our lads to taste the desolation because doing that was the only way we could set about re-launching the season in a meaningful way as opposed to just going through the motions.

We had four weeks to wait for the qualifiers and we worked extremely hard to get ourselves right. We had now lost five successive games – four in the League and the Ulster clash with Monaghan. A turning point for us was a weekend we spent in Galway where we were invited to play a challenge game to mark the opening of the redeveloped Pearse Stadium. Philip Loughran was outstanding in that game against Galway and I felt afterwards that, although we were facing a long haul in the qualifiers, the attitude was good. We were paired with Waterford in round one. From the outside, it might have looked like the ideal draw for, even though we had to travel down to Walsh Park, there was little real prospect of us being beaten. Waterford weren't as good then as now, so it really would have been some shock if they had beaten the previous year's All-Ireland champions, having earlier lost to Clare in the Munster Championship.

We won easily enough after a slow start but there was still no real sense that we were back on track. Maybe it was the venue and the opponents, there was something surreal about finding ourselves in Walsh Park playing before a small crowd the year after winning the All-Ireland but it was of our own making so we had to get on with it.

I have one particular memory of the Waterford game which still stands out. We took Francie Bellew off and, as he was making his way to the sideline, he got a standing ovation from the small band of Armagh supporters who had made the long trip. It was a lovely moment although, typical Francie, he turned the tables on me.

As he was running off the pitch to the sound of the Armagh supporters clapping in appreciation I said to him, "See, Francie, you're getting a standing ovation."

He looked at me with a mischievous glint in his eye and said, "No, Joe, they're clapping you for taking me off." Another Francie special.

Next up, was Antrim in Casement Park and, although it was a much, much tougher game, we made it through by three points. Still, the fire wasn't lit. We needed a big draw to get back into real Championship mood and it came immediately after the Antrim game when we were paired with Dublin in round three. What's more, it was to be played in Croke Park.

That's more like it. If this doesn't get us going, nothing will.

We would know soon enough if there was anything left in the tank and if we were ready to press on or if that poor form in the second half of the League, followed by the defeat against Monaghan, was really where we were at.

Dublin had lost to Laois in Leinster but got their season back on track with a good win over Derry and were beginning to look as if they were emerging as genuine contenders again. They took that approach into the game and played well in the first half. However, there were little signs that the spark was about to return to our play.

I remember one incident which gave a clear pointer that we certainly weren't a spent force. The ball broke near the sideline and, as two Dublin boys went for it, Tony McEntee arrived at pace and somehow managed to knock the pair of them down. A bit of a dust-up followed and, suddenly, you could sense that the spirit was right.

We were ready for war.

There was a bit of a dust-up on the way into the dressing room at half time, too, which raised the temperature even higher. One of Dublin's backroom shouldered one of our lads in the tunnel and things threatened to get out of hand for a while before simmering down.

Tommy Lyons had held his players back on their way down the tunnel to avoid clashing with our boys, which was the sensible thing to do, but, of course, when Dublin lost he was pilloried for it. I even read much later that Tommy's decision marked the beginning of a slide in Dublin's confidence which had long-lasting implications. Pure rubbish, of course, but then people will read anything they want into the smallest, most insignificant things.

We had Paddy McKeever sent off early in the second half and suddenly we were facing the challenge of our lives. It's in that type of situation that good teams make a statement about themselves and we did it that day. To be honest, we were lucky to be only four points behind at half time. We had played too much direct ball, which Dublin mopped up and then came back at us with pace and no little creativity. We talked about it at half time and were ready for a different approach in the second half, only to find ourselves a man down inside the first five minutes. Suddenly, we had to re-adjust all over again.

We had done a good psyching job on the lads at half time, using Ciaran Whelan as the target. He was Dublin captain that year so we got a life-size cardboard cut-out of him with the Sam Maguire Cup. I wanted our lads to visualise what it might be like in September if we lost to Dublin. Whelan waving the Sam Maguire Cup was the ideal way to do that.

We brought the Sam Maguire Cup along in a black plastic bag so that we could show the lads that it was still our property and could remain so if we did things right.

We positioned the Whelan cardboard cut-out in the dressing room so that it was the first thing the lads would see when they sat down at half time. Mind you, it nearly came unstuck. Our secretary, Paddy Og Nugent was in first and when he saw Whelan's face staring at him, he thought it was a ruse by Dublin to upset us. Paddy was about to tear it into bits but I quickly intervened.

"No, no, hang on… We've put it there."

It certainly had the desired effect and, by the time the lads were going back out for the second half, they were ready for anything. Mind you, Paddy McKeever's dismissal presented problems which we couldn't have legislated for. What happened from there on is still talked about, certainly in Dublin. For reasons which I'm sure he's still trying to fathom, Dublin goalkeeper, Stephen Cluxton, got himself sent off after lashing out at Stevie McDonnell. Dublin were left with no option but to bring in a sub keeper and remove one of their outfield players. Tommy Lyons took off Johnny Magee, a decision which drew much criticism from Dublin supporters afterwards but, then, people always look for scapegoats in defeat.

I don't think it would have made any difference who Dublin took off that day. It was as if we had suddenly rediscovered the energy and vibrancy of 2002 and weren't going to be denied. We trailed by 0-8 to 0-4 at half time but, once we got going in the second half, we overwhelmed Dublin physically and mentally, winning the second half, 0-11 to 0-3. John McEntee kicked four points from play and there were plenty of other outstanding performances in what was a massive team effort.

Beating Dublin for the third time in a year in Croke Park was the catalyst to move on to an even higher level while, all the time, keeping an eye on who was heading for the All-Ireland quarter-finals, via the provincial Championships.

I'd have to say that beating Dublin in the 2003 qualifier was one of the most satisfying days I had as Armagh manager. Over the years, we had watched the big stars of Gaelic football coming from the likes of Kerry, Dublin, Galway, Meath and Down but now Armagh were up there with the very best. That gave me huge satisfaction.

There was a lot of local pride for me, too, as no fewer than five of the side, Paul Hearty, Francie Bellew, Tony and John McEntee and Oisin McConville, were Cross men who had come through the ranks with me from Under-21 level. Now they were part of a great Armagh team alongside so many fine players from all over the county.

I remember meeting Patricia and our boys upstairs in Croke Park after the Dublin game and feeling really emotional. It was just one of those special occasions I will always treasure. The boys were obviously delighted and I remember chatting to Aaron and Stephen away from everybody else, at one stage, and saying, "I just love this – it's days like this that make it all worthwhile."

I was also relieved because I had made a decision during the game which might have backfired. Oisin McConville was a doubtful starter in the run-up to the game because of a back injury. We started him but he didn't look quite right so we took him off and sent in Ronan Clarke.

Taking Oisin off was risky because he was a proven big-day performer and I'm sure, if Armagh had lost, I would have taken some stick. Still, it worked out okay and it meant that we had Oisin for the rest of the campaign. If we had played him all through he might have aggravated the damage and missed the crucial games ahead.

The qualifying games were coming at two-week intervals, which was exactly the right rate, so we had a huge advantage in the next round where we were paired with Limerick who had only a week to recover from losing the Munster final to Kerry. Some losing provincial finalists had only a week before the fourth-round qualifiers back then, which was most unfair and, although Limerick protested, they were told to get on with it.

Given the circumstances, they never stood a chance against us. By now, we were fully back in the groove and with Stevie McDonnell scoring 3-4, more than all of the Limerick team put together, we ran out easy winners, 4-10 to 0-11 to qualify for the All-Ireland quarter-finals. Everyone tries to reach Croke Park in August and, ideally, teams like to get there unbeaten but you'll take what's going so we were thrilled to be back in serious All-Ireland contention after that early season scare.

We were into new territory against Laois who had finally delivered on their undoubted potential under Mick O'Dwyer by winning Leinster for the first time in fifty-seven years. He had done a great job with them and we knew full well that the crafty old fox would have them well primed for the quarter-final. They had beaten us by three points in the League semi-final so they wouldn't have been in any way psychologically fazed by the prospect of taking on the reigning All-Ireland champions.

They pushed us all the way too but, in the end, we nudged through by two points. We were criticised afterwards for delaying our return to the pitch for the second half. Laois arrived out five or six minutes before us and it was claimed that we were trying to play mind games with a team that was new to this level of Championship activity.

You would think from some of the over-the-top stuff that was written about it afterwards that we had done something scandalous, having decided to show bad manners just for the sake of gamesmanship. The truth – as is so often the case – was completely different and a lot less sinister. One of the lads was suffering from diarrhoea at half time and was in no position to go back out at the appointed time.

What were we to do, play with fourteen men for a while or replace him when we knew he would be okay in a few minutes? We locked the door, ignored the banging from various officials and waited until he was ready for action again. The Laois crowd booed us back out, thinking we were up to something devious when, in reality, our late arrival was down to nothing more than a call of nature.

I presume we were fined by Croke Park for being late out and, no doubt, we paid up. Citing diarrhoea as the reason for our delay would have been a novel defence and, although perfectly true, there are times when it's better to take your punishment and get on with things.

We expected to be playing Galway in the All-Ireland semi-final as they had looked quite impressive in winning Connacht again. They still had most of the 2001 All-Ireland winning set-up while a young Michael Meehan had forced his way onto the team so they really did look like big contenders.

It didn't work out that way. They were lucky to draw the quarter-final with Donegal in Croke Park and lost by three points in the replay in Castlebar. With Tyrone also qualifying for the semi-finals, it meant that Ulster had three teams in the last four for the first time in Championship history.

Like ourselves, Donegal had travelled the long haul through the qualifiers and, with Brian McEniff back at the helm, we were fully aware of the threat they would pose. We had beaten them in the 2002 Ulster final but this would be different. The Ulster final was in Clones but now we were heading for Croke Park and, while Armagh always like playing there, the same is true of Donegal as it suits their open style. Also, McEniff had vast experience of bringing sides to Croke Park so, despite what the pundits were saying in advance, this was always going to be a tricky test for us.

Even so, we should have beaten them out the gate but, instead, we got home by four points after Oisin McConville slotted a very late penalty. It was one of the worst shooting displays we gave during my six years in charge. The wide count was 21-3 in our favour – or, more accurately, to our embarrassment – and, on another day, this would probably have torpedoed us.

Donegal had full-back Raymond Sweeney sent off, probably unluckily, on a second yellow card early in the second half but they continued to play with incredible fire and determination and were a goal up at the three-quarter stage. We were winning more than enough possession to win two games but it took a Stevie McDonnell goal to settle things down and set us on our way.

There was some controversy afterwards amid claims that we had escaped lightly in contrast to Donegal who had had a man sent off. In particular, it was alleged that referee, Michael Monahan of Kildare, should have sent off John McEntee for one particular incident. Naturally, I didn't agree, the referee had consulted with his linesman and booked John but, with many scribes writing that he should have been sent off, there may have been a growing opinion that somehow Armagh were getting away with things. It's possible that impression came back to haunt us in the final when Diarmaid was sent off in the wrong. I got a lot of abusive letters after the Donegal game but, quite honestly, I couldn't see where the grounds for complaint lay. Believe me, plenty of our lads were pretty sore after that game but somehow Donegal were portrayed as being on the side of the angels.

It was around that stage that the whispering campaign began about Armagh's approach to the game. I have no doubt that it did us enormous damage in subsequent years because, once a rumour takes flight, it's virtually impossible to ground it and, over time, it becomes harder to separate the truth from the lies.

Tyrone had beaten Kerry the week before we played Donegal so it was going to be an all-Ulster final irrespective of who won our game. With respect to Donegal, I think the majority of football fans wanted an Armagh-Tyrone clash. The rivalry had always been intense but had become even more so over the previous few years so the prospect of us meeting with the All-Ireland title at stake sent pulses racing, certainly in our part of the world.

It was the first time that neighbouring counties from the same province had met in the final which added to the terrific sense of occasion. It was all so different to the barren years when Ulster teams went through a terrible run and couldn't even reach a final, especially if they were playing against Leinster or Munster champions. Who knows, it might never happen again that Armagh and Tyrone meet in the All-Ireland final and, even if they do, it's unlikely to replicate the atmosphere of 2003.

Unfortunately, the great dream of completing the two-in-a-row wasn't to be. It was an almighty occasion alright but, in the end, the GAA had first-time, All-Ireland winners once again. Still, all these years later, I doubt if that would have been the case had Diarmaid Marsden not been subjected to one of the greatest injustices I have ever witnessed in Croke Park.

CHAPTER 8

Prior to 2000–09, you had to go back to the 1960s to see a county win the Ulster title six times in one decade. The great Down team of that era achieved it but, throughout the next three decades, the titles were won mainly in singles.

Derry won the double in 1975–76 and Tyrone in 1995–96 but, other than that, defending the title proved beyond everybody's capabilities. Perhaps this isn't all that surprising as Ulster has long been the most competitive province where, on any given day, most of the nine counties would fancy their chances of beating anybody else.

It's different elsewhere. Leinster seed the previous year's semi-finalists into the quarter-finals so four teams steer clear of the first fence. Munster is usually a two-horse race between Kerry and Cork. The same goes for Connacht where Galway and Mayo win the majority of the titles. Ulster, however, is ultra-competitive all the way.

Winning the previous year's title – or even the All-Ireland final – bestows no favours for the following season. It's an open draw where everybody has the same chance of being drawn in the preliminary round. I have no problem with that. Every season is a new experience and what happened the year before shouldn't influence the draw in any way. Mind you, it's nice to avoid the preliminary round because life is hard enough without having to win four games just to get out of Ulster.

The sheer competitiveness of the Ulster Championship makes doubles or trebles most unusual but Armagh managed to win a double in 1999–2000, a treble in 2004–2005–2006 and singles in 2002 and 2008. It was a remarkable haul, especially in a decade when Tyrone were at their strongest ever, Derry won two NFL Division 1 titles while Donegal picked up their first. Fermanagh were at their most formidable for decades, too, while Monaghan re-emerged at their combative best under my good friend, Seamus 'Banty' McEnaney.

And, at the close of the decade, Antrim were playing better than they had for a very long time.

To dominate the Ulster Championship in such a competitive decade was quite an achievement and will always be fondly remembered in Armagh history for delivering a first All-Ireland and NFL title. For all that, we'd still be disappointed that it didn't yield quite a bit more.

Ironically, the closest we came to a second All-Ireland was in 2003 when we didn't even win Ulster. Rather disappointingly, the Ulster treble of the next three years didn't come to anything on the All-Ireland stage. No county had won the Ulster treble since Down in 1959–60–61, and they succeeded in winning two All-Irelands, whereas we didn't make it back to Croke Park on final day from our three attempts in 2004–2005–2006. That will always be a source of deep regret for me.

I have no doubt that it would have been very different under the old Championship system where one defeat meant the end of the road for that season while winning a provincial title brought direct entry to the All-Ireland semi-final. In 2004, we would have played Mayo in the semi-final, in 2005 it would have been Dublin and, in 2006, Cork would have been our opponents. In all probability, we would have won one or two of them and maybe even all three. Surely we'd have picked up an All-Ireland somewhere along the line, too.

There were many years prior to the introduction of the 'back door' in 2001 that a second chance would have re-energised Armagh but, ironically, its opening came at a bad time for us as it meant we had an extra fence to jump after winning Ulster. Meanwhile, some very dangerous campaigners were pouring back in.

The 'back door' has taken the pain out of defeat in the provincial Championships and, as a result, some of the glamour, too. Looking back on my own playing career, I think of the many close calls we had in Ulster, days when we just came up short and had to wait another full year to go again. In 1979, Monaghan beat us by two points in the Ulster semi-final and went on to win the final. In 1981 we lost the Ulster final to Down and, three years later, Frank McGuigan beat us on his own in the final. In 1985, we lost a semi-final replay by a point to Monaghan who went on to come very close to beating Kerry in the All-Ireland semi-final. In 1987 – my last year on the panel – we lost the final to Derry by two points.

They were all years when we might have made genuine progress through the 'back door' but we never even thought about second chances, because they didn't exist. Sudden death meant exactly that: winner take all, loser make way.

You play to whatever system is there so, while I would have been very happy to be crowned All-Ireland champions in 2003 after losing in Ulster, there's no doubt that winning the provincial and the All-Ireland in the one year is the purest form of success.

I am convinced that, under the old system, we would have won one – possibly two – All-Irelands in the 2004–2005–2006 period but, on each occasion, we were beaten by teams who had lost earlier on in the provinces. I'm not complaining about it but just pointing out that when the change came, in 2001, it was at exactly the wrong time in the life and times of Armagh football.

Take 2004. We ran a poor League campaign and were lucky enough to avoid relegation, finishing just a point above the drop zone after winning three and drawing one of our seven games. Still, I wasn't especially concerned about it. The 2003 Championship had been extremely busy as we carefully picked our way back through the qualifiers to reach the All-Ireland final, so we had no great appetite for a pressurised League campaign the following year.

No, regaining the Ulster Championship was everything and we were geared accordingly. We did it, too, beating Monaghan, Cavan and Donegal – two of them most impressively, the third much less so. We had Monaghan very much in our sights after what they had done to us a year earlier and, to be honest, we crushed them. When a team knows the identity of their first-round opponents for months it's easy to focus on them. Monaghan had thrown us offline in 2003 so we felt we owed them one. It wasn't hard to re-kindle the hurt we felt after losing to Monaghan. The memory of their supporters banging the side of the bus as we drove down through Clones that evening did the trick nicely.

We were out of sight by half time and raced to the easiest of wins, 2-19 to 0-10. Cavan, who had beaten Down in a replay, were next up and, although they had been relegated from Division 1 a few months earlier, they had given us a terrible hammering in Breffni Park. It was one of those days when everything they did produced a score and everything we did turned into a problem. They beat us by thirteen points and were worth every point of it!

The late Eamonn Coleman, a man who knew a thing or two about winning big games, was in charge of Cavan at the time and had them fired up for the Championship. However, they were a man down inside a minute after midfielder, Pearse McKenna, was sent off but, instead of allowing it to handicap them, they appeared to become inspired by the numerical disadvantage and the mounting odds.

It was a hot, sticky day in Clones so the extra man should definitely have counted but we never managed to exploit it. Remarkably, Cavan were two points up just after the hour mark but we held our nerve and managed to kick the vital points which took us home by two in the end. Once again, we had finished strongly, a characteristic that was now deeply embedded in the squad's psyche.

So, there you had it. From the heights of the Monaghan demolition to the realisation that we were damn lucky to have booked in for a unique occasion in Croke Park as the Ulster final was headed for Dublin for the first time since 1939.

It was thought that it would be an Armagh v Tyrone final but Donegal refused to act out their part of the script, beating the All-Ireland champions in the Ulster semi-final. The 2004 season had a sad undercurrent for Tyrone following the untimely death of Cormac McAnallen in the spring. It came as a terrible shock to the entire GAA community and, more especially, to those who knew Cormac. He was a wonderful player and a very likeable lad and his death really did strike a chord with people all over the country but, most especially, in Tyrone and Ulster where he was so well known and liked.

Understandably, Tyrone weren't quite themselves in the 2004 Championship, losing first to Donegal and later to Mayo in the All-Ireland quarter-finals.

The atmosphere around the Ulster final was special. It was a chance for Ulster to show off its wares in Croke Park and, since the previous two All-Ireland titles had come north, there was a real swagger to our Championship. To be honest, we loved going to Croke Park and saying to the rest of the country, "This is Ulster football and this is where we are right now".

We had had to work fierce hard to beat Donegal in the 2002 Ulster final but it was completely different two years later. In fact, I would regard our performance in the 2004 final as possibly our best in the years I was in charge. It was one of those days when all the jigsaw pieces slotted together early on and remained firmly in place. The points flowed early and then Diarmaid Marsden struck for a goal before half time. We were eight points up at the break and got even stronger in the second half to finish 3-15 to 0-11 winners. It was the highest score in an Ulster final since Down hit Cavan for 2-19 back in 1978. More than that, it re-established us as serious, All-Ireland contenders.

It's a lovely feeling standing on the sideline watching your side get everything just about right in a big game. The 2004 Ulster final was in that category. Paddy McKeever and Oisin McConville scored 1-3 each, Diarmaid Marsden landed 1-2 while Tony McEntee and Stevie McDonnell kicked 0-2 each.

Only one point in our total of 3-15 came from a free, whereas Donegal managed just five points from open play. Brian McEniff described our performance as awesome, a view with which I was happy to concur. What I liked most of all was the appetite for work and enterprise the lads were showing. A lot of them had been around the circuit for a long time but their ambitions were as finely tuned as ever. It was a contented bus that left Croke Park for Armagh with the Anglo-Celt Cup up front, on the evening of July 11, 2004.

There was an added satisfaction in having made such a positive statement in Croke Park. We had got used to winning there by now but it's a feeling you can never get enough of. All the more so for a county like Armagh, who had endured so many bad days in Croke Park over the years.

I genuinely believed we were in exactly the right place to launch a powerful bid for the All-Ireland. We had a month to wait for the quarter-final and, while I always thought it was too long, it was something we could cope with.

At least I thought we could.

How wrong can you be?

Four weeks later, we were on our way out of Croke Park and out of the All-Ireland, having lost to Fermanagh in a game which is still recalled with a sense of horror in Armagh. Fermanagh, who had run Tyrone close enough in the Ulster Championship, re-launched under Charlie Mulgrew and put in great performances in the qualifiers. We should have been warned by their wins over Meath, Cork and Donegal but clearly we weren't. They had beaten Meath and Donegal in extra-time and battled back against Cork in the second half to win by six points, all of which showed just how resilient they were.

I have no doubt whatsoever that over-confidence cost us that All-Ireland quarter-final. You can warn all you like about it in advance but sometimes a psyche sets in which is impossible to dismantle. Afterwards, I heard that as lads were getting on the bus to head for Croke Park they were asking our secretary Paddy Og Nugent if there were club championship games the following weekend. They were asking that with one eye on the All-Ireland semi-final. Earlier in the day, one particular player handed Paddy an expenses sheet. I also heard that some fellas were on their mobile phones on the way to the game. Put it all together and it comes down to this: our focus wasn't quite right and we all have to take responsibility for that. For whatever reason, we took our eye off the ball.

Nevertheless, we should have won. Early in the game, we led by four points and it was looking as if it might be as easy for us as Tyrone had found it a year earlier when they trimmed Fermanagh by nineteen points in the quarter-final. We seemed to be shaping up for a similar performance and then, inexplicably, a strange thing happened. We had a good goal chance but didn't take it, the ball was moved downfield, Fermanagh scored a point and the battle started.

Normally, we thrived on that type of challenge: Bring it on, boys, we're ready for anything. The more it was put up to us, the better we responded, but not this time. Normally, we would tighten the team ethic under pressure but this time we started to play as individuals and, minute by minute, the error count increased. It was as if lads didn't trust each other to get it right, which was the exact opposite of everything we stood for.

Fermanagh dug in, grew in confidence and became a totally different side to the one that had started so tentatively. We had Enda McNulty sent off just before half time but that wasn't the reason for our edginess. We'd usually sort that out – it's never easy having to play with fourteen men but it happens sometimes and you must get on with it.

We didn't start Oisin McConville due to injury but brought him on after fifty-five minutes, hoping that would ignite the spark.

It didn't.

I'm not, for one second, taking away from Fermanagh's success but we made mistakes that day which we'd never made before – or perhaps since. We lost by a point (0-12 to 0-11) in what was a sickening setback. On and off the field we were poor. I made a mistake in not bringing on John Mac, who had been out injured, while players made silly errors all over the place. Put it all together and you have a total mess, which may well have cost Armagh the All-Ireland.

Our defeat probably impacted on Tyrone, too. They were playing Mayo immediately after our game and would have expected us to win, leaving them with the chance to set up another clash against us in the semi-final. They would have loved that. You never know how a team's focus can be upset but, in any event, they also lost. The result was that, instead of Armagh v Tyrone in the semi-final, you had Fermanagh v Mayo. I doubt very much if anybody called that double right.

The sense of frustration after the Fermanagh game was unbelievable. Why did we seize up after such a good start? Why did Enda get himself sent off and, when he was sent off, why didn't we close ranks as we usually would? Why didn't we hold our shape and play to the strengths that had made us so formidable over previous years? We had been awarded only five frees in the first half, were Fermanagh really more disciplined or were we paying for some perception or other? Why hadn't I sent on John McEntee?

You can ask all the questions you like but the answers mean nothing in a desolate dressing room strewn with the debris of a season. The journey back home was sheer bloody hell. We felt like dashing back to Croke Park to get things right but it was all over. We had been the architects of our own problems and had to live with it. The season was moving on without us.

Fermanagh turned in two battling performances against Mayo in the semi-final but, in the end, came up just short which made it all the harder for us to take. We felt that if we'd been in a position to bring our 'A' game to the semi-final with Mayo, we would have beaten them without much fuss and their poor performance in the final against Kerry merely reinforced that view. Still, Mayo got to the final and we didn't, having wasted a glorious opportunity.

Inevitably, there were unspoken questions during interviews after the Fermanagh game. Nobody asks outright if the manager is going to stand down or if older players are about to quit but the sub-text was there. I told the players to watch the All-Ireland semi-finals and final and see how much they hurt. The greater the pain, the greater the likelihood they would be back the following year.

First, though, we had to suffer the pain and frustration which came with realising what we had thrown away. You can accept losing a game when you know you weren't as good as the opposition, but the fact is that we weren't just as good as Fermanagh, we were better. I have no doubt that if we had played them again a week later we would have won reasonably comfortably but, after the misery of the Fermanagh defeat, it was pointless even thinking like that.

In our heart of hearts we knew we had spurned the opportunity to build on the success of 2002.

CHAPTER 9

BOOM.

BOOM … BOOM.

BOOM … BOOM … BOOM.

We were stuck in traffic out near Whitehall Church, on our way out of Dublin city, and the Tyrone supporters in the car next to us couldn't believe their luck.

Tyrone had just beaten us in the 2005 All-Ireland semi-final and the Armagh bus was jammed solid in traffic. So, too, was the Tyrone car alongside us but the lads inside the car couldn't have cared less. In fact, they were having a ball.

BOOM … BOOM … BOOM.

How better to spend your time after a game than taunting the losers. All the better when the losers happen to be your neighbours who have beaten you earlier in the Championship. As opportunities go, this was too good to miss and the Tyrone boys weren't going to let it pass.

They were leaning out of the car and thumping the side of our bus. BOOM … BOOM.

It would have given us a severe headache if we hadn't already had one but, with the traffic packed so tightly, there was damn all we could do. Somehow I don't think that a polite request to call off the taunting would have made much difference.

As far as the Tyrone boys were concerned that particular evening was as close to heaven as they could get. They were back in the All-Ireland final and, to make it doubly sweet, they had knocked out Armagh.

BOOM!!!!

I spotted a Garda motorcyclist at the traffic lights near Whitehall Church and had a quick word with him.

"Guard, can ye do us a wee favour? Could ye pull them boys in and have a word? We're feeling bad enough without those boys taking the piss."

What the Tyrone boys were doing wasn't exactly the most serious crime committed in Dublin – or anywhere else – that day but, in fairness to the Garda, he understood just how bloody infuriating it was for a team to have the side of their bus repeatedly thumped by rival supporters. So, the next time traffic moved a few yards, he pulled the Tyrone car in and had a word. I'm not sure what he said but it got them off our case, and we didn't see them again.

Now, if only we had been able to do the same with the Tyrone team out on the field in Croke Park a little earlier.

As we faced the dejected journey home they were also making their way out of Dublin feeling that the world was, indeed, a beautiful place. They had beaten us by a point in yet another of those typical Armagh-Tyrone collisions which had provided so much fascination throughout most of the last decade.

Another year was over, one where we, again, reigned over Ulster only to see the team we had beaten in the provincial final heading for the All-Ireland final.

Christ, it was hard to take. Beaten by one point.

One, lousy point.

You think of incidents throughout the game where this or that happened and, while it might not have looked important at the time, it takes on a completely different complexion when the winning margin is one point. Our big chance was gone for another year.

The 2005 season had started in most unusual circumstances. A first round National League game in Wexford Park seemed to be under total control when we led by six points at half time. *Nothing to worry about here.* Paul Keenan and Brian Mallon hit two first-half goals and we hadn't a care in the world as we went out for the second half.

Then came the Wexford avalanche. They out-scored us by 2-9 to 0-2 in the second half with Matty Forde and midfielder, Diarmuid Kinsella, doing most of the damage. It meant we had signed off on 2004 – the All-Ireland quarter-final v Fermanagh – and started 2005 with two, bad second half performances. Is it any wonder some of the pundits were suggesting Armagh might be finished?

In hindsight, what happened against Wexford may have been a blessing. It focused us very quickly on the demands of the season, starting the following week with a clash against Galway in Crossmaglen. We mangled them, winning by ten points and were on our way. In fact, we wouldn't lose another game until the first Sunday of September when Tyrone beat us.

In between, we won the League (Division 1) and the Ulster titles which, in another era, would have made it a fantastic year. However, times had changed in Armagh and now the season was judged solely on how we did in the All-Ireland.

Still, it remains a great source of pride that as well as being the first team to win the All-Ireland for Armagh we also won the League title for the first time. It's a record which can never be taken away from that squad. After the Wexford setback we won all the other games to reach the semi-final against Mayo which was fixed for Dr Hyde Park, Roscommon.

The heavens opened a few hours before the game and the pitch was declared unplayable. We complained that we only heard about the problem on our way from Athlone and immediately started a campaign to have the re-fixture played in Croke Park. There was method in what we were trying to do. Mayo were far more familiar with Hyde Park so we wanted to get them out of there, if possible. Besides, we loved playing in Croke Park which, by now, was like a second home to us.

The timing couldn't have been better for us. The postponement came the day after GAA Congress had voted to open Croke Park to soccer and rugby so we talked up the need to play as many of our own games there too. Only the day before, Sean Kelly had spoken about bringing as many GAA games as possible to Croke Park so we felt there was a good chance our game with Mayo would be moved. It was and we made the most of it, winning by five points the following week.

Wexford had stunned Tyrone in the other League semi-final – that game had gone ahead in awful conditions in Portlaoise on the day ours was called off – winning by a point to set up a novel League final. Now, I know that there's a tendency to talk down the importance of the League but I can tell you we regarded it as very significant that year.

Armagh had never won it and, since I had played in two finals where we lost, in 1983 and '85, I certainly didn't want to complete an unfortunate treble as a player and manager.

Also, our Championship opener against Fermanagh (we were back in the Ulster preliminary round for the second time in three seasons) was coming up two weeks after the League final so we wanted to go into it off a winning run.

Besides, we owed Wexford after the February mauling and this time we made no mistakes. Wexford stayed with us for twenty minutes but we kicked on from there to win by seven points, without ever actually being extended. It was another master class from Stevie McDonnell who scored ten points, seven from open play. Really, he was a joy to behold that day.

There was a sense of satisfaction with a job well done but it was straight down to planning for the Fermanagh game. There certainly was no need for gimmicks this time – instead all it took to send the players into motivational orbit was a mention of the previous year's All-Ireland quarter-final.

As in 2004, we ran into an early lead and, once again, Fermanagh recovered and were only a point behind at half time. However, unlike 2004, we powered on in the second half to win by eight points. It was relief all round but, at the same time, it was hard to avoid reflecting on why the second half was so different this time. There could only be one answer – we got a lot of things wrong the previous August but had corrected them for the next season.

Indeed, what happened throughout the summer of 2005 was quite remarkable. Even now, when I look back on it, I can still feel the buzz, the excitement, the tension and the sheer drama. It really was one hell of an Ulster Championship on all fronts. Some cracking games, three replays, plenty of controversies and, in the end, we were back as champions.

We drew our quarter-final with Donegal, rather luckily it must be said and, while we each had a man sent off, it was tame when compared to the replay. This was the fifth Championship clash between us in four seasons so maybe there was a question of familiarity breeding a certain amount of contempt. Donegal hadn't beaten us in any of the previous four games and upped the physical stakes considerably, but to no avail. Instead, they had three players sent off to our one, but the more important figure was the result: Armagh 3-11 Donegal 1-10.

It was fiery stuff all through, even at half time.

Brian McEniff confronted the referee, Joe McQuillan of Cavan, as he left the pitch at half time so I joined in. I wasn't going to let Brian make his case on his own for fear it would impact on us in the second half. We had Francie Bellew sent off in what I would regard as a definite case of reputation influencing referees. Even the newspaper reports, which usually didn't do Francie any favours, admitted that he was hard done by. As far as I was concerned, Donegal played a far more physical game than usual and lost their focus as a result. Whatever problems we might have had, being out-muscled by the opposition wasn't one of them.

I was reported for intruding on the pitch and ordered to the stands for the next game which was against Derry in the semi-final eight days later. A John Toal goal proved the difference and we were on our way to the final against Tyrone who had to survive a replay against Cavan.

I believe that history will reflect very kindly on the Armagh-Tyrone rivalry of that era in terms of the quality of football and the entertainment it provided. Certainly, they were massive occasions, games that always seemed to produce something unexpected.

Take the first 2005 clash.

Tyrone would later admit that they thought they had one hand on the Anglo Celt Cup when they led by four points late in the game. Croke Park was rocking to a white and red beat, we had scored only 1-7 in sixty-five minutes and didn't look as if we could conjure up a game-saving finale. And yet, we always believed.

The great thing about that team was that they never knew when they were beaten. They proved it again that day. Somehow, from somewhere deep inside, they summoned reserves of mental strength which enabled them to work a goal finished by McDonnell. Right man in the right place, again. And then, in stoppage time, Paul McGrane hoofed a spectacular long-range equaliser to make him the toast of Armagh – not to mention the Ulster Council, who were in line for another bumper pay-day with the replay.

Having saved the day in such dramatic circumstances, we would normally have been in great form afterwards but, unfortunately, we had lost a midfielder: John Toal suffered a horrific knee injury just before half time. We didn't know the full extent of the damage immediately but it didn't take long for the worst to be confirmed.

He was lucky – if indeed you can use the word in these circumstances – that he didn't lose the leg altogether. It was held together only by skin and blood vessels. It was truly a remarkable medical feat that John's leg was put back together and, after that, his drive to play again took over. No man on earth worked harder on rehabilitation and the manner in which he kept putting in the effort was truly inspiring.

Unfortunately, despite his remarkable recovery, his inter-county career ended long before it should have, which was a terrible pity for him and Armagh. Indeed, I have no doubt that if he had been playing we would have won more over the coming seasons. It was only when he was gone that people realised exactly how valuable he was. He covered so many holes, got himself into positions where you'd never expect him to pop up and made crucial tackles which broke up many an opposition attack. He had a wonderful ability to be in the right place at the right time, whether it was sweeping in behind 'Geezer' at centre-back, or popping up in the full-back line. He was the ultimate Mr Honest, Mr Dependable.

Philip Loughran came in for John for the replay thirteen days later, a game that turned into the ultimate war of attrition. By now, the teams were so used to each other that little niggles built up from game to game so the tension was thick around Croke Park right from the start.

Tyrone led by four points at the end of the third quarter but, as in the drawn game, our boys settled in for another big finish. Point by point, Tyrone were pegged back and two late strikes from Oisin McConville clinched victory.

We had lost Ciaran McKeever to a red card while Peter Canavan and Stephen O'Neill had walked for Tyrone. O'Neill's dismissal was actually a mistake as it was only a yellow card offence but the referee thought he had been booked earlier and sent him off. McKeever and Canavan were sent off at the same time following a bust-up among several players just after Canavan came on as a sub.

Some of the nonsense written after the game was totally over the top. It was portrayed as some sort of faction fight when, in reality, there had been an awful lot of good football. Admittedly, much of it was of the defensive variety but it was no less enthralling for that.

Yes, it was tough but there was also a great sense of manliness to it. Besides, it produced only thirty-five frees – hardly a sign that the players had lost the run of themselves. Two weeks later commentators were eulogising about the free-flowing quality of the Cork-Galway All-Ireland quarter-final but it produced forty-eight frees. It goes to show that people see what they want to see and, around then, it was fashionable to decry Ulster teams, with Armagh as the main targets in the campaign.

To be honest, we didn't give a damn. Armagh were living through the most exciting and successful period in our history and we weren't going to be distracted by loose talk or begrudgery.

All that concerned us in mid-August 2005, was that we were heading for another All-Ireland quarter-final, having come through a six-game Ulster Championship. Laois were waiting for us for the second time in three seasons but, unlike 2003, we were provincial champions, while they were qualifier survivors after losing to Dublin in the Leinster final. We were far more assertive than we had been two years earlier and with McDonnell, McConville and Clarke scoring 2-11 between them, we galloped to an easy nine-point win.

A week later, we were booked in for yet another showdown with Tyrone after they beat Dublin in a quarter-final replay. I suppose, by the law of averages, it was their turn to win because clearly Armagh and Tyrone were so evenly matched at the time that there was never going to be much between us. And so it proved: Tyrone led at half time, we came back and led by two points after sixty-four minutes but they out-pointed us, 0-3 to 0-1, over the closing minutes. Peter Canavan kicked the winning point from a free deep in stoppage time.

It disappointed me that the winner came from a free because we prided ourselves on good tackling and would always be conscious of getting it right at such a key moment in a game. But, once Paddy Russell decided that Ciaran McKeever had fouled Stephen O'Neill, there was nothing we could do except watch as Canavan swung over the winning point.

Ten years earlier, Russell had broken Tyrone hearts by penalising Canavan late in the All-Ireland final against Dublin and now it was our turn to lose out to a borderline call. Tyrone won by 1-13 to 1-12, leaving us with a dreadfully empty feeling.

The 'What if?' syndrome kicks in very quickly when you lose by a point.

What if we had made better use of our chances? What if we had been awarded an extra free or two, as we felt we deserved? What if we had converted even two of our eleven wides into points? What if? What if?

All very natural but quite futile. We were Ulster champions but Tyrone were heading for the All-Ireland final which, of course, they won. Our semi-final clash with Tyrone had been one of the best games for quite a few seasons. It had just about everything: excitement, intensity, manliness plus an awful lot of excellent football. Everybody – partisan and neutral alike – was on the edge of their seats throughout.

It would be the last time that Armagh and Tyrone would meet in the Championship during my spell as manager. We played them six times in four seasons, with each of us winning twice, while two games were drawn. The aggregate score in the three 2005 games was: Armagh 3-33 (42pts) Tyrone 1-38 (41pts). Over three games, that was pretty close! I would suggest that the Armagh-Tyrone rivalry of that period was as intense and as interesting as anything Gaelic football has ever produced. The fact that four of the games were played in Croke Park added to the drama.

Unfortunately for Armagh, Tyrone's two wins came in the knock-out All-Ireland games, whereas ours were in the Ulster Championship.

There were many who thought that the 2005 defeat by Tyrone would spell the end for that Armagh team and that we would fall back while the re-building job was underway. That was to underestimate the spirit and drive which underpinned everything we did. The experienced lads had waited an awfully long time to get their big breaks and had no intention of drifting away until they had squeezed every last drop from their careers.

They kept it going superbly in 2006, winning a third Ulster title in a row and a sixth since 1999. Once again, we were taken on the long route in Ulster, drawing with Monaghan and Fermanagh before winning replays to set up yet another final clash with Donegal in Croke Park. We beat them again.

I came off the pitch to find a most unusual sight awaiting me – Francie Bellew was being shepherded into the interview room to receive the RTÉ Man-of-the-Match award. Had the world gone mad?

No bookings for Francie plus recognition of his talents, and all in one day!

We should have known it wouldn't last, and it didn't. After losing the Munster final to Cork, Kerry had re-invented themselves through the qualifiers by posting Kieran Donaghy at full-forward as a big target man. It worked brilliantly against Longford and, you'd have to say, it worked against us in the All-Ireland quarter-final, especially after Francie was booked by referee David Coldrick just before half time.

It was a harsh call but we'd come to expect that type of thing by then. Referees seemed to think that they hadn't done their job properly without booking Francie. It reached a stage where we were thinking of telling Francie to go to the referee before games and sign in with them just to save time later.

Marking Donaghy was tough enough in ordinary circumstances but doing it while on a booking was like playing with handcuffs. Francie did his best but was hit for a goal in the second half after slipping as Donaghy cut inside. If Francie hadn't slipped, Donaghy might never have got his shot away.

Kerry won by eight points, which was somewhat flattering as they were only two points ahead with five or six minutes remaining but, despite having Paul Galvin sent off, they hit us for 1-3 in the closing minutes.

Mind you, the main damage was done in the first half when we missed some very good chances. In the end we leaked 3-15 in what was the biggest Championship defeat in my time as manager. Yet again, we had lost as Ulster champions to a team that had come through the qualifier system. And, as in 2003 and 2005, we had lost to a team that went on to win the All-Ireland title.

Management is about making decisions. It's about backing your judgement and living with the consequences. It's about being strong enough to make the hard calls and not being swayed by a fear that you're going to get it wrong.

It's about being your own person, although not to the extent that you ignore what everybody else says. Indeed, as far as team selection or changes in Armagh were concerned, I never made a decision without discussing it with Paul Grimley, John McCloskey, and John Rafferty when he came on board. That's why they were there.

Of course, management will get decisions wrong, but so what? It's not an exact science and it's a mistake to try to turn it into one. You can bring all the experience, expertise and information you want to bear but, in the end, instinct plays a huge part in it, too.

Every manager makes hundreds of decisions in the course of a season so all he can do is hope that most of them are right. Each manager goes about things differently but they all share one common aim: to get it right.

One of the hardest calls I had to make during a game was in the 2005 All-Ireland semi-final against Tyrone. I took off Kieran McGeeney after sixty-three minutes and sent in Enda McNulty, a decision that I knew would have repercussions if we lost.

Geezer was more than just our captain, he was very much the on-field leader, the enforcer who got things done. The Armagh public loved him, his colleagues looked up to him and I trusted him implicitly, both as a player and as a man.

It was against that background that I found it very difficult to take him off the field. As it happened, we lost the semi-final by a point which, inevitably, left me open to accusations of getting it badly wrong. I know that Kieran was very put out about it, which was understandable. I got some stick for taking him off from some sections of the media and the Armagh supporters, but I still maintain it was the right thing to do. I have no regrets about it and, having looked back at events, I can state categorically that it certainly wasn't the reason we lost that game.

It was claimed afterwards – by some people who wanted to make mischief – that it was a decision I took on my own without reference to Paul Grimley and John McCloskey, but nothing could be further from the truth. Although the call was, ultimately, down to me they were both heavily involved in the decision.

The balance of power in that game had see-sawed over and back all afternoon, Tyrone making much of the running and us coming back at them. Indeed, we took the lead for the first time in the fifty-eighth minute when Stevie McDonnell scored a magnificent goal from the tightest of angles.

However, there was something else going on which was of concern to us. Geezer hadn't been in the game for quite some time and certainly wasn't making the impact that we needed at that stage. I spoke to John and Paul to see what they thought.

After our discussions, I felt it would be best to wait a few minutes and see how things developed. Besides, other things were happening which needed attention. Andy Mallon was beginning to have some problems with Peter Canavan so we needed to address that. Enda McNulty, who was sitting on the bench and eager for action, had a good record against Canavan so putting him into the full-back line and releasing Andy to the half-back line looked a decent option. Andy had plenty of pace which he could use to our advantage from the half-back line.

Geezer still hadn't got into the game, so I went back to speak to Paul and John.

"Things haven't changed lads … what should we do about it?"

We talked for a little while about bringing Enda into the full-back line, switching out Andy and taking off Geezer.

"Get Enda ready," I told John.

When we lost, it was claimed in some quarters that taking Geezer off had cost us the game. I expected that people might make that connection but I don't believe it to be true. People seem to forget that we led by two points after he went off. Opening up a two-point gap looked like a decisive break in what had been an epic struggle, but Tyrone plugged on and landed three late points to win the game by a point. In the end, it was down to one borderline call by the referee which gave Tyrone the chance to kick the winning point.

Lots of great players have been taken off over the years and, while it's always a tough decision to make, that's what management are there for.

Kieran has been managing Kildare for the past few years and now knows how lonely and difficult a role it can be. I'm sure he will be in management for a long time to come and will probably find himself faced with the sort of decision I had to take in that 2005 All-Ireland semi-final. What's more, it will hurt him just as much as it hurt me when I took him off that day.

All I can say is that it was done with the right intentions.

Even Mickey Harte acknowledged there was method in what I was doing and pointed out in his autobiography, which was released several years later, that it would have been regarded as a masterstroke if we had won. But we didn't, so I took the flak.

Kieran was understandably disappointed, but then, so were we all because we'd lost a game we seemed to be on our way towards winning. I have always felt that the absence of John Toal, who had wrecked his knee in the drawn Ulster final, was a crucial factor in our defeat that day. He was on top of his game that year and would have given us an extra dimension when the battle with Tyrone was at its most intense.

Kieran's resilience was one of his greatest strengths. He was a true warrior spirit on whom you could always rely for the big effort. He was a hard man who put his body on the line all the time and, boy, did he take some hits. He seemed to be fair game for the opposition who quite often targeted him. But, just as Francie Bellew was a marked man with referees even before he walked onto the pitch, Geezer couldn't get a free whatever belts he took.

He took some terrible stick in the 2006 All-Ireland quarter-final against Kerry but hardly ever got a free. Meanwhile, Bellew had the handcuffs put on him with a first-half yellow card for daring to try and mark Kieran Donaghy.

Kerry have a reputation for being pure footballers but when an opponent has to be slowed down or they feel someone needs special attention to prevent them from exerting too much influence on a game, there's no better team to do it. As for Armagh ... well, we had to put up with an awful lot of unfair stuff being written about us.

Somewhere along the line we got a reputation for playing just over the edge and, once that happens, it's very hard for a team to shake off. The suspicion is that you're always up to something. I was disappointed to learn that, at one point, referees were studying videos of Armagh games at their meetings because they considered that elements of our games were useful examples of what they should watch out for. The idea that we were villains and all the others were saints simply didn't tally with the truth, but we had to live with it.

Sport isn't divided into angels and devils. There's a bit of both in all teams but, for a period, we were dumped into hell with the devils and made to believe that certain other counties were on first-name terms with the angels.

Sections of the media didn't help our cause either. Some scurrilous articles were written about us by, what I would call, the 'hit and run' brigade, the journalists you never see around a dressing room after a game, who never talk to players, managers or anybody actually involved in the game.

It's easy to pontificate in front of a microphone or into a laptop if you're never going to meet the people you're writing about. We were often victims of that over the years. For the most part, I couldn't care less what was said about us, but as time went by I began to believe the criticism was influencing referees.

I remember one period, during the 2004 All-Ireland quarter-final against Fermanagh, when we were repeatedly penalised for next to nothing. We went four points up early on and then Fermanagh started to get the softest of frees which brought them back into the game.

I'm not saying referees were ganging up on us, but there was a certain amount of conditioning going on and, being human, referees were influenced by it. Nothing typified that more than how they dealt with Francie Bellew.

The opposition could do just about anything they wanted with him and nobody would be booked or sent off, but if Francie raised his little finger he was in trouble. That's not paranoia, it's a fact, and there's video evidence there for anybody who wants to look back. I've never heard a player complaining about being marked by Francie – in fact, all his peers held him in high regard.

Maybe we did too well for too long. It's okay for the likes of Kerry to be successful all the time but when a new force comes along they're only supposed to stay around for a certain length of time. That's the impression I had about our situation and, to be fair to Tyrone, the same thing happened to them.

It also happened to other teams who made the breakthrough, such as Galway hurlers in the 1980s and Clare hurlers in the 1990s. Ger Loughnane once said to me that everyone supports a team when they win the first All-Ireland, but then they want you gone. We were great lads in Armagh when we kept getting beaten. We'd be told we were grand altogether and, sure, we'll see you again next year. It wasn't nice but that's the way it was.

I have looked back at 'incidents' during Armagh games which were deemed worthy of highlighting on TV, whereas, by contrast, similar events from other games went unmentioned. We were accused, among other things, of body-checking players who had parted with the ball and of tackling with the closed fist.

Proper tackling is allowed in Gaelic football and we, as a team, worked hard at getting it right. It's about regaining possession so you have to work hard at it. We brought in various referees from time to time to make sure that our tackling was okay from their viewpoint.

As for fouling the off-the-ball runner? We didn't do it. We stayed with him but the instruction at all times was not to foul him because that would be stupid. Why concede a free so needlessly? The same goes for tackling with the fist. If you do it, you're guaranteed to be pulled up since it's happening right in front of the referee. However, you are allowed to punch the ball out of an opponent's hand, which was something we worked on.

If one of our players stepped out of line and got caught, I had no problem with a sending off. I did, however, have a difficulty when referees made decisions based on misconceptions. Let's put it this way – if an opponent went to ground anywhere in the vicinity of Francie Bellew, the chances were that he would get a free even if he had taken a dive.

Unfortunately, cheating has crept into the game in recent times, yet very few referees take any action against it. A word of warning from the referee to the cheat would help sort out the problem but, for some reason, it rarely happens. It's an issue that needs to be addressed because if cheating is allowed to become an integral part of our game, we're in serious trouble.

More generally, if a referee makes a mistake – especially if the incident leads to a player being sent off – I would like to see him have the courage to come forward and admit that he has made a mistake. Anybody can make a wrong decision, especially at the pace at which games are played nowadays, so surely it should be possible for a referee to own up to his error? That wouldn't, in any way, undermine referees or the important job they do. On the contrary, it would reflect very positively on them but, for reasons I simply don't understand, they never do it. Maybe the powers-that-be wouldn't allow referees to admit to making mistakes but, if that's the case, it makes a bad situation worse.

Players will accept punishment if they're guilty of a serious offence. What's more, as a manager, I wouldn't make a case for any player who has stepped out of line. However, if a player is punished in the wrong, then I would go as far as it takes to have him cleared. I just wish that referees would be more prepared to admit it when they get a decision wrong. Changing their minds afterwards would be a sign of strength, not weakness.

Speaking of strength, I found out fairly early on in my days as Cross manager just how important it is to assert your authority. In March 1996, we were invited down to Ballincollig in Cork for a tournament (Crossmaglen has had a great relationship with Ballincollig for over 30 years) but I delayed travelling because I wanted to see Armagh U-21s play Longford.

I brought some of the Cross U-21s to Longford while the seniors – and my two selectors, Donal McKenna and Ollie McEntee – travelled to Cork on the Saturday afternoon. I didn't get down until around ten o'clock and didn't like what I saw on my arrival.

The younger lads were sitting around drinking orange and looking bored stiff while some of the older boys were, shall we say, enjoying something stronger in the bar. So, too, were my right-hand men, Donal and Ollie!

The first player I bumped into was Joe Fitzpatrick, a great club man and a good friend, and it was clear that he had been enjoying himself. Clutching a frothy pint, he said: "Don't worry, Joe, I've only had six of seven". I presume he was exaggerating but since I had left instructions that there was to be no drinking on the trip, I wasn't at all happy.

I was even less so when I saw that our captain, Jim McConville, was also showing all the signs of a man who hadn't quite managed to resist the lure of the bar. I reared up on Donal and Ollie, demanding to know how they had allowed this to happen.

The reply was a classic. "Joe, we arrived down too early. We had too much time on our hands." I didn't know whether to laugh or cry!

I decided to say no more about it until the next morning. I gave Ollie and Donal a right lecture and, shortly afterwards, I met Jim in the car park. I told him how disappointed I was in him, how, as captain, he was expected to set the standards and, how, when I said 'no drinking', I meant it. I also told him that I was stripping him of the captaincy for the tournament.

John Mac took over and we went on to win the trophy. And who got man of the tournament? Jim McConville! He played brilliantly, quite how I don't know. Still, I had made my point.

I had sent out a message that we had a code of conduct that wasn't optional if we were to give ourselves the best chance of advancing as a club and a group. One of the Ballincollig officials said at the presentation how he hoped to see us back down the following year to defend the title, but Ollie piped up: "We won't be here, we'll be in Croke Park winning the All-Ireland club final."

He was right. What's more, Jim was captain for that remarkable run through Armagh, Ulster and All-Ireland in 1996-'97. I reinstated him when we got back from Ballincollig and he went on to do a great job. Neither of us mentioned the incident again but we both knew where we stood from there on. So, too, did everybody else.

I had the made the right decision and it worked. I was less sure about a decision in the 2003 All-Ireland qualifiers against Dublin, in Croke Park. Oisin McConville had a bit of back trouble around then and while we started him against Dublin, he hadn't got into the game. So, around the twenty-five minute mark, we decided to take him off. It was a big call but we believed that his back problem was preventing him from being as effective as usual.

However, as he passed by me on his way off, he said quietly: "Joe, I'm okay." That worried me a bit. *Have we made the right decision? Maybe, he would have got into the game if we'd left him on.*

We were trailing by four points at half time but came back to win by four so everything worked out, but I'd have got some stick for taking Oisin off if we had lost. He was fully fit for the next game and resumed normal service but maybe if we'd left him on, he might have aggravated the injury and missed the rest of the campaign. Those are the type of calculations you have to make all the time.

We were thinking of the future when we left Geezer off for the 2005 All-Ireland quarter-final against Laois. He had a hamstring problem but, being Geezer, he'd play on one leg if he was allowed. The medical advice was that to play him risked losing him for several weeks and since I always went with what the medics said, we left him out. Again, it worked as we beat Laois quite easily and he was fit for the next game.

Of course, if we had lost to Laois, we would have been hammered for leaving him out.

Taking off our Stephen in the 2006 Ulster semi-final replay against Fermanagh was obviously a tough call, personally, but when you're in it as a team – on and off the field – you have to put personal considerations aside. Several of the players didn't play well in the first half that day so, in hindsight, we were probably a bit hard on Stephen by taking him off first, because he was going as well as some others.

It was his senior Championship debut so, naturally, he was very disappointed and I didn't exactly feel good about it myself, even if we did win.

But that's management for you. It's a lonely world at times but you have to be true to what you believe in – otherwise you shouldn't be there.

CHAPTER 11
FRAYING AROUND THE EDGES

It was the greatest day in Armagh football history, an occasion which will be recalled, celebrated and commemorated for evermore. Sam Maguire, the Holy Grail for every kid who ever put on a pair of football boots, was in Armagh hands after decades of gloom, doom and misery.

I wanted time to stand still so that the perfection of it all could remain in place but that was impossible. Even before we had returned home to Armagh I had a hunch that things would never be the same after 5pm on the evening of Sunday, September 22, 2002.

A few hours later, as the team bus was winding its way up the long avenue leading to the Citywest Hotel, I turned to Eamonn Mackle and said, "Amazing feeling, isn't it? But, do you know what? I can't help wondering if we will be able to control the monster that's after being created. Coping with success is sometimes harder than dealing with failure."

He looked at me in surprise.

"What do you mean? What sort of monster?"

"Well, it's like this. Up until today, nobody in Armagh knew what it was like to win the All-Ireland. No player ... no manager ... no County Board member and no supporter had the faintest idea what it felt like. It's completely different now. From today on, there won't be a person in Armagh – young or old – who doesn't become an expert on how to win All-Irelands and everything that goes with them! Mark my words ... that's certain to happen and it won't be easy to deal with."

Eamonn paused for a second, as if considering what I'd said, but quickly decided this was no time for anything but celebration.

"Let's get in here and enjoy the night and the next few weeks and let the future look after itself," he said.

He was right, of course. That was a night to party and party we did. It was a night to savour and enjoy and, while the heroic men who had finally taken Armagh where they'd never been before deserved all the credit, it was also a time to pay respect to those who had done so much for Armagh over the years.

None more so than the team of 1953 who came closest of all to winning Armagh's first All-Ireland. Their heart-breaking defeat by Kerry in the final was still talked of in Armagh, much more than the loss to Dublin in 1977. We were well beaten by Dublin in '77 whereas the team of '53, which included my cousin Frank, were unlucky losers.

It was all the more fitting, then, that Kerry were the opposition when we won the All-Ireland forty-nine years later. Certainly, nobody could say we won it the easy way. Eight games, two replays, several close calls but, in the end, we were champions.

Winning a first All-Ireland title changes the dynamic in a county and, while we managed to keep things under reasonable control, it was far from easy. By the time we reached the end of 2006, things had changed in a way I never thought possible.

By then, information was leaking from our camp as if through a sieve. Details of things we were doing in training were being passed on to others outside the county. We had always prided ourselves on keeping a tight ship but now all had changed.

You might ask, how did I know?

I live in Crossmaglen where we've always been pretty good at keeping our ear to the ground, so not much happened in Armagh football that I didn't know about. Besides, I was told by a few people, including one County Manager who asked me, bluntly: "Joe, do you know that everything is being leaked?"

I had heard it from other people, too, which was hardly surprising since football is something of a goldfish bowl in any county and certainly in Armagh at a time when the great era was coming to an end.

The damage extended right across the camp and to the very heart of Armagh football. What was it I said to Eamonn Mackle about not being able to control the monster we had created? By the end of 2006, there was damn all I – or anybody else – could do about it.

Okay, so it wasn't classified information which impacted on national security but there was an important principle at stake.

All my managerial life with Crossmaglen and Armagh had been based on keeping things tight within the group. What happens in camp stays in camp. That's easy enough to achieve when things are going well but it tends to loosen once the cracks begin to appear.

I had experience of how upsetting leaks can be from an incident a few years earlier, which was totally of my own making. I have always believed that the more you talk to people who know the game, the more you pick up. It's a policy that has served me well over the years. Nobody ever knows the full story so there's no harm in listening to an alternative view. Martin McHugh is a man whose views I have respected over many years and whose opinion I would have had no hesitation in seeking on any issue at any time, just as he would have been happy to seek mine.

Anyway, on one occasion some of what we talked about in a squad discussion came out, indirectly, in one of Martin's newspaper columns. I have no doubt it was an inadvertent slip by Martin as he's a very honourable guy, but it was noticed in our camp. Paul Grimley came to me and told me I'd better clear it up.

He was right, so I held my hands up, explained what had happened and apologised to the lads. When you're wrong the only thing to do is apologise.

But in 2006 we had enough problems without moles burrowing away in the background. We were three-in-a-row Ulster champions but, in squad terms, things were moving on. John and Tony McEntee announced their retirements in April and we also had a spate of injury problems which made things extra difficult. We were lucky enough to escape relegation from Division 1 after winning only three games, which left us joint sixth on the table with Westmeath, just one point ahead of Louth who were relegated.

Armagh were heading into a period of transition but the basics were solid. There was a strong core who were still young enough to continue into a new phase, while the Under-21s had won the 2004 All-Ireland title in what was another first for the county. What's more, it was a seriously good team.

As for me, my appetite was as strong as ever although certain things were going on in the background that were making things a bit tricky. It was at that stage I began to fully realise just how difficult it was becoming for me to manage a county squad where my own sons were involved.

Aaron and Stephen had both been on the Under-21 All-Ireland winning team in 2004 and made their Championship debut a year later. Aaron started out as a corner-forward in a challenge game against Meath, switched to right half-back for the League semi-final against Mayo and held his place from there on. Stephen came on as a sub against Derry in the Ulster semi-final and against Laois in the All-Ireland quarter-final.

Two years later, with two other sons, Tony and Paul, also pressing for places, it was becoming very difficult to balance things. Whatever a manager does in that situation, he's in trouble. Play your own sons and you'll be accused of favouring them, don't play them and they'll want to know why they're not being given the same chance as everybody else, which is perfectly understandable.

That's one of the worst aspects of the GAA. A manager can play anybody else's sons but not his own. How unfair is that? Surely, nobody believes that a manager who's doing his job properly will pick his own son simply because of who he is. Would he put him through that if he weren't up to the job?

Right down through GAA history, a lot of great players have taken a long time to settle into their careers. Not everybody is an instant hit. If a manager plays his son and the lad is taking time to find his feet, is it fair to single him out? Isn't he as entitled to get a decent chance as anybody else?

Now that I'm no longer involved with the Armagh team (other than as a proud father and a loyal supporter) I have to say that the attitude to fathers playing their sons is very destructive. There are always people prepared to pick holes in even the best-run set-up and the father/son situation is manna from heaven for their mean-spirited little minds.

It could stem from jealousy, ignorance or maybe even malice, but it's one of the very few things that disgust me about the Association I hold so dear. I wasn't the first manager and, no doubt, I won't be the last to experience it but it's something I wouldn't wish on my worst enemy.

Mickey Harte had it in Tyrone when his son Mark was on the team. They both took some awful abuse at times. Indeed, at one particular Tyrone game where I was among the crowd, I took on a man who seemed more interested in abusing the Hartes than he did in supporting Tyrone. The man clearly had a pre-conceived notion in his head that young Harte was there because of his father and it probably wouldn't have made any difference if he had scored three goals. I told him, in no uncertain terms, that he should be ashamed of himself. The people around me in the stand agreed and 'mouth almighty' didn't like it when he became the focus of attention, although he clearly considered it acceptable to abuse others. He shut up straightaway but I'm sure he wasn't silenced for good.

He probably went away saying that I was defending the Hartes because of my own situation but I didn't give a damn. He deserved to be told a few home truths. There's no doubt that my own family involvement with Armagh made me more sensitive to the father/son dilemma but I just couldn't stand by and watch that kind of bloody stupidity. That really is a downside to the GAA where some bitter, vindictive types don't want to see other people's sons making it, especially if it's a manager/son situation.

Aaron made the No. 5 jersey his own from 2005 onwards but it was much tougher for Stephen. The truth is that I was probably harder on him than anybody else on the squad but it was twice as difficult for him watching his dad doing something he knew wasn't quite right. As for me, I regret to this day replacing him against Fermanagh in the 2006 Ulster semi-final replay.

He didn't deserve to be taken off but, conscious of the risk of being accused of favouring my own, I watched his game in an overly-critical way. His mistakes were magnified whereas others got away with theirs. Far from giving him an easy ride, I was too tough on him. It must have been hugely frustrating for him: it's hard enough to survive at top level without your father judging you by higher standards than he applies to others.

I got a call from another County Manager after the Fermanagh game telling me that I had been wrong to take Stephen off and that there were two others who should have been withdrawn first.

In terms of off-pitch dealings, I treated my lads like everybody else on the panel. I didn't ask them what was being said by other players when I wasn't around and they didn't tell me. I was the manager, they were players and I wanted a clear demarcation line to remain in place. It's not easy when you're all sleeping under the same roof but it can be done and I think we managed it quite well.

As far as I was concerned, the lads were involved because they were good enough. For some, that's okay while things are going well but, the day fortunes begin to change, is the day the gossip starts.

Nobody said it directly to me but, eventually, I got the distinct feeling that a few of the lads on the panel didn't like the fact that two Kernans were on the team. Stephen's presence would have been the main issue. Every player wants to be on the team so it's inevitable that there will be a bit of bitching over being left out, but it got more serious than that in Stephen's case.

It pains me to say it but I'm convinced there were occasions when colleagues didn't pass to him, not because he was in a bad position but because there was certain resentment towards him being on the team. We needed a centre-forward who would spray the ball around after John McEntee retired and, as far as I was concerned, Stephen was the best man for the job.

Unfortunately, a few on the team obviously didn't agree. There were some occasions when I wondered what the hell was going on. Stephen would be free and waiting for a pass but the ball would go elsewhere or be given away. At first, I put it down to a lack of vision but when it happened on a regular basis, I began to wonder. It's a simple fact of football life, from kids' level up, that if you're free in space the ball goes to you. Stephen is good at losing his man but wasn't always picked out. All I can say is that if people were ignoring him they weren't doing themselves or Armagh football justice.

It was clear that he wasn't getting as much ball as he should. I brought it up in a general sort of way, once or twice, emphasising the need to be more aware of men in space. That's the sort of thing you tell six year olds but it was as much as I could do. After all, I could hardly say, "Lads, will you cut out the messing and pass to our Stephen".

In my last game as manager, against Derry in the 2007 qualifiers, there were at least three occasions when Stephen was free inside the Derry full-back line but the ball wasn't played to him. Why not? What made it all the more frustrating was that we ended up losing by a point. That's how close it was, so you can see how every decision made on the pitch was crucial.

The fact that this sort of situation arose at all suggested that the team ethic was disintegrating. Once that started happening, I knew my days in Armagh were numbered. Apart from anything else, it wasn't fair on my own sons and with the younger boys also trying to make the breakthrough, it was only going to get worse.

For all that, we were unlucky to lose to Donegal in the first round of the 2007 Championship. They had won the League title for the first time a month earlier and were on a high as they prepared for their clash with us in Ballybofey.

Despite going for an Ulster four-in-a-row, having remained unbeaten in Ulster since May 2003 and having lost none of our seven previous meetings with Donegal, the Armagh public were harbouring doubts. More than 2,000 of the 8,000 tickets sent to Armagh by the Ulster Council had to be sent back unsold so not only did Donegal have home advantage but they out-numbered our supporters by at least two to one.

Granted, things had changed in Armagh. The McEntees had retired and we were without Francie Bellew, Ronan Clarke and Brian Mallon due to injury so, clearly, the supporters had doubts about our ability to beat Donegal. Either that or they didn't fancy the trip to Ballybofey and were waiting for the semi-final.

On the plus side, we had Diarmaid Marsden back onboard. Diarmaid had come out of retirement and still had plenty to offer. We were 7/4 outsiders, which showed how much the perception of us had changed, but we certainly didn't play like that. We were two points up heading into the final minute of normal time when a high, speculative lob for a point by Brendan Devenney deceived Paul Hearty, allowing Kevin Cassidy to score what turned out to be the winning goal (1-9 to 1-8).

Should referee John Bannon have disallowed it for a 'square' infringement? Definitely in my view, but then we had won many a game with a late flourish so we weren't complaining. If any team deserved to beat us it was Donegal who had suffered terribly at our hands over previous seasons. Trouble was, they went out next time and were eaten alive by Tyrone, which didn't exactly thrill us. Whatever problems we might have had, there was no way Tyrone would have beaten us by eleven points.

It was back to the All-Ireland qualifiers for us where we were paired with Derry, which wasn't the easiest draw we could have had. We needed a gentler return and not another dogfight with one of our great Ulster rivals. Once again, the winning margin was a single point and, once again, we were on the wrong side. Truly, the gods were telling us something which sounded remarkably like: "Your time is up".

The amazing thing was that we conceded just 1-9 against Donegal and 0-10 against Derry, giveaway rates you'd take if you were offered them in advance. Unfortunately, our strike rate had dropped alarmingly.

Still, we came back from a two-point deficit late on against Derry and the game seemed to be heading into extra time when they conjured up the winning point. Our season was finished in early-July for the first time in several years.

But it wasn't just the end of another season, it was the end of an era.

I took a few weeks before announcing that I would be standing down after six of the most enjoyable years of my life. I wanted to be absolutely sure I was doing the right thing but the more I looked at it the more I knew it was time to go.

Had I stayed on, there would have been a big transformation for 2008. We had made big changes over the years bringing in lots of new players but now it was time to re-build at a different level and, while I would have had the energy and the enthusiasm for the challenge, I felt it was right to go. Sometimes, you can overstay your welcome and I certainly didn't want to do that.

And then there was the question of my sons' involvement. However I handled it, it would have been next to impossible to get it right so the best thing all round was to slip away quietly and leave the future to somebody else. Of course it was a wrench but, at the same time, I probably needed a break.

Things had changed and, as I had predicted to Eamonn Mackle back in 2002, everybody in Armagh now thought they knew what it took to win an

All-Ireland so, when the titles didn't keep coming, cracks began to appear.

After the Kerry defeat in the 2006 All-Ireland quarter-final, I met with John (McCloskey) and Paul (Grimley) in the City Hotel, Armagh. We needed a change and I felt it was my time to go. In my opinion, Paul was the next man for the job. We had a good chat at the meeting and I decided to speak to the County Board about Paul taking over and me stepping down.

However, a few days later I was disappointed to learn from reading the paper that Paul was stepping down from Armagh. Later in the day, I heard on the grapevine that he was joining Cavan. I still hadn't talked to the County Board. I was disappointed with the turn of events which left me with no option but to stay on for another year. I also had to look for a new assistant.

Several of the players who had been on the great adventure, including Kieran McGeeney, Paul McGrane, Enda McNulty, Steven McDonnell and Oisin McConville, were all set to carry on into 2007, so I decided to stick with it.

It would be easy to be wise in hindsight and say I stayed too long but, when you're in the middle of something with so many people who have done so much for so long, it's difficult to walk away.

Whatever about staying for a season too long, my real regret was that the scene had changed so much by the end of 2006.

CHAPTER 12
GROWING PAINS

It's more than forty-five years since my father died but I can remember it as clearly as if it were yesterday. Every Saturday evening we would watch TV, sometimes a Western, sometimes 'Dixon of Dock Green', and then he would give me some money to go across the road to the shop.

This particular Saturday evening, in January 1966, started out the same as every other. We had watched TV, he had handed me money and I was just about to close the front door without a care in the world when I heard my mother screaming. I ran back into the living room to find my father collapsed. We knew immediately that it was serious.

I ran out to find Dr Crummie and then galloped over to the church to Fr McFadden. He was hearing confessions but I burst through the queue to tell him what had happened. He came over to the house straightaway but, even by the time he and the doctor arrived, Dad was dead, having suffered a massive heart attack.

Joseph Kernan senior was sixty-one years old at the time; Joseph Kernan junior was eleven.

Dad had probably had a heart condition for some time but would have told nobody. Men of that era didn't talk about things like that. They were tough to the point of being indestructible, or at least they thought they were.

The hours and days after my father's death passed in a blur. People coming and going, the house full all the time, the removal on the Sunday evening, the burial on Monday and then the horrible sense of emptiness and loss. I just couldn't understand how a man who was in perfect health one minute could be dead the next. Looking through eleven-year-old eyes, it made no sense. Your dad is the rock, the man that knows the answer to everything, the man who fixes everything, the man who doesn't even get sick, let alone die.

I just kept thinking, what happened to him? Why did it have to be Dad?

Was there nothing anybody could have done?

I was too young to have any real appreciation of how my mother, Joan, was feeling. One minute she had been living an ordinary life in Crossmaglen, County Armagh and the next she was left in charge of four children: my older sisters, Olivia and Annette, and my younger brother, Raymond.

My mother was Dad's second wife, the first, Bridie Fitzpatrick, died giving birth to my half-brother, Patrick, who is some years older than me. It wasn't the first – or indeed the last time – that tragedy visited the extended Kernan family.

My Uncle Jamesy, a member of the 1926 Armagh team that won the All-Ireland junior title, died in 1929 from an injury sustained in a football game. He was playing for Armagh against Cavan in the Ulster senior semi-final in Belturbet when he took a knee to the stomach area in the second half. He was in terrible pain and was replaced. Medical care wasn't anywhere near as sophisticated back then but, in any event, it was thought that Jamesy was okay afterwards and he was allowed to return home, as usual.

However, things took a drastic turn for the worse later and he was rushed to the Armagh County Infirmary on the Sunday night. He had suffered a serious intestinal injury and died two days later. It emerged at the inquest, which was held later the same day, that there was a large perforation of his intestine. That, in turn, raised the question of how he had sustained such a serious injury on the pitch and whether or not there was anything deliberate in the incident.

Inevitably, opinions differed and, while the Armagh County Board accepted that it was an accident, a Cavan player later faced a charge at Cavan District Court that he did "feloniously kill and slay James Kernan".

However, after some preliminary evidence was offered, the judge found that there was no case to answer. According to newspaper reports, there was as much relief at the verdict in Armagh as in Cavan, because nobody wanted to go down that particular road. Indeed, there was widespread surprise, on both sides of the border, that the charge was ever brought.

Jamesy's death – he was only twenty-eight years old at the time – cast a terrible pall over Crossmaglen and it would be several months before anybody in the town played football again.

The untimely death of my father and, before that, his first wife were two dreadful blows to the family and, later, there would be added grief when my brother, Raymond, took his own life in Australia.

The tragedy of losing a child was visited on Patricia and I when our first son, Joseph, died a week after being born in 1979. He was born perfectly healthy but he contracted septicaemia in Daisy Hill Hospital in Newry and died a few days later in Craigavon Hospital.

Patricia would later have an ectopic pregnancy, which very nearly led to her death. After that we feared we might have no family but, thanks be to God, everything was okay and we went on to have five strapping sons. The tragedies didn't end, however, as Patricia's brother, Thomas, was killed in a road accident in 1987 and my first cousin, Hank, who played for Armagh at all levels, died of multiple sclerosis.

That's an awful lot of tragedy for one family to endure but there was nothing anybody could do about it. Fate had dealt us a heavy hand, leaving us to get on with life as best we could. Personally, football always played a major part in helping me get through things and gave me so many joyous days for which I'm very grateful. Oddly enough, my father wasn't much into football. He left that to his brother, Jamesy, who was reputed to have had a great left foot.

He was at left half-forward on the Armagh team that made history by becoming the first Ulster side to win an All-Ireland title in August, 1927. It was actually for the 1926 junior Championship but I'm sure the year's delay didn't matter to the Armagh lads who created history. They beat Dublin by nineteen points in the final and, in what would become the norm for Armagh, the team was well stocked with Crossmaglen players.

Apart from Jamesy, other Crossmaglen players in the squad were Gene Hanratty, who captained the team, Harry Cumiskey, John Donaghy, John McCusker and James McEntee. Judging by what I've read about it, winning that All-Ireland had a massive impact on Armagh people. Some might have regarded winning a junior All-Ireland as scarcely an occasion to get over-excited but the fact that it was a first for Armagh and Ulster gave it a massive sense of importance. I'm sure Jamesy and his colleagues didn't think, back then, that it would take another seventy-six years for Armagh to win the senior All-Ireland.

Jamesy's tragic death knocked the heart out of Crossmaglen. It seems nobody had any appetite for football. Besides, there must have been a huge sense of shock that a young footballer, especially one who was a local hero, could die in such unusual circumstances. Indeed, it wasn't until my grandfather threw a football out to a few lads who were standing outside his hardware shop some months later that things got going again.

Horses were my father's life. Buying, selling, dealing – if there were horses around so were my father and his brother, Frank. Dad was into the wheeling and dealing while Frank was more into the showjumping side. Indeed, the Kernan name would become synonymous with showjumping over future years and remains so to this day. My cousin, James, was one of Ireland's top showjumpers for several years. We travelled the country together to various shows and, while I loved the buzz and excitement of the sport, it always came second to football in my eyes. I rode from time to time but clearly God hadn't intended me to be a horseman – otherwise he would hardly have grown me to be well over six feet tall by the time I was sixteen years old.

Still, horses played a major part in the Kernan way of life and, indeed, without them I might not even be on this earth. It was on a horse-trading foray that Dad met his second wife. Ballinasloe has always hosted one of the country's really big horse fairs and it was while my father and Frank were there one year that events took an unexpected turn.

Clearly, my father had his eyes peeled on more than horses and, when a young woman by the name of Joan Ward caught his fancy, he took time out from the horses to indulge in a bit of romance. A relationship was formed and, in due course, the pair got married. Joan Ward said goodbye to Ballinasloe and came to live in Crossmaglen where she remained until her death in 2007.

Despite being from Galway, she had no great interest in football, other than keeping an eye on how I was doing. She was at the 1977 All-Ireland final but, other than that, she wouldn't have seen me play very often. By 2002, her health was deteriorating so she wasn't at the All-Ireland final. Instead, she watched it on TV at home. She probably had her rosary beads out so, who knows, maybe she was the one who provided the divine inspiration that enabled the lads to kick on in the second half.

Her good friend, Kay McArdle – another Galway woman – brought her up to the pitch on the night we returned home with the Sam Maguire Cup and I'm sure there wasn't a prouder woman in Ireland. It was great to have her there but, sadly, my father never got to see the big day. Had he lived, he would have been ninety-seven years old in 2002. It has always been one of my great regrets that he wasn't around to see us growing up and follow my fortunes on the football field. While he might not have been all that keen on playing football himself, he would have been an ardent supporter once I got to wear the county jersey.

I felt that loss deeply. I envied other players who had their fathers to talk to after games and always felt there was something missing. As with everything in life, you only miss what you don't have.

My own interest in football was fostered in Newry Street where we lived. Crossmaglen was exclusively a Gaelic football town, unchallenged by such distractions as soccer, rugby or even hurling. This was football territory, pure and simple. We'd kick a ball up and down the street, up against walls, gable ends, gates or whatever. Nor was it unusual for the odd wayward shot to clang through a window, a shooting error which was immediately followed by an attempt at the 100 yard record as we sprinted from the scene.

On summer Sundays, young and old would gather outside Tommy Burns' house to listen to Micheal O Hehir's commentaries on Radio Éireann. Tommy would leave the radio on the window and turn the volume up as loudly as was required for whatever sized audience turned up on a particular day. It was in that environment that I became exposed to football and footballers outside Crossmaglen.

The 1960s weren't especially productive for Armagh football. They brought home no Ulster senior titles and the only appearance in the final was against Down, in 1961. Down were the big shots of Gaelic football at the time, having won the first of their All-Irelands the previous year. Nonetheless, Armagh gave them a right good run, losing by just three points. Sadly, that was as good as it got for Armagh. Down went on to win a second All-Ireland in 1961 but, unfortunately, Armagh went into decline. They won only two Ulster Championship games throughout the rest of the decade, which left them very close to the bottom of the ladder.

It meant we had few Armagh heroes to look up to. Jimmy Whan would have been the main man in terms of profile as he was a regular on the Ulster team for much of the 1960s. Our own Crossmaglen clubman, Tom McCreesh, came into the Ulster team around 1970 but a look back at the teams of that era shows just how little impact Armagh players were making among their contemporaries.

Instead, it was the exploits of Galway, Kerry, Dublin, Meath and Down that blasted out on Tommy's radio during the 1960s. If Down were the history-makers in the early-'60s by becoming the first team to bring Sam Maguire across the border, Galway replaced them as the glamour side, winning three successive All-Irelands in 1964, '65 and '66. Midway through their great run, I discovered that I had more in common with them than merely dreaming of being Mattie McDonagh, Enda Colleran, Seamus Leydon, or whoever. Much to my delight, I learned that I was a third cousin on my mother's side to John and Pat Donnellan from Dunmore who were also key players on that brilliant squad. Little did I know, back then, that forty-five years later I would manage Galway.

During those early years, I had no control over the way in which my devotion to Gaelic football was taking hold of me. Not that I wanted to control it, I was fascinated by every aspect of the game and just couldn't spend enough time playing. At that time, the street leagues were big in Crossmaglen and it was in those tense, feisty battles that I won my first medal.

The passion for football continued through my primary school days in St Patrick's, the local primary school, and later in St Michael's, Omeath, where I was sent as a boarder. Now, I have to admit that books and study didn't appeal to me. I'd go further and say that there was never much danger I would get a 'Student of the Year' award for diligence and devotion, unless of course it was on the football field. That was where I expressed myself best. It was where I felt at home. As for the classroom, it was some place to be endured until I could get out on the football field again.

I found it hard being a boarder in Omeath. In fact, I hated it.

On the first morning, I woke up with forty or fifty other young lads in the dormitory and nearly flipped. This wasn't me at all. Others settled into it quite easily, but not me. I have no idea how I would have survived without football. Looking forward to the next game kept me sane even if it didn't do much to help my concentration in class or at study time. Fr Kenny was a great football man and made sure we got plenty of chances to show what skills we had, but it still wasn't enough to improve my relationship with boarding school.

My football talents provided me with welcome benefits in the form of unscheduled trips home. Sometimes, I would be allowed out at weekends to play for Crossmaglen, outings which I welcomed by counting the days and hours until my release. Back home, I kept up the pressure to be permanently freed from Omeath and, eventually, my mother agreed. The poor woman was probably demented listening to my moaning. I switched to Abbey CBS in Newry and now I was in a different world altogether.

I travelled in and out to Newry every day, which put a pep in my step, even if it didn't do a whole lot to increase my interest in studying. More important, from my perspective, was that I would get as much football as I wanted, only now at a higher standard than I'd been used to in St Michael's. This was McRory Cup territory where colleges such as St Colman's, Newry; St Michael's, Enniskillen; St Patrick's, Cavan; St Mary's CBS, Belfast and, of course, Abbey CBS, were among the powerhouses.

It was during my time in Abbey CBS that I experienced my first great setback, one which still ranks high up there on my list of disappointments.

It came in the 1972 McRory Cup final in Dundalk when we lost to St Patrick's, Cavan, by two points. Abbey were going for their first title since 1964 while St Patrick's hadn't won it since 1962, so there was a real edge to the final.

We had come through a marathon semi-final against our great rivals, St Colman's, winning by five points in extra time in Carrickcruppin. I scored two goals that day, while the top scorer and captain for St Colman's was none other than Pete McGrath – who would, of course, go on to manage Down to All-Ireland minor and senior titles. There was a huge sense of achievement in beating our local rivals, all the more so because it went to extra time in a replay. It was a really close affair until, midway through the second half of extra time, I punched a goal that made all the difference. We won by 3-10 to 2-8 but, to be honest, St Colman's didn't deserve to be five points behind.

Gerry Brown and Brian McKevitt were in charge of our team and did the good cop/bad cop routine very well. Gerry was quiet and polished while Brian was the hard one who would let you know, in no uncertain terms, if you did something wrong. Still, they worked very well together and got the team playing a lovely brand of football.

There was an air of real excitement going into the final which drew a massive crowd to Dowdallshill in Dundalk. For reasons which I couldn't understand – then or now – college games were thirteen-a-side affairs in the first half of the 1970s. Maybe it was something to do with leaving more room for young players to indulge their skills, but that made no difference in the 1972 McRory Cup final because the players had to vie for space with many of the crowd who regularly encroached onto the pitch from a packed sideline.

The stewarding, if indeed it existed, wasn't wholly successful. With four or five thousand people there, it was inevitable that some would nudge their way over the sidelines and end lines.

We had a really good side, while Ollie Brady, Sean Leddy and captain, Niall Brennan, were among the stars for St Patrick's. I was playing midfield against a lad called Ciaran O'Keeffe, a fine player who would later go on to play for both Cavan and Sligo.

We lost by two points (1-9 to 2-4) after missing a lot of chances. We played against the wind in the first half but still led by a point at half time so it looked as if we were on our way to glory. It was a different story in the second half where we scored just one point while St Pat's kicked four points. We were very unhappy with the performance of the referee, Tommy Johnson from Fermanagh, although, in fairness to him, it was never going to be easy to referee a game with the crowd spilling over the sideline. Losing that game left us shattered because it happened in a year we could have gone on to win the All-Ireland title. St Patricks's walloped St Jarlath's, Tuam, in the semi-final

– which was no small feat – and went on to clinch the Hogan Cup beating a St Brendan's, Killarney, team which, if memory serves me correctly, featured lads by the name of Pat Spillane and Paidi O Se who went on to become pretty decent footballers!

Playing in that McRory Cup final was as good as it got for me at that time because Armagh wasn't making any impression at minor or U-21 level. Come to think of it, they weren't doing much at senior level either. It was a different world back then in terms of how the county organised itself. Indeed, it would be quite a few years before things changed for the better.

CHAPTER 13
GOOD TIMES AND BAD

It was one of those moments when you feel your head is going to burst. It's as if you're caught in some horrible nightmare and there's no way out. Surely this can't be real, it can't be happening. How could it be?

I put the phone down. My sisters in Australia, Olivia and Annette, had just told me that our younger brother, Raymond, had committed suicide. It was more than I could take in and I stared blankly at the wall, my mind flooding with questions.

Why did he do it? Why wasn't I told he had been ill? Why? Why? Why?

When the initial sense of numbness subsided I was overcome by frustration and my sisters were very much in the firing line: Why hadn't they told me that Raymond was suffering from depression?

He had moved to Australia, where they had settled some years earlier, so they had known about his condition. I was back in Crossmaglen and hadn't a clue what was going on until I got that heart-breaking phone call telling me that Raymond, who was two years younger than me, was gone.

He had moved to Canberra because there weren't many job opportunities around Crossmaglen in the 1980s. Olivia and Annette were already over there. They had married two brothers, Adrian and Gene Quinn from Cullyhanna, who had relations in Australia. It was the start of a new life for the two girls and they have remained Down Under ever since.

Unlike me with my obsession for sport, Raymond wasn't much into it. So, when the chance came to go to Australia, he didn't have the pull of Crossmaglen Rangers or any other team to keep him at home. As far as he was concerned, going to Australia was an adventure which offered him the chance of a different way of life in a far-flung country.

Times were different back then so, to a large degree, I lost touch with him. Nowadays, you can dial the far side of the world on your mobile phone in seconds but, back then, phoning Australia was a big, and expensive, operation. And, since neither Raymond nor I were much into writing letters, we didn't have a whole lot of contact. We'd talk every six months or so and, when we did, it was about fairly casual stuff.

He was okay before he left for Australia. Certainly, I have no memory of him being down or depressed. That's what made the shocking news that he had committed suicide all the harder to take. It seems he had tried to commit suicide a couple of times before and I felt I should have been told then, if not long before.

At the very least, I could have spoken to him on the phone or maybe even arranged a trip to Australia. To be honest, I'm not sure what I would have done but at least it would have been my decision to make. Instead of that, I heard nothing until his death in 1988.

In fairness to my sisters, they felt there was no point in telling me, believing there was nothing I could have done at several thousands miles' range. In a way, they were protecting me because they knew I'd be worried if I had heard Raymond wasn't getting on too well. Still, I felt keeping me in the dark wasn't their decision to make.

Being told that a close family member has committed suicide is about as hard as it gets on the human condition. I took it very badly, especially since it was mixed with the anger of not knowing he had been suffering from depression. A combination of confusion, helplessness and anger were swirling around in my head and, however hard I tried to unravel them, I couldn't. They kept tangling up in each other, leaving me more and more frustrated.

If it was tough on me, it was harder on my mother. She was completely devastated. A bit of her died when she heard the shocking news and, while I did what I could for her, there was nothing anybody could do to take away the awful pain she was feeling.

Raymond's body was cremated in Australia and the ashes flown home to Crossmaglen for burial. Those were dark, dark days. Even now, all these years later, none of it makes sense. Afterwards, I would often go over to the graveyard where we'd buried Raymond's ashes, say a silent prayer and then start asking him why he had done it and why he hadn't told me he was unwell. Pointless though my questions were, it was my way of coping, my way of trying to make sense of it all. But, of course, there was no sense to be found. Raymond had gone to Australia to start a new life and now he was dead.

I might well have emigrated to Australia myself if it hadn't been for football and a certain girl from Jonesborough. Patricia would always say it was the football that kept me here but that's only partially true.

I first met her in a bar in Crossmaglen on the night after a showjumping event out in my cousin Frank's place. Patricia's parents kept horses and she used to do some work for the local show. Anyway, this particular night she was talking to a friend of mine, Sligo man Cecil Mahon, who worked for her father. He asked her if she was going out with anybody and, as the joking started, he said, "Tell you what, I'll pick out a fella for you."

With that, I walked into the bar and Cecil announced, "There's the man for you."

We were introduced and, by the end of the year, Patricia Morgan was Mrs Joe Kernan. We got married in the church in Dublin Airport on December 29, 1976. She was eighteen years old and I was twenty-two.

My mother used to divide her time between Crossmaglen and my sisters' places in Australia so none of them were around for the wedding, which was a small affair with around thirty guests. As I recall, the food at the airport hotel was terrible but the craic was mighty. I went down to Dublin the night before the wedding with my best man, Tony Morris, and we had a few drinks just to settle the nerves. The following morning, we got ourselves to the church in good time and were waiting patiently inside when Patricia and her entourage pulled up outside.

Her father must have been a bit wary of me because he said to one of the lads, "Run in and see if yer man is there."

I was!

The wedding went ahead and now, more than thirty-four years later, Patricia and I are still together and more rock solid now than at any other time.

Even if Patricia and I hadn't met, I would still have found it very hard to leave Crossmaglen. I loved being part of the football scene, both with the club and Armagh. I played soccer in wintertime when there was a lull on the GAA scene. Still, with all the family in Australia, I might have tried it Down Under for a while and, who knows, I might have taken up Aussie Rules and stayed.

The strange thing is that I've still never been to Australia. I've seen the rest of the world but not Australia. Our sons gave us a present of a holiday in Australia two years ago but there was a lot happening at the time and we still haven't made it. We'll get there, one day.

Raymond's death wasn't the only tragedy to hit our family. We lost our first son, Joseph junior, five days after he was born. Patricia gave birth to a fine, healthy boy in Daisy Hill Hospital, Newry, on a Friday and everything went fine for a few days. In fact, he was the healthiest looking child in the unit and, with everything going well, I joined up with the Armagh panel to play a National League game against Sligo the following Sunday.

However, on the Monday morning we got a terrible shock. We were told that our strong, thriving son had contracted septicaemia (poisoning of the blood) and that it was extremely serious. We were absolutely stunned. Why would a perfectly healthy child develop such a serious condition so quickly? We never did get a satisfactory answer.

You put your trust in the medical world and hope things turn out right.

The next week was sheer hell. We felt totally helpless as the doctors battled to save our son. They did their best but, in the end, the poisoning proved too much and he died a week after being diagnosed. It had been the toughest, most awful time of our lives as we watched the little fella battling to survive but, in the end, he didn't make it.

Burying a child is the worst thing any parents can go through.

A few days after Joseph junior was buried, Sean O'Neill rang me. Ulster were playing a Railway Cup game the following Sunday and he suggested I might come along.

"Joe, I know you've had an awful week and it's entirely up to you but we'd love to have you with us. You know that," said Sean.

I asked him to leave it with me and I talked to Patricia about it. She told me to go ahead so I rang Sean back and told him I'd give it a go but also reminded him that I might not be any good to him or the team.

"You let me worry about that," he replied.

It was typical of Sean. He knew the trauma we were going through but felt that it might do me some good to meet up with the Ulster lads. What's more, he picked me for the team. I got through the game okay (we even won) but I'll never know how I managed it. Apart from the shock and the devastation of the previous week, I had hardly slept at all but, somehow, I got the energy to play from somewhere. Maybe young Joseph was giving me some inspiration.

Being asked to play for Ulster gave me a great lift. All the lads were very supportive and, with Sean knowing exactly the right things to say, I felt at home among friends. It was a classic example of the GAA family rallying around one of their own, as they always do. Indeed, it's one of the great strengths of our association that, in a time of need, everybody gets behind the person who needs a bit of help.

Losing our first-born son was a shocking experience for Patricia and me but, sadly, it wouldn't be the last family setback we suffered. A few years later, Patricia had an ectopic pregnancy which very nearly killed her. Indeed, if it hadn't been for our dog, Bruno, it might well have.

At that time, my job took me around the country and I was staying overnight in Roscommon. I'd always hook up with my good friend John O'Gara when I was in that neck of the woods and, since it was a few weeks before Christmas 1981, we went for a couple of drinks.

What I didn't realise was that Patricia had taken a bad turn in the middle of the night. The ectopic pregnancy was causing all sorts of problems and she started losing blood at an alarming rate. Bruno, our lovely old Labrador, loved to jump up on the bed if he got a chance and, as Patricia's body temperature started dropping, he kept moving closer to her as if sensing that there was something seriously wrong.

The following morning when she managed to call the doctor, Bruno was still in protective mode. He kept jumping up on the bed when the doctor arrived and was trying to stay between him and Patricia. He was trying to protect her and didn't like the idea of a stranger coming anywhere near her.

He had always been a smart dog. I remember going to the front door one morning to put the bins out and, for some reason, it slammed shut. Patricia was at work and I had no way of getting back in. Now, in normal circumstances, it wouldn't have been a big problem but on this particular morning I had gone to the door wearing nothing but my underpants.

So, there I was, early on a Crossmaglen morning, locked outside the front door of my house with nothing on but my underpants. Prowling around in that state isn't exactly recommended behaviour at any time, least of all first thing in the morning, so it was time to see just how smart Bruno really was. I opened up the letterbox, called him to the door and started urging him to fetch the bunch of keys on the hall table. He was well versed in collecting my slippers which he would fetch one by one and throw at my feet, but this was a new challenge even for such a clever dog.

So, there I was, down on my hunkers, trying to let Bruno know exactly what I wanted. I feared that I would be arrested at any minute and I wasn't sure if the explanation I was negotiating with my dog would be much of a defence. Come to think of it, it would have sounded pretty lame.

It took a while to get the message through but, eventually, Bruno copped on, ran to the table, collected the keys and dropped them just inside the letterbox. I put my hand through, collected them and opened the door. Boy, was I relieved. As for Bruno, he was on treats for a month.

Bruno used to keep a close watch on me in other ways, too. Sometimes, on Saturdays, I'd nip down to the pub for a drink and a chat with the lads and, after a while, Bruno would come looking for me. He'd arrive at the door but, before he came in, I'd nip out to the keg room to avoid him. Intelligent beast that he was, he wouldn't be put off that easily, he'd sniff the seat where I was sitting and then follow the trail to the door of the keg room and start barking.

No chance of a quiet drink!

To this day, Patricia remains convinced that Bruno was doing his best to keep her body temperature up the night she started losing blood. The following morning, she was rushed to hospital in a very serious condition. She needed six pints of blood before even being sent to theatre. I was eventually tracked down in Roscommon and drove back like a madman and straight to the hospital. When I arrived at her room and saw her hooked up to so many machines and tubes, I genuinely thought she was dying. It was all too much for me and I keeled over.

Patricia could hardly speak but she had a bell so she rang it, bringing doctors and nurses running immediately because they were very concerned about her condition. Of course, when they opened the door, it was me they found spark-out on the floor. They made an awful laugh of me afterwards: There was Patricia, in a serious condition but holding her own, while this big, strong fella had fainted.

The doctors were extremely concerned about her for a while but they did a fantastic job and, after a few days, she began to get stronger. She came home on Christmas Eve, which was the best possible present after what had been an awful time.

At that stage we began to wonder if we would ever have a family. The ectopic pregnancy had been very serious and, for a while, the doctors couldn't say if Patricia would be able to have any children. It was a very worrying time but, in due course, thank God, Patricia became pregnant again. Naturally, we were concerned after what had happened the last time but everything went fine and Stephen was born in January 1983. The Kernan brood were on their way. By Christmas 1983, we had two sons. Aaron was born in mid-December so we had no kids one Christmas and two lads the following one.

Despite being born in the same year, there's a world of difference in football terms between a January and a December birthday. With January 1 as the cut off point in the various underage grades the earlier in the year you're born, the better. Stephen got full use of every year whereas Aaron was always fifteen days short of being eligible for the following year.

It got to him on one occasion when Crossmaglen were in an Under-14 final the year after he was eligible. They were struggling a bit so he decided he'd take it out on Patricia.

"It's all you're fault," he complained. "If you had held on to me for another two weeks, I'd be playing and we'd be winning."

CHAPTER THIRTEEN   GOOD TIMES AND BAD

Tony was born in 1986, Paul in 1987 and Ross followed four years later. It really is a great blessing to have five strong, healthy lads, especially after fearing we might never have a family.

Sadly, we had another family tragedy a few months after Paul was born when Patricia's brother, Thomas, was killed in a car accident. Patricia's brother-in-law, Martin McKenna, heard about it before us and let me know so that she would hear it from me.

I was making frequent trips to New York to play football at that time and, while I was out at training that night, Patricia had taken a call for me inviting me over again.

She told me about the call when I came home but I said I wouldn't be going. That surprised her because she knew how much I enjoyed travelling to New York. Then I told her the news that Thomas had been in an accident.

My mother looked after the children while we drove to Patricia's family home in Jonesborough. I didn't tell Patricia how serious it was until we were almost there, and then I had to break the awful news that he was dead. Thomas had been Paul's Godfather at the Christening just a few months earlier and now he was dead, at the age of twenty-seven.

His car had been in a collision with an oncoming lorry.

Just over a year later, Raymond died so it was a really tough time for us. There's nothing you can do in these situations except get on with life as best you can and, since we had a very young family, we immersed ourselves in caring for them.

Times were tough on the business front, too, in the 1980s so it was a matter of being as resourceful as you could in whatever area you were involved. I had always longed to have my own business so Patricia and I decided to have a go at the pub business.

In 1988, we bought the Welcome Inn in Crossmaglen, re-named it the Cross Bar in honour of the town and the football club, and set about building up business. It wasn't easy. There were a lot of bars in the town and only a certain amount of money to be shared between them all. Interest rates shot up so, all in all, it was the wrong time to become involved.

I suppose I thought that my football connections would boost trade but it didn't turn out that way. I often thought afterwards that we might have done better if we had bought a pub away from Crossmaglen but, then, hindsight tells us lots of things. We certainly made no money running the Cross Bar but it brought us closer as a couple because we were working together all the time. That mightn't work for everyone but it did for us.

In the end, though, we realised that we were effectively working for nothing so we decided to get out of the pub business. We sold the license but kept the premises which has remained our home to the present day and we actually got more money than we had paid for the license and the premises in the first place.

Owning a pub was a great experience in terms of getting to know people and how they think. It also gave me an idea for another business so I set up as an insurance brokerage and later went into property. Nowadays, two of the lads, Aaron and Stephen, work with me.

Back in the good old days, I made a few dollars playing football in America, mostly New York. It was big business at the time and we had great craic, too.

I went to America nine times in eight years on those famous weekend trips. Back then, the National League started in October so there were times when it was hard to juggle the two. You couldn't let it be known that you had missed a League game because you were playing in America, but it happened from time to time.

When I look back on it now, some of the schedules I bought into were crazy. I remember one time when I trained with Armagh on the Tuesday and Thursday nights before flying out of Dublin to New York on the Friday morning. I played a match on the Sunday which finished level and was due to be replayed the following week. I flew home on Monday night, arriving home on Tuesday morning and went to Armagh training that night.

More training on Thursday night and then off to Dublin airport on the

Friday morning to head over to New York again. The Armagh boys didn't know I was taking on such a daft schedule but I never thought twice about it. It was all very exciting and, on top of that, I'd have a few hundred dollars in my pocket when I got back, which was very welcome at the time.

I made a lot of friends on those trips. Ger Power, Paidi O Se, Mikey Sheehy and John Egan were regular weekend 'wild geese' and I also got very friendly with Mick Dempsey of Laois who does such a great job as Kilkenny hurling trainer nowadays. We usually played for Cavan although, God forgive me, I played for Tyrone a few times, too.

There was one year we were playing against Donegal who had Pat Spillane aboard and, before the game, Paidi O Se made his intentions clear.

"Leave Spillane to me, boys," said Paidi with a glint in his eye.

We were quite happy to do that and even more intrigued to see what he had in store although, in fairness, we had a good idea. The first ball came in between them and Paidi hit Pat an unmerciful bang on the nose and walked away smiling. We didn't see much of Pat for the rest of the day.

Those games could be very tough because there was a lot of personal pride at stake but anything that happened on the pitch was usually put to one side with a good old session in Rosie O'Grady's. Billy Morgan and Fran Ryder were working there for a while so it became the real hub for New York's Irish GAA community. There was always a fantastic atmosphere and, as well as that, it was a great place when it came to fixing lads up with work.

The All Stars tours were wonderful experiences, too. Airline travel wasn't nearly as common then because of the high costs so it was a real experience to be brought to places like San Francisco.

There were many in the GAA who frowned on weekend trips to the US but, in reality, it was a perk that lads enjoyed. If there were clubs in America who were prepared to fly us over, look after us for the weekend and stuff some dollars into our pockets before we left we were hardly going to say no. There was a huge social side to those trips where players from all around the country got to know each other, something that would never happen back home.

When I look back now at all the time I have devoted to football, I often wonder how much better I would have done in business if I hadn't been so involved. Football has always come first, since I was a teenager. Work and business hinged on football, not the other way around.

I don't even know how I kept the show on the road at times. I certainly wouldn't have done it without the wonderful support I got from Patricia. She was, and is, incredibly supportive of me and the efforts I put into football. Without her backing, I couldn't possibly have been so involved for so long.

It was bad enough when I was playing but it got far more demanding when I became involved in management, first with Crossmaglen, then with Armagh and, of course, later for a brief period with Galway. If Patricia hadn't been one hundred per cent behind me, it just wouldn't have worked. Thankfully, she was and it did!

CHAPTER 14
A QUESTION OF STYLE

As was his style, Thomas Cassidy didn't beat around the bush. A club and county colleague of mine for many years, there wasn't much he didn't know about me. I had also soldiered for many years with his brother, Benny, and am proud to call them two of my best and most-trusted friends, to this day.

Thomas had played long enough for club and county to know that, when he spoke, others listened. His stature as a warrior figure had earned him the right to express his view as forcibly as he thought necessary and the respect to have them carefully considered.

He'd call it as he saw it and to hell with the niceties and, as the 1990s ticked on towards their mid-point, he clearly didn't like what his eyes and instincts were telling him about the direction in which his beloved Crossmaglen Rangers were heading under his friend and neighbour. A big man, and a mechanic by trade, he had a huge pair of hands so, when he thumped the table after training one night, the legs shook as if hit by a lump hammer.

"Joe, do you mind me asking you something? Could you tell us what's Plan B?"

"What do you mean?" I replied, bemused.

"It's simple enough, Joe. Plan A just isn't working, we can all see that, so where's Plan B? Whatever it is, we need to give it a go … and the sooner the better!"

Thomas and the rest of the squad were feeling deeply frustrated by the failure of Cross to build on the club's fine Championship tradition which had been established and maintained so consistently over the years – well, up until 1986, anyway, when we'd won our last county title.

Mind you, the manager wasn't feeling too good about how things were turning out either. County senior titles flowed in the '60s and '70s – eight, in all, between the two decades – and we won two more in 1983 and '86. I had won five senior medals myself, including two in the '80s, so I knew as well as anyone, and better than most, the joy and pride that winning the county title brings not just to those directly involved but to a whole community.

But, as we headed towards the mid-'90s, we had to face the fact that Cross were no longer the top dogs in Armagh: good pups, maybe, but still not claiming our own lamp posts. Clan na Gael, Harps, Pearse Og, Sarsfields and Mullaghbawn had shared the more recent senior titles and, while Cross had made fantastic progress at underage level, reeling off a string of Under-21 successes, there was an impatience around the club over the failure to develop that talent at senior level.

Understandably so. What we did on the football field identified us as a people. It cemented the community together in a very special way, so, while others around the country might have had their own view, uninformed or otherwise, of what Crossmaglen stood for, we had no doubts about the honour and integrity of who and what we were as a people.

Gaelic football was precious to us, a gift that we felt obliged to use to the very best of our ability. It was our way of expressing ourselves. County titles had rolled in on a regular basis over the decades, starting as far back as 1906. Indeed, the only decade we missed out on was the 1950s so, obviously, the club knew what it took to be winners. By 1970, Cross had won twenty county titles, an impressive haul by any standard.

The introduction of the provincial and All-Ireland Club Championships in 1970/71 changed the dynamic for county champions all over the country as it gave them a chance to look beyond local boundaries and to test themselves against their counterparts from elsewhere. It was a great idea but, for some strange reason, there was opposition to its introduction from certain counties. Forty years on, I presume they would admit they were wrong.

I played in five Ulster Club Championships between 1970 and 1986 but we never got very far. That was disappointing, but you don't win unless you're good enough and obviously we didn't pass the test. Still, those Ulster Championship games gave me a feel for what was involved and how playing against clubs from other counties could broaden horizons.

The trouble was that, as we approached the mid-'90s, I was in charge of the Cross team that couldn't even win an Armagh title, let alone progress in

The joy of defeating Kerry and finally landing a first All-Ireland Senior title for Armagh in 2002 was almost overwhelming for me.

The Armagh team stand for the national anthem before the 2002 All-Ireland semi-final against Dublin.

A mighty catch from our captain, Kieran McGeeney.

All-Ireland final here we come! Justin McNulty and Diarmaid Marsden celebrate after our narrow victory against Dublin.

A proud Armagh team before the 2002 All-Ireland final against Kerry.

Francie Bellew wins the ball in his own inimitable style against Colm 'Gooch' Cooper.

Kerry 'keeper Declan O'Keeffe saves Oisin McConville's penalty.

In the second half, Oisin turns the tables on O'Keeffe and celebrates after scoring the goal which sealed Armagh's greatest victory of all time.

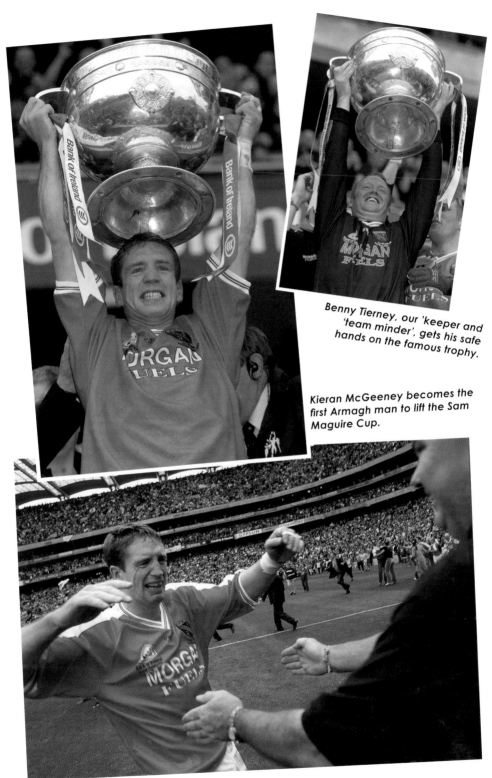

Benny Tierney, our 'keeper and 'team minder', gets his safe hands on the famous trophy.

Kieran McGeeney becomes the first Armagh man to lift the Sam Maguire Cup.

Kieran and I embrace at the final whistle of the 2002 triumph.

Paul Hearty celebrates our victory over Donegal in the 2003 All-Ireland semi-final.

With Mickey Harte at a pre-All-Ireland press conference in 2003. Our rivalry with Tyrone was incredibly intense for several years.

*The Armagh team before the
2003 All-Ireland final.*

*The strength of character in our team was demonstrated by the likes of Kieran McGeeney,
Diarmaid Marsden, Stevie McDonnell, Oisin McConville and John McEntee, lined up to meet
President Mary McAleese before the 2003 All-Ireland final against Tyrone.*

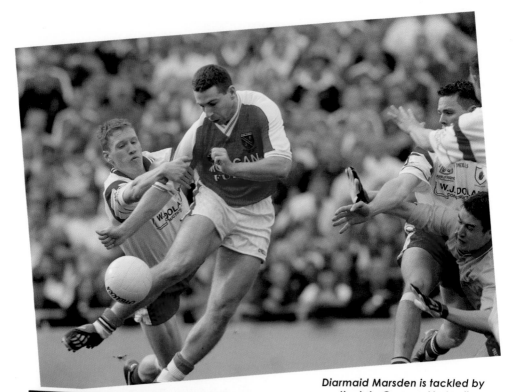

Diarmaid Marsden is tackled by the late Cormac McAnallen.

The game was hugely disappointing for Diarmaid as he was sent off by referee, Brian White, a decision that was later overturned.

An outstanding catch, so typical of Paul McGrane in the middle of the field.

The sideline is a lonely place if you're watching an All-Ireland title drifting away, as happened to us in 2003.

I congratulate Tyrone manager Mickey Harte on Tyrone's first All-Ireland title success.

Kieran McGeeney with the Anglo Celt Cup held aloft after our
victory over Donegal in the 2004 Ulster final at Croke Park.

The lads huddle in for a final talk before our shock defeat
to Fermanagh in the All-Ireland quarter-final.

Enda McNulty gets his marching orders from referee, John Bannon, in the 2004 All-Ireland quarter-final against Fermanagh.

Ryan McCluskey keeps a tight watch on Stevie McDonnell.

I congratulate Fermanagh team boss, Charlie Mulgrew, after a fiercely disappointing defeat.

Back on the sideline with Mickey Harte in 2005, during the Ulster final replay in Croke Park.

BAINISTEOIR

It's special to have your sons play for the county. My lads have always done the family and Armagh proud. Here, Aaron celebrates the 2005 Ulster final win.

Despite the attention of Conor Gormley and Pascal McConnell, Stevie McDonnell scores a great goal in the All-Ireland semi-final against Tyrone in 2005.

Paul McGrane can only watch from up close as Tyrone's genius, Peter Canavan, scores the winning point in the 2005 All-Ireland semi-final.

Aaron tackles Kerry's Paul Galvin during the 2006 All-Ireland quarter-final.

The lads celebrate another Ulster final victory over Donegal in 2006.

Kieran Donaghy and Francie Bellew go head to head in the 2006 All-Ireland quarter-final. I felt Francie got a raw deal that day.

In the end, Donaghy helped Kerry to victory and here he has something to say to Paul Hearty after scoring a crucial goal.

My last Championship match as Armagh manager, after losing to Derry in 2007 in the All-Ireland 'qualifiers'.

Our Stephen joined Aaron on the Armagh team and is seen here playing against Donegal in the 2007 Ulster Championship, a game we lost to a late goal by Kevin Cassidy.

Out west! In my brief spell as Galway manager in 2010, I got to meet up with some old friends like Mayo manager, John O'Mahony.

But my season in Galway turned out to be deeply frustrating.

Ulster or beyond. And now, in front of the rest of the panel, my great pal, Thomas Cassidy, was inviting me to bin Plan A in favour of another route.

It came as a bit of a shock, to be honest, but that's how he felt and he was dead right to have his say.

The question was, how should I respond?

If I had known it was coming, I'd have planned an answer but, now, I had to think on my feet. I thought I'd better say my piece because, if I didn't, I'd lose them all.

These lads needed to be convinced so, I started talking...

"It's like this, boys," I said. "I'll teach you Plan B when ye fully learn Plan A! It's all very fine changing course now just for the sake of it but what if we go to Plan B and it doesn't work? Where do we go then? Back to Plan A? On to Plan C, whatever that is?

"No, let's stick with what we're doing, only let's get it right. There's nothing wrong with Plan A, it's just that we're not doing it right.

"That's the challenge for everybody. It's my challenge but it's yours, too. You're the ones on the pitch. This will work if we make it work.

"And, anyway, doing it the old way has got us nowhere since 1986, so why should it be any better now? We've got to have the confidence to back ourselves on this one."

Then I took a deep breath, and waited.

I'm not sure my explanation satisfied the lads but it was the best I could come up with. Besides, I also believed it to be true. Afterwards, I asked Thomas where exactly he was coming from.

"Jesus Christ, you put me under fierce pressure there. What's this about?"

"Joe, we're frustrated, can't you see that? Where the hell are we going with all this?"

It was a fair enough question and coming from a man like Thomas Cassidy, whose very soul was steeped in the best traditions of the Crossmaglen club, it demanded an answer. From my perspective, it came down to this: we needed to fine-tune our approach and philosophy on how Gaelic football should be played.

Yes, there was a Crossmaglen way, based essentially on catch-and-kick. And, since it had taken Cross comfortably to the top of the Armagh Championship honours list, many in the club regarded it as heresy to tinker with what had been a winning formula over the years. Trouble was, it had run its course.

All over the country, and most especially in the successful counties, the game was changing, evolving, developing – quite rapidly as it happens – and my view was that we had to move with the times. We had a lot of young, mobile players in the squad who possessed the skills and temperament to adapt to any type of game and I was convinced that they were made for the new era.

It wasn't that I was proposing to totally abandon a style of football that had been bred into us as kids, but I felt that we needed to refine it so that we mixed the long and short game: play short to get out of trouble, go long when the space is available and the kicker and his intended target are on the same wavelength. In other words, play with your head up and your mind in gear. Play sensible, play smart. It had worked well at Under-21 level where Cross piled up the Championships but, naturally, it would take time to bed in with the senior scene where it was new to many players and where the opposition was better at counteracting it.

I wasn't the first manager who would find that meddling with what was seen as the traditional way of doing business didn't always impress people. Before Mick O'Dwyer went in as Kerry manager, they were regarded as the catch-and-kick kings. He changed that and was resented for it. Eventually, of course, it was forgotten as the All-Irelands rolled in, but a lot of Kerry fans weren't exactly eulogising him after a second successive Championship defeat by Dublin in 1977. Indeed, many wanted him out.

Still, Micko stood by his beliefs and principles, got the backing of key people on the County Executive, and the rest is history. So, while I was aware that there was a high degree of scepticism around Cross when we failed in the 1995 Championship, I remained convinced that we were playing with a style which would eventually bring us success.

While we waited for that success, there were always going to be frustrations and disappointments and it was during a severe outbreak of such sentiments that Thomas Cassidy had his say. But, typical of him, once he had made his point and had listened to mine, he bought into what I was trying to do – even if, perhaps, he continued to harbour doubts over whether it would ever lead to anything other than more misery.

Unfortunately, by the time we made the county breakthrough in 1996, Thomas and his brother, Benny, who had captained Cross to our last county title ten years earlier, had retired. They had been outstanding campaigners for a great many years and, although they weren't playing in 1996, they took just as much satisfaction from the win as everyone else in the club. Both of them were on the backroom team and worked as hard as they could to make sure everything was done right.

Benny had stopped playing for us after shipping a bad injury in the famous 1995 Championship clash with Mullaghbawn – a day we suffered a defeat that helped transform us over the seasons which followed. We thought we had covered every base, every angle and every possibility on that June evening, but Mullaghbawn still beat us by two points. We were completely shattered. Mullaghbawn were a good team but we thought we had their measure. We were all sick after that defeat. Patricia told me afterwards that she got chatting to the father of one of the Mullaghbawn players just after the game and he told her, cheerily, that Crossmaglen would win nothing with that team. The records show things a bit differently.

I took the defeat badly. Stephen, who was twelve years old at the time, often tells the story of how I arrived home late that night having been out with the lads drowning our sorrows. I sat at the end of his bed and got all emotional, telling him that nobody was listening to me or taking onboard what I was trying to do. I had a vision for where I wanted to take Crossmaglen but was finding it hard to bring people with me.

It's claimed that the birds didn't sing for a week around Crossmaglen after the defeat by Mullaghbawn. Nor were they too chirpy some weeks later when Mullaghbawn won the county title for the first time in over thirty years. And, to crown it all, they went on to win the Ulster title. That made it harder for us all to take.

Watching Mullaghbawn steam into the All-Ireland semi-final in February

1996 meant we had several months to keep reminding ourselves of how costly our defeat had really been. There's no way of knowing how we would have done if we had beaten Mullaghbawn but, in our own minds, the county title was there for the taking and, if we had won that, Ulster was waiting to be conquered. Mullaghbawn's run eventually came to an end against Eire Og of Carlow in the All-Ireland semi-final, by which time we were up and running for the new season.

The 1996 County Championship was always going to be crucial for Cross as a club and me as a manager. With so many young talents aboard, it was time to make a statement. As for me, the club had tolerated my methods (just about) but, if we lost in 1996, their patience was going to run out.

Granted, I had my supporters who believed in what I was doing but a manager is judged on results. There had been a bid to get me out at the end of 1995 but it was sorted out at a player meeting where the vote in favour of me staying was won by 19-3. In any event, I had the backing of the Club Executive who were very keen for me to stay. That was the end of it and I was left to get on with planning for 1996.

And, guess what? We came mighty close to being dumped out of the 1996 Championship.

We were cruising to what should have been a comfortable win over Sarsfields in the first round of the Championship in the Athletic Grounds but conceded two goals and held on to win by just one point. If the game had gone on another few minutes, who knows what might have happened?

Heads were down afterwards.

We had scored a miserable nine points and lads were feeling that if we couldn't be more impressive against Sarsfields what chance had we against Mullaghbawn in the quarter-final? I didn't see it that way at all. We had played poorly against Sarsfields but still scraped through. The game had served its purpose – now forget about it and move on.

I built up the Mullaghbawn thing as big as I could in the weeks before the game.

"Lads, haven't we waited a year for this? Remember how we felt when they beat us last year? We felt that if we played them every day for a week afterwards we'd have won them all, so what's different a year on? We're a better team now.

"Don't mind the Sarsfields game, it's gone. Think of Mullaghbawn. Are we afraid of them? No. So, let's be positive in every way from here on. This is the big chance we've been waiting for."

We had put in an unbelievable amount of hard work and built our entire year around winning the county title, so playing poorly in the first round was no reason to lose confidence in ourselves. Our time was coming and we weren't going to let Mullaghbawn delay its arrival. Not this time.

The game was played in Silverbridge in mid-July. The tension was incredible and even people from other clubs have admitted since that it was one of those special occasions that county Championships throw up from time to time. It was the last of the quarter-finals and, while three other clubs were safely through to the last four, the general view was that whoever won between ourselves and Mullaghbawn would end up as county champions.

The atmosphere was as tense and edgy as you would ever get in a County Championship game. Not surprisingly, it was one hell of a tough hour, complete with the odd bust-up and scuffle, but that was to be expected given that it was our second big Championship clash in a year. The pot was sweetened by a generous sprinkling of animosity, too. There was no comparison whatsoever between our performance that day and the first-round game. It was as if the sight of the Mullaghbawn jersey lit a fire which would continue to burn for a very long time.

We won by five points and were on the road. We beat Maghery comfortably in the semi-final to set up a final against Clan na Gael, who had won the title in 1993 and '94. They were far more experienced than us but it counted for nothing once we got our game going, and we won quite easily.

In the end, we had fourteen points to spare on a day when Jim and Oisin McConville and Cathal Short did most of the scoring.

Cross were back as county champions. A new team playing in a new way had delivered.

It was only after we won that I began to realise the full extent of the opposition to the style of play we were using. In the course of the year, a few people had come up to me and said: "Joe, you can't be playing this type of football. It's not the Crossmaglen way." I'd reply that it mightn't be the Crossmaglen way but it was the way that would eventually bring us to where we wanted to be and that was all that mattered.

It was particularly difficult when lads would go home to their parents and friends and tell them what we were doing in training only to be told how 'un-Crossmaglen' the style was. Naturally, that put doubts in their heads. I could cover every base except what players were being told once they left training. All I could do was stick by what I believed and hope the panel stayed with me.

On the night we won the county title in 1996, quite a few of the doubting brigade came up to me and openly admitted that they had thought we'd never win anything with the game we were playing. I appreciated their honesty. At least they were prepared to admit they got it wrong.

I didn't see winning the title as any great vindication for what I or my selectors, Donal McKenna and Ollie McEntee, were doing. It was more a relief than anything. I had always thought that with the talent we had in Cross at the time we should be thinking far beyond our own county scene and, while it was great to end a ten-year, title-free run, it was only the start of a much more exciting adventure. After we won the county title I asked everyone except the team and management to leave the dressing room. I wanted to get the lads thinking ahead to the Ulster Championship straightaway, as did Donal and Ollie. I really enjoyed working with them. They lived and breathed Crossmaglen and would have done anything for the club. Donal was the calm one, always quietly reflecting on how we could get more out of the team, while Ollie told it as it was. No better man to thump the table if the occasion demanded and no better man to know when the table needed to be thumped.

We had nearly two months to wait between winning the county final and our first Ulster Championship game against Burren of Down. There's always a risk of lads switching off after winning a county final but this lot were different. They were young, ambitious and knew no fear. They were now winners at all levels within the county and couldn't wait to drive on in pursuit of something that no other team from Cross had ever achieved.

In fact, they were so determined, that they nearly came unstuck in the very first round.

We led Burren by six points at half time but they used the wind to telling effect in the second half to draw level with seven minutes to go. Down teams play with a great swagger when things are going their way and, since Burren were previous Ulster and All-Ireland club winners, they would have been quite confident of closing the game out in the final minutes.

They didn't. As the game moved into injury time, we launched an attack. As a shot for a point hung in the wind, Burren 'keeper, Gary Walsh – Donegal's No. 1 when they won the All-Ireland four years earlier – was odds-on favourite to claim the ball. But, out of nowhere, Jim McConville, all 5'5" of him, arrived on the scene and got his fist to the ball and knocked it over the bar. Typical Jim – always poaching, always menacing and with a hawk's eye for being in the right place at the right time.

Burren had one last chance to level it up when they were awarded a 21-yard free but, for some odd reason, 'Shorty' Trainor, who had nailed several kicks in the second half, didn't take it. Instead, Rory Mussen lined it up but his kick was short and dropped into the hands of our goalkeeper, Jarlath McConville.

At the end of any successful campaign, you look back on games, parts of games and even moments in games that made a crucial difference and there's no doubt that the last seven or eight minutes of the clash with Burren was very important in terms of showing that Cross could hack it in the most difficult of circumstances. It wouldn't be the last time that our ability to dig out a victory in the closing minutes would stand to us.

The win over Burren made the team. We now realised that we could prosper outside Armagh, too. It was much easier in the Ulster semi-final where we were far too good for Castleblayney, hitting them for 1-19 to set up our first appearance in the Ulster final against Bellaghy. Oisin McConville kicked ten points that day.

Now, we were getting somewhere. My goal all along was not to regain the Armagh title and be satisfied with that. Lots of Cross teams had won Armagh Championships and, rewarding as it was, we had to be thinking a lot bigger now that there were Ulster – and maybe even All-Ireland – tests to be taken on. Besides, if Mullaghbawn could win an Ulster title, why not Crossmaglen?

I have to admit, we were lucky to survive against Bellaghy in the drawn Ulster final. It was played on one of those dark, wet Sundays that December tends to deliver so often and we certainly didn't play well. We led by six points coming up to half time but Bellaghy battled back and, in the end, it took a late point by John McEntee to get us a draw. John took a heavy knock to the leg that day but, typically, he played in the replay after getting an injection before the game.

The replay was always going to be a tough affair. So much so, that I warned the lads what to expect, little realising that, when the big bust-up came, it would be me who took the heaviest punch of all. It came after we had scored our second goal late in the second half. A free-for-all broke out and I ran in to make peace (honestly!), when some Bellaghy boy gave me a good clip from behind. I didn't see it coming and it landed just below my ear. Down I went in a heap and, as the chaos continued, young Aaron dashed in to see if I was alright.

That was all I needed. There I was lying on the Clones mud with mayhem all around me and my young son standing over me asking me if I was alright. With tempers out of control he was in danger of getting a dig himself so I shouted at him: "Away with you, I'm fine."

It was a right brawl and, I suppose, not unexpected given the tensions that had built up over the two games. However, I never thought that I'd be the only one eating grass. God, was that one sweet win. Bellaghy had an outstanding record in finals and looked set to extend it that day, too. They led by four points late in the first half but we fought like dogs in the second half, and a goal by Oisin McConville brought us right back into contention: Bellaghy got a free which was dropped short in front of our goal and we worked the ball all the way upfield and Oisin took his goal in great style. Still, we were trailing by a point late in the game when some superb combination play gave Cathal Short a goal chance, which he took. Oisin kicked another point and we were Ulster champions for the first time.

The brawl made the headlines the following day but we didn't care. In the space of seventeen months we had gone from the depths of despair after losing to Mullaghbawn, to winning Ulster.

Not only that, but we had won Ulster the hard way, surviving against Burren by a point, winning comfortably against Castleblayney, before beating Bellaghy in a replay. You could see the squad maturing with every game, and while there may have been a view outside Armagh that we wouldn't be good enough once we came up against the big boys from down South, I knew that wouldn't be the case.

Our boys had an unbelievable sense of self-worth. Nothing bothered them. In fact, the more it was put up to them, the more they responded. What's more, they were playing a style of football which made them very hard to beat. Once we'd won the Armagh title, I heard no more about catch-and-kick or betraying the Cross heritage and, by the time we'd won Ulster, everybody was well and truly aboard.

We had conquered at county and provincial level and were now moving on to the All-Ireland stage. The average age of the team was just over twenty-three years. Jim and Jarlath McConville were the only over-30s while Francie Bellew, Patrick McKeown, John and Tony McEntee, Anthony Cunningham, Cathal Short, Oisin McConville and Gavin Cummiskey were twenty-one, or younger.

I was really excited by the set-up. This squad could only get better, provided we all continued to do the right things.

Once Ulster was won, Croke Park on St Patrick's Day became the new target. A year earlier that would have seemed ridiculously ambitious, but we had gone unbeaten right through 1996 and were now a far different outfit from the one that lost to Mullaghbawn in 1995.

Knockmore (Mayo) had won the Connacht title, Eire Og (Carlow) had landed another Leinster crown, while Laune Rangers (Kerry) had made it two in a row in Munster. Laune Rangers were also the reigning All-Ireland champions, making them the opponents everybody wanted to avoid in the All-Ireland semi-final.

But the rota had spoken. The novices from Crossmaglen were heading south to take on the Kerrymen.

A few weeks before the 1997 All-Ireland club final I invited Colm O'Rourke to talk to the Crossmaglen panel. I'd known him well for many years and, operating on the basis that you can always learn from people who know what they're talking about, I would have asked his opinion on various things from time to time.

Colm would tell you exactly what he thought and, while it wasn't always what you wanted to hear, you listened and, in fact, it made his advice all the more valuable. I can still remember the lads sitting there watching him as he talked. Many of our boys were, effectively, at the start of their careers whereas Colm had been through it all.

What's more, he knew the good days, the bad days, the in-between days. Meath had gone through many disappointing years in the late-1970s and well into the '80s before finally winning a Leinster title in 1986. That was the start and they went on to win two successive All-Ireland titles over the next few seasons. However, the older players knew that nothing comes easy and, if it does, there's usually something flawed about it. O'Rourke was a winner but had to fight for years for everything he got, which made him an ideal man to talk to Cross in the spring of 1997.

I could tell the Cross boys what it was like to come close to winning an All-Ireland medal. I knew the misery and the sense of disappointment that always remains with teams who don't quite seal the deal. My story had its place in our build-up but so did O'Rourke's, only, in his case, he could complete the story.

He was one of the best players of his era and had achieved everything possible at inter-county level but, as he sat there talking to the Cross lads, they knew that they had a chance to reach a summit which he never did. He told them how he would have given anything to be in the position in which they found themselves.

Together with his Meath team-mate, Liam Hayes, he had played for a very long time with his club and, while they had won a few county titles, Skryne hadn't made much of an impression on the provincial scene. Now, as the Cross panel were preparing for the All-Ireland final, they were listening to one of football's greats telling them just how much he regretted never having had the opportunity to enjoy Croke Park on All-Ireland club final day as a player.

I think it helped to bring home to our lads just how privileged they really were. But then, they had made it happen for themselves and deserved every break they got. We had gone in as outsiders in most of the big games in 1996 and things didn't change at the start of 1997. Laune Rangers were not only the reigning All-Ireland champions, they were also from Kerry so they carried themselves with all the natural confidence and swagger you'd expect from players with such a pedigree.

It did not, however, involve bringing anything like as many supporters to Portlaoise as we did for the All-Ireland semi-final. I have no doubt that the sight of so many black and amber flags, the noise of the excited supporters and the unmistakable sense of occasion gave our lads a shot of inspiration which might well have proved crucial in such a close game. When the margins are tight, every little helps to produce that vital burst of extra energy just when it's most needed.

Mike Hassett, Billy O'Shea and a young Mike Frank Russell were the best-known players in what was a very evenly-balanced Laune team. They were managed, of course, by John Evans, who's now doing a fine job with Tipperary. We had heard a lot about Russell in particular, so I delegated Paddy McKeown to mark him. Paddy was a real terrier who loved jobs like that. He'd be snorting and grunting behind his opponent making sure that his presence was always felt. Still, to help the cause along, I'm afraid I may have given him a bit of dodgy advice.

"Paddy, you'll need to get stuck into this boy Russell. Let him know you're there ... maybe even the odd wee slap if you have to."

I know, I know, not very nice but, hey, it happens. Always has and always will. Besides, Paddy knew what I meant.

After a while I saw Paddy on the ground holding his jaw. Now, that wasn't in the script so at half time I asked him what had happened. Still rubbing his jaw, he shot me a look which suggested he wasn't best pleased with the pre-match advice.

"That boy was no softie, Joe."

It seems the Laune forwards had switched around and the opponent with whom Paddy had engaged rather vigorously wasn't a young, stylish Russell at all, but a far more experienced boyo who didn't take kindly to Paddy's attentions. Paddy was still holding his jaw all the way back to Crossmaglen that night.

Still, we had won by a point so the pain didn't matter.

It was a marvellous win for us. We had played a very sensible game in difficult conditions and edged home by the minimum. We were outside Armagh and Ulster but had held on to the principles we believed in and they didn't let us down. There was a huge level of confidence in the way we played and, as we left O'Moore Park that evening, I was convinced that Croke Park would suit us better than anywhere else we had played. We got a bit of a shock when we heard the result from the other semi-final where Knockmore had beaten Eire Og, who had lost to Laune Rangers in the final a year earlier. What's more, the Mayo boys had put 3-14 on Eire Og and given away just five points.

It was some statement by Knockmore and may, in hindsight, have been very much to our benefit. Suddenly, all the talk was about Knockmore and their lethal full-forward line of Kevin O'Neill, Padraig Brogan and Ray Dempsey. Of course, however good they were, they couldn't do any damage without the ball and, besides, we knew their defence would get a much tougher grilling than they might have expected in the wide-open spaces of Croke Park.

The atmosphere around Cross coming up to the final was something none of us who were directly involved with the team will ever forget. I know it has become something of a cliché to claim that playing a club final is the most personal event in a player's life but it's no less true for that.

At county level, the responsibility is divided across all the clubs and parishes but the club scene is as close and personal as it gets. You're playing for yourself, your family, your neighbours, your street, your area. And, when that area is Crossmaglen, complete with all the trouble and strife it had endured for so long, there is an incredible sense of belonging. We had tapped into something that was new and exciting and had no intention of letting go.

There was also a fierce responsibility on those of us – on and off the field – who were charged with delivering the goods. Who knows, this might be the only chance Cross would ever get to win the All-Ireland title? That's the way we approached it so everything had to be right on the big day. And it was. Well, it must have been because we won far more easily than we could ever have expected.

I suppose we sensed it was going to be our day when the Knockmore goalkeeper dropped a long-range effort from Oisin McConville into his net early on. It was the perfect start and we built on that, powering to a 2-6 to 0-5 lead at half time, before holding strong throughout the second half to win by eight points. Between them, Oisin and Jim McConville scored 2-8 of our 2-13 total.

It's unlikely that anything will ever come close to the feeling experienced by every Crossmaglen person – at home and abroad – when referee, Brian White, sounded the final whistle. A community which had suffered so much over the years and who had to battle so very hard to keep its GAA club going had produced the best team in the country. We had done it with a nice brand of football and, while it might have been new to Cross, it was certainly effective. Funny, I heard no complaints about the demise of the catch-and-kick approach after that.

The only downside on a splendid day was the injury to John McEntee. John had a very open style of soloing the ball and, late in the game, a Knockmore boy cleaned him out as he ran at their defence. John took an awful crack to the head and had to be carried off. He was sitting on the sideline at the final whistle with a blanket around him and I went to him and said: "John, John you're after winning the All-Ireland," but he couldn't take it in. For all he knew, he might as well have been asleep back home. He spent the night in a Dublin hospital, which was very unfortunate for him, but he was released the following day and got the most unbelievable reception when he arrived home in Cross.

There's no doubt that the return home and the sheer emotion of being back in Cross as All-Ireland champions will always be hugely special for the entire community. We had completed the first stage of a journey which would go on for a long time but, I suppose, nothing can ever match the first time a team wins an All-Ireland.

It was such a well-balanced set-up – from goalkeeper, Jarlath McConville, the oldest man on the team, to No. 15, Colm O'Neill. And then there was our 'super-sub', Michael Moley, who was at his most effective coming off the bench. For some reason, he tended not to do so well when he started but he certainly had the knack of switching on to the pace and tempo of a game as a sub. He got a huge number of crucial scores for us after coming on in tight games.

It was fitting that Jim McConville was captain. He had been one of the real stalwarts who had bridged the ten-year gap between winning county titles in 1986 and 1996, and who was still poaching away in his own inimitable fashion when we moved to a higher level in Ulster and on to Croke Park. He had a tremendous knack of popping up for crucial scores when they were most needed and was also a very positive influence on his more youthful team-mates, including his brother, Oisin, who was about ten years younger. Oisin's strike rate had been phenomenal all through the campaign, including in the All-Ireland final, when he scored 1-7.

Oisin, the McEntees, Cathal Short, Gavin Cumiskey, Anthony Cunningham, Francie Bellew and Paddy McKeown were all young fellas who grew up winning titles and who had now taken it to a new level.

Martin Califf, Donal Murtagh, Joe Fitzpatrick and Gary McShane had been around a bit longer but were still quite young so there was no apparent reason why Cross couldn't win an awful lot more. As it transpired, we did, but not before being re-united with the unchanging reality that once you've reached No. 1, you must be prepared for bigger challenges all the time.

We talked about future challenges in great detail as we headed into the following season's Ulster Championship but still came unstuck against Errigal Ciaran of Tyrone in the semi-final. We had played them in a challenge game a few months earlier and won quite easily. In hindsight, they probably learned more from that game than we did, as they were ready for us next time around: Shades of Armagh in 1997 when we played Dublin in a challenge game a few months before the All-Ireland, giving them an insight into how we played.

It wasn't even Peter Canavan who did most of the damage for Errigal. As usual, he brought his own particular threat to the mix but it was Eoin Gormley who wrecked us. He kicked 1-9 to set Errigal on their way to a six-point lead in the second half and, while we pared back four points, we ran out of time. I'm convinced we would have won if we'd had a few more minutes, but we couldn't complain because we hadn't done enough over the full hour.

It was our first defeat in a long time and it was all the more disappointing for that.

I closed the dressing room door afterwards and told the players that, whatever else they were doing come St Patrick's Day, they were to make sure they watched the All-Ireland final. That was late October and we had no idea who would be in the final, but it wasn't going to make any difference – we were to watch it anyway, just to remind ourselves of what we had thrown away.

I reckoned that we had to take something from the Errigal defeat and all that remained was to store up as much hurt as we could to use as a spur at a later date. As it happened, Errigal lost the Ulster final to Dungiven who, in turn, lost to Corofin of Galway in the All-Ireland semi-final, so we couldn't even say we were beaten by the team that went on to win Ulster, let alone the All-Ireland.

I have always felt that losing to Errigal was a key factor in the transformation of our team into one that could win an All-Ireland title and then go back and take two more. Of course, we had to keep winning in Armagh, too, which we did. We struggled to beat Mullaghbawn by a point in the 1997 county final, but had a much easier win over Madden a year later to set us up for – what we regarded as – a redemption mission in Ulster and, potentially, on to the All-Ireland.

Mind you, we came close enough to falling at the first Ulster fence in 1998 where it took a late point against Mullahoran of Cavan to earn us a draw. We won the replay easily and then beat St John's of Antrim with more to spare, setting us up for another Ulster final clash with Bellaghy.

After the drama of the 1996 final, there was huge interest and, as expected, it turned into another tight, dour affair. We had Gary McShane sent off in the second half but still managed to hang on in there and pounce for a late-winning point from Michael Moley. 'Super-sub' had struck again.

It was no accident that we had won another big game by the narrowest of margins. By now, we had such belief in ourselves that we felt we could always make it home through the tight finishes. Someone always pulled something out of the bag and, even if things were going against us, there was no sense of panic.

That was a major plus on two fronts: we believed we could always sort things out while the opposition suspected the worst and, even if they had built up a decent lead, they tended to start looking over their shoulders to see where we were. They expected us to come back at them and, more often than not, we didn't disappoint. It's a fantastic feeling when your confidence levels are so high that you don't harbour even the tiniest doubts.

The 1999 All-Ireland semi-final was another example of confidence at work. Eire Og were back as Leinster champions and although winning the All-Ireland title had proved beyond them, they had been incredibly consistent for several years. We met them in Navan on a horrible February day where, once again, our ability to press on in the second half proved decisive.

We led by three points at half time after playing with a very strong wind, then, when Eire Og put it up to us in the second half, it called for real character to survive. A great goal by John McEntee settled it our way. I can still remember him lining up his shot before sending a thundering drive whizzing to the net. It sent the water shimmering off the net in what was an inspiring sight for us, and a real downer for Eire Og. We won by five points – which was more than we deserved – but it was in keeping with our self-belief and ambition at the time.

Amazingly, we were back in another final and, once again, it was Mayo who provided the opposition, this time in the form of Ballina Stephenites complete with fine footballers such as Liam McHale and David and Ger

Brady. This time we were favourites but we certainly didn't play that way.

In fact, I would be the first to admit that our one-point win was among the grandest larcenies ever pulled off in Croke Park. We were beaten all over the field – and maybe on the sideline, too. We were five points down after fifteen minutes and didn't get a shot at the Ballina posts for twenty minutes. It was excruciating to watch, unless, of course, you were from Ballina. A lad in Stephenites colours was banging the drums down behind the Hill 16 goal, thumping louder and louder as the first half progressed. On a normal day, it would have been the drum that would have given you a headache, but what was happening out on the pitch was doing that all by itself.

Somehow, we hung on against all the odds, not to mention the laws of possession, but we were still four points down early in the second half and not really looking as if we could close the gap. Until, gradually, it dawned on us that this game wasn't beyond rescuing because Ballina kept kicking wides. Despite producing what might have been our worst performance in over two years, we turned it around – a point here, a point there and, ever so slowly, we were back in business.

In the end, a point by John McEntee put us in front for the first time and, shortly afterwards, referee, John Bannon, was signalling the end. We had won by a point, 0-9 to 0-8. How the hell we conceded only eight points I will never know. I was genuinely embarrassed going into the Ballina dressing room afterwards. It had to be done, but what do you say to a team who had all but handed you the cup? The last thing they needed was me telling them that I knew how they felt. I didn't, and even if I did it was no consolation to them, so I said a few words and left. They needed to be on their own.

If the 1999 final was daylight robbery in what was a poor game, the 2000 final was the very opposite on all fronts. In fact, I would argue that our win over Na Fianna was the best performance by any club team in Croke Park. That was the day that we put down a marker which, I have no doubt, was hugely helpful in generating the spirit and the confidence which would be part of Armagh's armoury two years later.

Mind you, we were lucky enough to survive in Ulster in late-1999, having had close calls against Gowna of Cavan, Cargin of Antrim and Enniskillen in the final. All those games remain fresh in my mind because, by then, we were caught up in our great journey and just wanted it to go on and on.

The final against Enniskillen in Clones was especially memorable as we won it after being down to fourteen men for all of the second half after Gavin Cumiskey was sent off just before half time. Our character and ambition were tested and, once again, we responded, winning by a late point from John McEntee. Yes, him again, always good for the important score.

I went down to Limerick to watch the Munster final between UCC and Doonbeg of Clare two weeks later. They were clubs I knew very little about and, since we were due to play one of them in the semi-final, I needed to check them out. UCC won easily but I noticed something which I reckoned we could exploit. Every time a high ball went into their goal area, they seemed unsettled. Doonbeg didn't exploit it but I decided we'd have a right good try.

Nothing changed in the semi-final. UCC were still vulnerable to high balls. We put two goals past them in the first twelve minutes, led by twelve points at half time and ran out seven point winners. We conceded three goals in the last ten minutes which was probably down to a lack of concentration but, inevitably, it led to questions in the media over whether our defence was all it was cracked up to be.

Perhaps because our opponents in the final were to be Na Fianna of Dublin, the issue came under particular scrutiny. After all, this was going to be one of those games which had a wider than usual appeal due, in no small way, to the presence of two of Armagh's finest, Kieran McGeeney and Des Mackin on Na Fianna's team.

They had plenty other big names aboard, too, including Jason Sherlock, Dessie Farrell, Mick Galvin and Senan Connell, while Paul Caffrey was manager. Na Fianna were regarded as one of the glamour outfits and got the usual Dublin hype behind them, which, in fairness, was good for the final.

It was the ultimate city v country clash and, since we were reigning champions, the media focused on the build-up to the game much more than usual. For reasons I could never figure out, Na Fianna were favourites but then that suited us down to the ground. I knew it annoyed our lads that people still didn't seem to rate us despite having won two of the previous three All-Ireland titles. That was why we all got such huge satisfaction out of beating Na Fianna.

We played some outstanding football that day, took whatever was thrown at us and came back with much more. We lost Jim McConville to injury before half time and, despite it being a blow to be without such a sharp finisher, it might have brought an up-side, too.

Jim had been such a central figure in our team for so long that Na Fianna might have thought we would drop the heads when he went off. If anything, it had the opposite effect. The lads now had another reason for wanting to win and upped their game considerably. Besides, we were able to bring on Michael Moley, and 'super-sub' went on to score two valuable points in the second half.

One incident just before half time still sticks out for me. Colm O'Neill made a fantastic fetch over Jason Sherlock in our own square and we worked the ball all the way upfield before John McEntee, who was immense all day, kicked a point. It was training-ground stuff coming to fruition on the biggest day of all. A joy to behold.

We were five points up at half time and went on to lead by eight points in the second half. Oisin hit a stunning goal to maintain his great record in finals and, at 1-10 to 0-5, it looked as if we might win easily.

But, then, it seems that wasn't in our nature and, point by point, Na Fianna reeled us in until they were only two points behind with around ten minutes to go. It's at times like that the value of character becomes apparent in a team. It can be hard to break up momentum when it's flowing so powerfully against you but, somehow, we did it, scoring the last three points of the game to win by five points.

It took a long time for the extent of what we had achieved to sink in. In the space of a few years Crossmaglen had won three All-Ireland titles, something which had seemed a long way off the radar on that infamous June evening in 1995 when we lost to Mullaghbawn.

Nemo Rangers were the only club to have won more than us, and now we were in joint-second place with St Finbarr's of Cork on the honours table.

Since then, of course, Crossmaglen have won a fourth All-Ireland so, currently, we're on our own in second place. I watched the 2007 final from the stands which was even more difficult than being in charge of the team, especially as my four sons, Aaron, Paul, Stephen and Tony were all involved.

Donal Murtagh and Martin Califf, two of our full-back stalwarts in the three previous All-Ireland wins, were in charge of the team in 2007, further underlining the togetherness and continuity which is so important in the life of any club.

As the saying goes: 'One life, one club'. That explains why I resisted the invitation to take over as manager of Carrickmore in 2000. They were very anxious that I join them and were certainly the sort of ambitious, progressive club that would have interested me in different circumstances.

But, home is home and Cross is special to me. I doubt if the club or the town would have forgiven me if I had toddled off to Tyrone to manage Carrickmore. I did feel, however, that it was time to leave the Cross job. I had put my heart and soul into it for so long, but now it was time to step back.

Managing Cross provided me with a wonderful range of experiences and memories which I will keep with me for the rest of my life. It had also given me the best possible education which stood to me when I moved on to the county scene with Armagh. Most importantly of all, it showed me what it was like to win All-Ireland titles and when I looked around the dressing room, I saw the faces of lads who had a lot more to give.

They knew it, too.

What's more, there were others like them sitting in less-successful dressing rooms in other clubs around Armagh. Put them all together and you'd never know where it might lead.

As for Crossmaglen, there was another joyous St Patrick's Day in 2011 when the lads – who again included four Kernans – won the All-Ireland for the fifth time. Tony Mac had a different role this time, now showing his skills in management together with Gareth O'Neill who, of course, enjoyed a fine playing career with Louth and Armagh.

CHAPTER 16
THE PHRASE THAT PAYS

I have often been asked, especially since Armagh finally ended the All-Ireland famine in 2002, if I would like to be twenty years old and starting out all over again.

The answer is, no. I would never want to go back.

All I'm interested in is the present and the future. Keep healthy, keep active, keep alive. I've had a great life in football, for which I'm very grateful. I'm known through football and that's how I'm viewed by most people. Those close to me, however, see me as the person I am, rather than somebody who has been wrapped up in football since I was big enough to kick a ball around the streets of Crossmaglen.

I suppose we'd all go back in life if we could, to pick out the good things and re-live them while avoiding the bad times. If only it were that simple. Life deals everybody some crushing blows at times and I've certainly had my share. I've come through them all with the help of some very strong people, none more so than my wife, Patricia, who has been there with me, through thick and thin, for the past thirty-four years.

Nobody ever knows what's going on in somebody else's life and, when you have a high profile in sport, the world sees you only as a player, manager or whatever. Your family don't really count in the public mind. All the public sees is the players, the managers, the performances. Yet, quite often, there might be something going on in your private life which is infinitely more important than whether or not you win or lose the next game.

In late July 2002, the only thing being talked of in Armagh was how we'd do in the All-Ireland Championship. The Ulster title had been secured and now we were setting out on the Croke Park trail again. The Armagh players and management were public property, charged with taking the county on a great adventure. It was as if we were pulling the whole county behind us and, if we stopped, they stopped. Those of us inside the bubble were so focused on driving things forward that we tried to put everything else to one side in pursuit of the great dream.

As team manager, it was occupying my every, waking moment. This was our big chance and we had to make sure we put ourselves in the very best position to exploit it. We played Sligo in the All-Ireland quarter-final in Croke Park and came very close to losing which, inevitably, led to some criticism. Normally, I couldn't care less about criticism but this time was different. If only people had known what was going through my mind in the days before the drawn game and right up to the Friday before the replay, they would have understood that there was more to my life than worrying about why Armagh had been held to a draw by Sligo.

Patricia was in the middle of a breast cancer scare at the time and, for two weeks, we didn't know whether the news would be good or bad. It was a terrifying period and, though we appeared to be carrying on as if nothing was happening, we were living with the constant fear that the diagnosis would be bad. We decided not to tell our own sons because we felt there was no point worrying them over something which, in the end, might turn out okay. But for those two weeks, all sorts of fears were coursing through our minds.

She finally got the all-clear in Craigavon Hospital two days before we played Sligo in the replay. The sense of relief was unbelievable. Suddenly, we could return to enjoying the whole excitement of the Championship again, having spent two weeks trying to act normal while this massive black cloud hung overhead.

Mind you, it was a great lesson in perspective. At any time after that when there were problems or stresses in the Armagh camp, I'd think back to those two weeks when I was facing a real problem, as opposed to something involving a football.

Whoever said 'Your health is your wealth' certainly got it right. I had a health scare myself a few months after Crossmaglen won the first All-Ireland club title and, to make it all the more frightening, it happened while we were on a team holiday in Florida.

We had been on the Terminator ride in Disney World and when I got off I starting sweating as if I'd been running for an hour. Some of the lads were heading on to another attraction but I began to feel terrible and told them to go without me.

My old friend, John McArdle, was with me and he sensed things weren't too good, so we got a taxi and went back to our hotel.

When we got there, John decided he had the answer to my predicament.

"Joe, what you need now is a wee brandy. I'll go get you one."

Now, I'm no medical expert but if you have pains in your chest, you're sweating heavily and you're feeling weak, I doubt if brandy is on the list of recommended cures.

"Thanks, John, but I don't think brandy will solve this. I'll need to see a doctor."

John went to the hotel manager who organised a taxi to take me to a clinic where I was handed about ten pages of forms to fill in. Bloody hell, I thought, I have pains in my chest and they want every detail about me since I was about five years old. Should I tell them how we lost the 1977 All-Ireland? It seemed to be about the only thing missing from the list of questions.

I went over to the desk and said: "I'm sure this is all very important but my chest is killing me."

Suddenly, doctors appeared from everywhere and started examining me. They did everything short of fitting jump leads before deciding it was a job for the hospital. An ambulance was called and John and I were off to the hospital where they had been told to expect us.

At the time, John was in his 70s and I was in my early-40s, so he thought it all wrong that I, rather than he, was in a bit of trouble.

"Joe, if I could change places with you, you know I would," he said in the ambulance.

Know what? He meant it. That's the sort of fella he was.

We were greeted at the door by a red-headed nurse, waving a clipboard.

"You Mr Kernan?"

"That's me."

"Very good, sir, we're going to take right good care of you."

"Thanks very much, that's great to hear."

She paused for a second, looked at John and myself, and then came the crunch question.

"Just one small thing, Mr Kernan. You got any insurance?"

"All the insurance you need, nurse. I'll have the details here in thirty minutes."

"Very good sir … step right this way."

The club had organised insurance for the trip, which was just as well because without it I have no doubt that the red-headed Florence Nightingale would have shown me and my painful chest the door. Maybe not that callously but, in 'The Land of the Free and the Home of the Brave', they have a way of letting strangers know that having no health insurance is bad news.

They kept me in for a few days, running various tests and, thankfully, all they discovered was that I had high blood pressure. The stay still cost US$9,000 so, the moral of the story is, if you're travelling to America – or anywhere else – make sure your insurance is in order.

Lying in a Florida hospital wasn't exactly how I had planned to spend the holiday but I had no choice. I was stuck in a room with an elderly Japanese man who looked, for all the world, as if he might have been a sumo wrestler in his younger days. The groans and the grunts out of him every night would drive you mad so I couldn't wait to get out of the place.

Only a few boys knew I was in hospital. John McArdle, Fr Clarke and Eddie Hughes knew but I didn't want the whole squad to know because, inevitably, word would get back to Crossmaglen where, no doubt, reports of my condition would be greatly exaggerated. Besides, I hadn't told Patricia because I didn't want to worry her.

John was like a mother hen fussing over me and we often laughed afterwards about his suggestion that I have a shot of brandy to cure the pain. Mind you, he always insisted that it would have done the trick. He was a lovely character and a great friend for many years so it came as a big shock when he died on Christmas Day, 2000. It was a sad day for me and everybody in Crossmaglen. On the evening of his removal, the lights went out in the town just as the funeral cortege was passing through and I couldn't help thinking how John would have enjoyed the moment. It was as if even the streetlights were mourning his passing and had to take time out to mark it.

Crossmaglen was very much the poorer for John's death, while on a personal level I really missed him.

He certainly was a big help to me when I had the scare in Florida. He would quite happily have taken it himself if he could, rather than see a friend in trouble. In hospital, I waited until I got the all-clear before I rang Patricia to tell her what had happened. I knew she would be in a panic so I also rang Thomas and Benny Cassidy to explain the situation. Of course, as soon as she put the phone down to me, she was off to see the two lads who were able to reassure her that they, too, had been talking to me and that I sounded fine.

It took the lads in Florida a few days to find out I was in hospital. Donal McKenna was so worried about me that he drank for three days wondering where the hell I was! He eventually found out and arrived at the hospital with a few other boys and, once he saw I was okay, the sympathy ended.

"Joe, will you get the hell out of that bed and let in a man who IS sick," he said. I took a look at him and replied: "You're dead right, Donal ... you look a lot worse than me!"

The whole incident was a blessing in disguise. You would prefer it to happen at home but, in the end, all was well. I went to my own doctor when I got home and he put me on blood pressure tablets and I haven't had a bother since.

I did learn a few lessons, though. I had taken far too much out of myself with Crossmaglen. I used to do daft things like pick lads up in Belfast or Dublin, take them to training and then drive them back. I was also flat-out with my business at the time so I paid no attention whatsoever when my body started telling me I was overdoing it. One night, shortly before we went to Florida, I felt a twinge in the chest after pushing a van that had cut out while I was moving furniture but I was so busy I didn't bother going to the doctor. I had a thousand things to do before I went to Florida and, when we got there, I suppose we had one or two too many drinks. I should have gone to the doctor when I felt the initial twinge. It was a mistake I will never make again.

I changed things around a bit when I got back so that I didn't have as much to do. Of course, it was my own fault that I had taken on so much, but it was one of those situations where I started out in a certain way and just kept adding to the workload.

I had two excellent selectors in Donal McKenna and Ollie McEntee and plenty of other supports, too, but I suppose I wanted to try to do everything myself. Luckily, I got the warning in Florida and, from then on, I was more careful about how I pushed myself. Some years later, when I took over Armagh, I knew that it couldn't be a one-man show and I became better at delegating.

Mention of Donal and Ollie reminds me of a poem written by John Fearon after Crossmaglen won the 1996 county title. It seems Donal, Ollie and I all had our own sayings and, while we probably weren't even aware of them, everybody else was.

Donal's catchphrase was, "We've won nothing yet". You would need to have the cup at the front of the bus before Donal's special brand of caution would allow him to acknowledge that we'd actually won. It was no bad thing either because his "We've won nothing yet" reminder had an important place in the scheme of things.

Ollie's well-worn phrase was, "Up on your toes". As far as he was concerned, it was all about being alive and alert from the start to the finish of every game. Again, it was sound advice, something he never stopped dispensing down the years.

As for me, I adopted, "By hook or by crook" as my motto. It's pretty self-explanatory. Whatever must be done, will be done, otherwise you won't get anywhere.

John Fearon decided to put all three mottos into a poem to mark our 1996 Armagh title success.

Entitled 'The Phrase That Pays', the poem ran to four verses, with the final one as follows:

> *Well by hook or by crook, we are champions at last,*
> *And "we've won nothing yet" is a phrase from the past,*
> *So, we'll keep on playing and God only knows,*
> *We could be Ulster champions if we keep on our toes.*

Sure enough, we went on to win Ulster and All-Ireland titles so 'The Phrase That Pays' got several outings.

Mind you, I can't help thinking back to John McArdle and me, standing there in that Florida hospital, with the nurse asking if I had health insurance. "All the insurance you need," – now there was a phrase that really paid because, otherwise, I would have been out on my ear, pain or no pain.

CHAPTER 17
LITTLE ACORNS

Things were pretty grim in the Armagh football world into which I graduated in the early-1970s. Down and Cavan had dominated Ulster in the 1960s and, while others offered the occasional threat to their empires, Armagh were stuck in a rut from which there seemed to be no escape.

It was just the way things were. Success was for other counties and Armagh appeared happy enough to live their lives as second-class citizens, just fulfilling the fixtures and muddling along.

I was promoted to the senior team as a seventeen-year-old for a Dr McKenna Cup game against Donegal in 1971 and my career went from there. Earlier in the year, I had been on the minor team which went into the Ulster quarter-final against Down with reasonably high hopes.

I was playing at midfield and won a lot of ball early on, but we couldn't turn possession into scores and trailed by three points at half time. The second half was an absolute nightmare. Down ran in four goals to win by 5-8 to 1-6. I have often wondered to what degree Down's senior successes over the previous decade impacted on that minor game.

The young Down lads believed that they were good footballers just because they were from a county that had enjoyed so much senior success since 1960. They regarded their county as winners, whereas we had nothing to fall back on except tales of how Armagh were unlucky to lose the 1953 All-Ireland senior final to Kerry. As it happened, Down minors obviously weren't all that good at the time because they didn't even get to the Ulster final. Even so, they were a lot better than us.

When a county team is really struggling, players tend to live their lives through the club scene, which was very much the case in Armagh in the early '70s. Crossmaglen had won the Armagh senior county title in 1970 and, shortly afterwards, I was brought into the squad for the Ulster Championship.

I was on the fringes of the senior squad all year but since our minors were going well I was left mostly with them. Besides, the county minor and senior finals were on the same day so I could hardly line out in both.

However, a few weeks later, I was brought into the senior squad for the Ulster club Championships which were in their first year as an official competition. Crossmaglen were drawn away to Castleblayney of Monaghan in the first round but, for some reason that I can't recall, I missed the team bus. I was only sixteen years old at the time, so I suppose there was no great concern when I didn't turn up. I must have got the wrong take-off time and was very disappointed to discover they had gone without me, but it was my own fault and something I learned from for the future.

Cross drew the game, and I can only assume that they weren't satisfied with how the attack performed because I was selected in the half-forward line for the replay. It turned into a mighty tough game but I kept out of trouble as best I could and kicked a few points in the first half.

An almighty row broke out in the second half, after which I was temporarily taken off. The boys who were in charge of the team obviously deemed it no place for a sixteen-year-old and decided to remove me from the scene for a while. It was a cute move because, by the time I came back on, things had calmed down and I had got my second wind.

Making the transition to senior level was quite a challenge, even for a tall sixteen year old like me, but I had plenty of 'minders' on the team. I had played for the seniors earlier in the year and I can still recall one of my first games, which was against Clann Eireann. I was at right half-forward and Paddy Fitzpatrick was the right half-back.

He liked to go forward when he got the chance and, on one occasion as he made a run upfield, I spotted my opponent galloping over to cut off the attack. I went to block him and, in return for my attempt to help Paddy, I was hit an unmerciful box in the jaw which sent me sprawling to the ground.

Paddy saw what happened out of the corner of his eye but had some business to conduct before he dealt with the situation. He ran on, kicked the ball over the bar and, as he came back, he spotted me lying on the ground trying not to cry with the pain.

"What happened?" said Paddy, as if confirming the evidence before he took action. Feeling my jaw, I said nothing but pointed to the Clann Eireann man who thought he was Muhammad Ali.

Paddy sauntered over to him. "Hey you, don't you touch that garsun again," he warned, before delivering a haymaker. I had no more trouble in that particular game.

Obviously, the older lads thought I needed their protection – which I probably did – but they must also have felt I had something to offer and, as the Ulster Championship progressed in 1970, I held on to my place. We reached the semi-final against Bryansford of Down but lost by three points in Newry.

Gene Larkin made a comeback for one game and played alongside me at midfield. It was a real case of the veteran and the youngster. Gene had been on the Cross team for many years but had opted out some time earlier, only to make a dramatic return for the Bryansford game. The All-Ireland Club Championship might have been in its infancy but it quickly gained the attention of the public and would go from strength to strength. In time, it would play a major role in the history of Crossmaglen Rangers.

It would appear I did well against Bryansford. The following day's *Irish Press* noted that, "Sixteen-year-old, Joe Kernan, who played at midfield, showed flashes of promise for the future."

The *Irish News* was even more generous: "Brightest star on the heavy pitch was sixteen-year-old, Joe Kernan. Captain of St Michael's, Omeath, senior team, Joe was taking part in his second outing on the club's senior team and after yesterday's performance there's no doubt we will hear more from this extremely high-potential player."

We had lost but it was nice for a young fella to be recognised as one to watch.

Armagh weren't making much progress at any grade but it was still a huge thrill to get the call to join the senior squad in late-1971. It was during Gerry O'Neill's first stint in charge and, although he would go on to preside over some thrilling times later, not much happened in the early-1970s.

I can still recall wearing the Armagh senior jersey for the first time in a

Dr McKenna Cup game against Donegal in the Athletic Grounds. I played at corner-forward but my debut ended, as would most of the games in my early years, in defeat. It would be difficult for the current crop of young Armagh people to understand just how bad things were on the county scene back then.

I remember going through a full season without winning a single game, in any grade. God, that was depressing. We just kept playing and losing, playing and losing. Here's an example of how bad things were: On the day I played for Abbey CBS against St Patrick's of Cavan in the 1972 McRory Cup final, Armagh seniors conceded the National League points to Tyrone. For some reason, Armagh couldn't field a full team at the beginning of the game but, after agreeing to concede the points, they played Tyrone in a challenge game and drew. Can you imagine that happening now?

With work scarce around Crossmaglen – and all of Northern Ireland – I headed for England after finishing secondary school. Local man, Barney Hughes had a building business in Birmingham and I worked there for a couple of years. Then I moved to London to work with a company called Frankipile. Some local men – like Tommy Leneghan, the Dooley brothers from Inniskeen in Monaghan and the Kelly family from Crossmaglen – were involved, which opened a few doors for lads from the North. I might have been working in England but my heart was always back home in Crossmaglen and Armagh. And, of course, that's where the football was – well, the football I wanted to play, anyway. I would travel home for weekends when Armagh had games, but we'd lose nearly every time and I'd go back to London, on a Sunday night, to face the usual jibes on Monday morning.

Gerry Fagan, who was then Armagh County Secretary, would pick me up from Belfast Airport on Friday nights to bring me home to Crossmaglen. Gerry was a fast driver and neither the cars nor the roads were as good as they are now. Between the hard driving and the cigarette smoke those journeys were quite an experience, I can tell you.

Gerry was a great Armagh man and a great GAA man. Football was a way of life for him and, even when things were going terribly for Armagh, he always held out hope for the future. That was just the way he was, so nobody enjoyed the turnaround in 1977 more than he did.

I worked with lads from all over Ireland who found it very amusing that, when they'd be out having the craic in London at weekends, I'd be back home trying to be an inter-county footballer on a poor team. The questions would be the same every Monday, game after game.

"So, who hammered ye this time?"

"Ye must be shocking bad altogether."

"Would ye beat a women's team?"

All very funny and, to be honest, very accurate. At one point, we were rated 31st out of the 32 counties in a newspaper's end-of-year review. Only Kilkenny were behind us and they didn't give a damn about football, so you can see how poorly Armagh were regarded.

Despite the defeats, I kept coming home whenever we had a game because I just loved the buzz of being involved with the county team. Then, every Sunday evening, I'd make a mad dash from somewhere around the country to Dublin airport to get the last flight back to London – back to the hard work and the slagging on Monday morning. There was one year when I played on teams that lost nine games at senior and Under-21 level.

In the end, I got sick of travelling back and forth and decided that London wasn't for me. In fact, I baled out so suddenly that I left some of my clothes behind. One Sunday night, I decided I wasn't making that return journey. Unfortunately, although I had made my decision about coming home to Armagh, the football scene wasn't getting any better.

At the time, Armagh football was suffering from a lack of proper organisation and a shortage of men interested in playing for the county. We were still struggling to field a full team – there was one particular League game in Leitrim where we had to take a lad in from the terrace to make up the fifteen. How depressing was that?

There were lots of good players in Armagh but there was no clear focus on the county team and, as a result, a lot of boys only gave their allegiance to the club scene, on the basis that it was more enjoyable and more rewarding.

That view seemed to be accepted at official level. It became a case of fulfilling our obligations to the League and Championship programme and then concentrating our real efforts on the club scene.

You'd even look at the Ulster Championship draw to work out exactly when you'd be free for holidays or to travel to play abroad, say, in New York: you wouldn't go too far wrong by choosing any date from the Monday after the first round game. Making plans around playing in Clones in an Ulster final in late-July was for others – we were just bit players making up the numbers.

After my homecoming in 1974, I was lucky enough to get a job with FB Sherry Motors in Armagh as a rep, selling car components. I loved it because it took me all over Ulster. I'd call in to fellas with their small, wee garages out in the country and I'd get the conversation going by talking about football. Armagh might not have been doing very well but being a county footballer gave me a huge advantage. Even today, I come across people I dealt with all those years ago, so it just goes to show that you never lose contacts made through the GAA.

Things were moving very slowly with Armagh but, every so often, we'd show flashes of what we could do. In 1973 we ran Down to a point in a first round Ulster Championship game in Newry (2-10 to 2-9).

It was a good performance but, as was typical of Armagh football at the time, we gave away a stupid goal. Around ten minutes from the end, Sean O'Neill fed Mickey Cole, who sent in a speculative shot from forty yards, which somehow bounced into our net. That goal proved to be the difference, and we were left to wait another year.

I came on as a sub that day and was named in the next day's papers as Joe 'Keran'. The number of different spellings of my name at that time was unbelievable: they ranged from Kiernan to Keran and from Cernan to Carnan. There were times I thought I had multiple identities!

The close call in the 1973 Championship didn't exactly light a fire in Armagh; in fact, we won no games in the subsequent National League and were trimmed by Down in the 1974 Championship. The great Sean O'Neill was still pulling the strings for Down and we were no match for them, losing by seven points in Lurgan. I played at left half-back that day, with Colm

McKinstry and my clubmate, Larry Kearns, at midfield.

A key turning point for Armagh football was the arrival of Fr Sean Hegarty and Peter Makem. They had a vision which extended beyond fulfilling the fixtures. Makem had a belief that, as a county, we could achieve much more. Indeed, he was convinced that there was no reason why Armagh couldn't match the other Ulster counties. He took a very serious and systematic approach to the job and brought a fresh, innovative outlook on how things should be done.

He drove around the county visiting all the squads on an individual basis, telling us exactly what he had in mind and what he required from us. I recall him saying that he wanted me to be part of the Armagh scene for the next ten years, which was very flattering for a young fella. He had short-, medium- and long-term goals and was good at convincing players that, with proper effort and planning, we could all be a whole lot more successful. Given our starting point, things couldn't get much worse.

We hammered Fermanagh (4-6 to 0-10) in the Ulster first round in 1975 on a day when Sean 'Dingle' Daly scored 2-5. A new beginning? Not at all. We took a terrible tanking from Derry in the quarter-final in Omagh and were back to square one. Sean O'Connell, who was thirty-eight years old at the time, ran rings around us. We were seven points down at half time and ended up losing by 2-15 to 1-7. One small step forward, one giant step back. Same old story – another season down the drain.

I played directly against Tom McGuinness in our games with Derry in 1975 and '76, which was very enjoyable, if tough. Tom, a brother of Sinn Fein's Martin McGuinness, was one of the best fielders of the ball in the game at the time. If you came close to matching him, you were having a very good day.

I played a lot of soccer during my earlier years as a county player, largely because I had time on my hands. Crossmaglen didn't win any county senior titles between 1970 and '75, so there were lots of weekends when I had no football game. I played soccer in Dundalk with a club called El Toro in the summer League and had some smashing times with them. I also played with

Milburn FC, which featured a lot of Crossmaglen and Burren GAA players who wanted to keep busy. We had great craic in those games.

However, it was while I was playing with Newry Town at a higher level that I came to the attention of Dundalk manager, Jim McLaughlin.

Jim was one of the most outstanding managers in League of Ireland history, and a lovely man with it. He brought me into the Dundalk panel for a Leinster senior Cup game against Drogheda United in Oriel Park. I was promised a few quid, which was quite a change from the GAA scene so I decided to give it a go: a fiver was a lot of money at the time.

Dundalk were going well and would get even better over time, so I was delighted with the chance to test myself at a much higher level than I had been used to alongside fine players like Tommy and Brian McConville, Synan Braddish, Richie Blackmore, Jimmy Dainty and various others. I played as a striker against Drogheda but Jim always said I would have been better as a defender and, had I stayed around and worked on the soccer, I think he would have turned me into a centre-half. Nevertheless, I loved trying to score goals and, since I was only playing soccer to fill in the gaps when there was no Gaelic football, I didn't bother too much with the defensive side of the game. I saw myself as the old-style bustling centre-forward which was a most enjoyable role to play, especially at the lower end of the scale where plenty of goal-scoring chances tended to come my way.

I did okay in the game against Drogheda but, shortly afterwards, I injured my groin and that was the end of soccer at that high level. I was out for a while and never made any attempt to get back with Dundalk. By the time I was fit again, there were Gaelic football games to be played, so soccer was off the agenda.

At one stage, I had the opportunity to go to Oxford United for a trial but, strange as it might seem, I couldn't be bothered. I loved playing soccer but there was never the remotest chance it would become my first choice. As for rugby, it simply didn't exist for me other than as a spectator, watching the International games on TV. I would have loved to have played rugby at some stage but the chance never arose.

Soccer knew its place in the Kernan affections. The soccer boys knew that I was only using it as a means of staying fit when I wasn't playing Gaelic football and they accepted that, even if they couldn't understand why I was putting in so much hard work with Armagh when we never seemed to win a game.

Funnily enough, it was a question I had never asked myself. I just adored the game and everything that went with it and, even if we weren't in Clones or Croke Park on the big days, the thrill of being an Armagh player kept me going.

Gradually, signs began to emerge that things were beginning to pick up for Armagh. Gerry O'Neill was back in charge and we made what turned out to be a significant advance in the 1975/76 National League. Granted, it was down in Division 3 but, at long last, we started getting some consistency into our game. More importantly, we strung a series of wins together and began to run up big scores.

We beat Leitrim, Longford, Westmeath, Louth, Laois and Donegal in Division 3A to reach the final. What's more, we were scoring goals for fun, amassing no fewer than seventeen in six games, which was probably as many as we had scored over the previous two years. The final in early March was against Clare and was played in Croke Park as a curtain-raiser to a Derry-Galway, Division 1 play-off. It was the first time in several years that Armagh had been to Croke Park and, coming after a string of wins, it sparked plenty of interest in the county.

Still, the crowd was pretty small and, of those, most were there to see Galway play Derry. Coincidentally, one of the men playing for Galway that day was Tom Naughton, who was a selector with me during my year in Galway.

Our game with Clare ended in a draw so we were back in Croke Park the following Sunday for a replay, which we won. Our win might have gone largely unnoticed in the rest of the country but it meant an awful lot to us. At long last, Armagh had some silverware. What's more, we had won it in Croke Park. I was at left half-back that day, with Jimmy Smyth, our inspirational captain, in the centre and Noel Marley at right-half.

When we won Ulster and reached the All-Ireland final the following year, I was at midfield, while Jimmy and Noel were in the half-forwards. Quite a change but then the team was only beginning to come together in 1976. We lost the League quarter-final to Cork but it had still been an excellent campaign when compared to our recent past.

It raised hopes for the Championship and although we struggled to beat Fermanagh by a point in the first round we still felt we were in with a decent chance of putting it up to Derry in the semi-final. They were the reigning Ulster champions and were downright unlucky when losing the League final to Dublin by a point but, at the same time, we were beginning to get ambitious thoughts about ourselves.

They didn't last long.

We played Derry in Omagh and it was all over in twenty minutes. We were nine points down and looking like a junior team that had gone to the wrong venue. Derry had nine different scorers, drawn from every outfield line, as they powered to an embarrassingly easy win, 1-19 to 2-1. How a team could go a full seventy minutes without scoring more than one point is a mystery, but it happened to us that day.

There we were again: one step forward, one step back. Derry had a very good team but we shouldn't have been that far off the pace. It was the second year they had beaten us out the gate, so it was difficult to find grounds for optimism at the end of that season, even if we had made some progress in the League.

Little did we know that, within a year, we would be back in Croke Park on All-Ireland final day trying to win the title for the first time in our history.

CHAPTER 18

ORANGE LEFT WITH THE BLUES

The GAA would never admit it, but I suspect they decided to make the 1977 All-Ireland final an all-ticket affair because they were afraid that all those mad orange men coming down from the North might wreck the place.

Not the twelfth of July type of Orangemen, you understand, but orange men (and women) nonetheless. There was a new breed of them in Armagh that year, singing Armagh songs and ready to make their presence felt around Croke Park in August and September.

Up until then, the Hogan and Cusack Stands were ticket-only for All-Ireland finals while you could pay into Hill 16 and the Canal End on the day. While that would be unthinkable nowadays, it was the way things were back then. In theory, the gates were supposed to be closed when the place was full but health and safety regulations weren't quite as strict as they are now. As long as there were fans outside with cash in their hands, the stile men tended to find a way to squeeze them in, whether or not there was room. It had been normal practice over many years.

Then suddenly, out of the blue, when Armagh were back in the final and taking on Dublin, the GAA thought they had a problem and made it their first all-ticket fixture.

The last time Armagh had been in the All-Ireland final, back in 1953, thousands of people couldn't get into Croke Park. Instead, they were forced to hang around outside listening to Micheal O Hehir's commentary. Apparently, it passed off quite peacefully but, twenty-four years on, the GAA were taking no chances.

They reckoned that, with Dublin in the final and Armagh returning after so long, bedlam would break out if it wasn't ticketed.

However, there were plenty of people in Armagh who believed it was done out of fear that rampaging hordes would go down to Dublin just to cause trouble. It was a view that showed the disconnect that existed between North and South at the time. The relationship and understanding wasn't anything like it is today, but then things were very different back in 1977.

Turning the final into an all-ticket affair for the first time led to a farcical situation where touts managed to get their hands on batches of them. I have no idea how that happened but tickets were freely available on the black market outside Croke Park on the day of the final while many genuine fans, in Armagh and elsewhere, couldn't get any.

Afterwards, it was estimated that as many as 2,000 Hill 16 and Canal End tickets found their way into the hands of touts, but there were plenty of stand tickets on the black market, too. The face value was IR£4.50 but touts were looking for IR£10, only to find that the market wouldn't bear such extortion. And as the clock ticked towards throw-in time, they were being sold for less than face value as touts tried to cut their losses.

It was a mistake by the GAA to impose the all-ticket ruling so abruptly but it seems they panicked when Armagh reached the final.

Whatever about a lack of understanding between North and South, an awful lot of people all over the country had difficulty coming to terms with the fact that Armagh were in the All-Ireland final. How the hell had they got there? Hadn't they been beaten out the gate in Ulster over the previous few seasons? To say people were stunned by Armagh's dramatic surge would be an understatement. And, if we'd been brutally honest, we would have had to admit that we were a little bit surprised by our progress, too.

After all, we had been well beaten by Derry in 1975 and '76, so it was difficult to fathom how we had improved to such an extent that we had become All-Ireland contenders in 1977. It was true that we had a lot of very good players but, for some reason, we just hadn't been gelling the way we should. Or, at least, not until a June Sunday in 1977 when we played Cavan in the first round of the Ulster Championship in the Athletic Grounds.

Cavan were hot favourites, having only lost to Derry after extra-time in a replay in the 1976 Ulster final. Given that Derry had slaughtered us in 1976, there was no reason to believe we could match Cavan the following season.

When they ran-in seven points without reply in the first seventeen minutes, it seemed as if our fifteen-point drubbing by Derry the previous season might look like a close call. Cavan were walking through us, over us and around us. We were completely out of our depth. I was at midfield with Colm McKinstry and, if memory serves me correctly, we were up against Ollie Leddy and Ciaran O'Keeffe.

Cavan were leading by nine points just before half time when we got a penalty, taken by Paddy Moriarty. Cavan goalkeeper, Aidan Elliot, blocked the shot but Paddy finished off the rebound to the net to leave us six points down at half time. Although this was a bit more respectable, nobody would have given us the remotest chance of coming back to win the game.

However, what happened next was quite remarkable and proved just how quickly things can change for a team if the attitude is right. In the second half, the transformation apparent in the whole Armagh team was unbelievable. Man-for-man, line-for-line, we overwhelmed Cavan to such a degree that we were seven points up with a few minutes to go and, while Steve Duggan pulled a goal back with a penalty, we went on to win by five points, 2-14 to 1-12. We had won the second half by 1-12 to 1-1, which was about as comprehensive as it gets.

The atmosphere right through the thirty-five minutes was something else. The noise and the sheer enthusiasm from the Armagh supporters transferred to us on the field and we began to feel that something special was happening, at last. It was as if we were awakening as a squad and a county.

I will never forget that game. It was the first time, while wearing an Armagh jersey, that I felt there was something different about the whole set-up. It was as if, somehow, we had been freed from the shackles which had seemed to tie us down in the past. We were making a statement about ourselves and we didn't give a damn what anybody else thought.

That win electrified Armagh.

Suddenly, we were thinking differently as individuals and as a team. We beat Monaghan by four points in the semi-final in Dungannon but we should have won by a lot more. The only downside for us was that Tom McCreesh, our lion-hearted centre-back, suffered a dislocated shoulder in the second half which left him very doubtful for the final.

We were devastated by the thought of him missing a chance to win an Ulster medal. Tom was a father-figure to the squad, the man who had played with Armagh for years and won damn all, except the respect of colleagues and opponents alike. He was an inspirational character, the sort who would do two men's work if he had to. When Tom thumped the dressing room table during a team talk, he'd scare the shite out of us. He'd always talk as if the game we were about to play would be his last, which seemed a damn good reason to do everything possible to win.

He believed in Armagh when a lot of others didn't. He was living in Virginia at the time, but never gave up on the Armagh dream.

As strong as an ox and as brave as a lion, he was also an exceptionally skilful player, especially when it came to high fielding. He was the real engine of the team and the thought of being without him for the 1977 Ulster final was not appealing. We need not have worried. After playing for Armagh for what seemed like all his life, he wasn't going to miss out.

And so, when we took to the field in Clones on July 24, 1977 for the Ulster final against Derry, T. McCreesh was at No. 6. Derry knew that he had recently recovered from a shoulder injury and did all they could to test just how sound it was. In fact, they tore into Tom from all angles but they were picking on the wrong man. He stood up to every challenge and, with the rest of us annoyed at what Derry were trying to do, it certainly got the adrenaline flowing. The exchanges were, shall we say, rather frothy.

The memory of the big defeats by Derry over the previous two years was a considerable motivation for us. Whatever the mix of factors, we got it just right. We were eight points ahead at half time and went on to win the second half, too, running out 3-10 to 1-5 winners. It was the biggest winning margin in the Ulster final for years and the fact that we had done it against a Derry team which was going for the three-in-a-row made it all the sweeter.

The after-match scenes in Clones that day were something I will never forget. There were troubled times in Armagh, so winning an Ulster title after a twenty-four year wait brought a joy to the GAA community that would last for a very long time. Ulster titles may have come to be taken for granted over the last decade but it was a different world back then, one where Armagh had gone for nearly a quarter of a century without any success.

Not only that, but we had gone from being something of a joke in the early-'70s to winning the Ulster title later that decade. Suddenly, we began to see ourselves in a different light. Equally importantly, so did others.

Having won Ulster, we genuinely thought we could go all the way and take Sam Maguire. Two months later, we realised that it wasn't really on. We were good but not as good as the Dublin team of that era, which has gone down in history as one of the best of all time. What's more, 1977 was probably their prime year so, from our perspective, we got them at the worst possible time.

Mind you, we came mighty close to not reaching the final at all.

Roscommon had emerged as a powerful force in Connacht and, like ourselves, were bidding for a place in the All-Ireland final after a long absence. Around then – and indeed for several years afterwards – there was a view that the only chance Ulster or Connacht champions had of reaching the All-Ireland final was when the semi-final rota pitted them against each other. It was backed up by facts so, every three years, when it was an Ulster-Connacht semi-final, the teams involved knew how important it was to take the chance.

It was generally assumed in 1977 that whoever won the Dublin-Kerry semi-final would take the All-Ireland but, when you're as immersed in it as the Armagh and Roscommon players were, you don't think like that. It's about taking one step at a time and seeing where the adventure takes you.

It took us into an All-Ireland semi-final that's still remembered for a number of reasons. First, it was the day that we came back from a seven-point deficit in the final fifteen minutes to snatch a draw. Roscommon had been the better team for three-quarters of the way but a Paddy Moriarty goal from a penalty was the launch pad for a revival, which brought us level.

Of course the famous incident right at the end is still talked about when Dermot Earley was lining up a long-range free kick which, if pointed, would probably have won the game for Roscommon. Our manager, Gerry O'Neill, ran across him and appeared to pass some comment to Dermot just as he was about to begin his run-up. Now, if he had pointed the free nobody would have drawn any attention to Gerry's apparent intervention. However, Dermot failed to make a proper connection and the ball flew wide, immediately sparking the question: "So, what did Gerry say to him?"

Gerry claimed that he had said nothing while Dermot insisted that, if Gerry had spoken, he didn't know what he said. Dermot also maintained nothing Gerry did or said had affected his kicking, instead blaming a wrong run-up for the wide. It was typical of Dermot, who was never one to make excuses. He was a fantastic footballer and a lovely man whose untimely death was mourned by everybody who ever met him. We all have fond memories of a great man.

He always insisted he didn't hear Gerry saying anything before he took that crucial kick, back in 1977. All I can say is that if he didn't hear anything, it wouldn't have been for want of Gerry trying! He was wearing a pink shirt that day so it wasn't as if you could have missed him and there would be no better man for a word at the right or (in Roscommon's case) wrong time. You'd get away with wearing pink nowadays but not many managers did it back then – Gerry always was his own man.

He brought great organisation to the scene and definitely played a huge role in moving us forward in a very measured way. His brother, Martin, who was playing with Nottingham Forest, would come along to training from time to time. I presume Gerry picked up a few tips from Martin as to how they were doing things at Nottingham Forest. He certainly had a very advanced approach to everything we did and we benefited immensely from it.

We were starting to take shape as a team. Gerry's approach was impacting on the players and you could see the benefit that individuals were beginning to reap.

I'd say that the drawn All-Ireland semi-final was as good a game as Jimmy Smyth ever played for Armagh. Jimmy was an outstanding player, captain and leader, well ahead of his time in lots of departments. Mentally, he was switched on to the game in a way that most players weren't. I loved playing with him because he had such outstanding vision.

He was one of very few boys I ever saw who was able to solo the ball with one hand and point to where he wanted you to be with the other. He'd do that all the time. Off he'd go on a solo run, so the trick was to join in his slipstream and wait for him to start pointing.

Since I was a big fella, we worked well together. Jimmy would know the best running angle and, if I timed my run at pace and arrived at his shoulder at precisely the right second, he would thread the pass through to me. I'd be on full throttle and the accuracy of his pass, combined with his ability to read exactly where it should go, often gave me a clear run on goal. We conjured up many a score that way.

Incidentally, John Egan of Kerry was another man who had a brilliant style of soloing the ball with one hand but he was so cute he'd be holding you off with the other. A delight to watch but a nightmare for defenders.

Smyth, Paddy Mo, Peter Loughran and Peter Trainor did most of the scoring in the drawn semi-final with Roscommon. Loughran was one of the best corner-forwards in the business but, unlike many of his counterparts, he loved tackling. He had some great battles with Harry Keegan of Roscommon, including indeed in the 1977 semi-final. As tough as they came, Harry had a good footballing brain, too, so any forward who had a good day against him knew he was on his game.

The drawn game produced a total of 5-21 (Armagh 3-9 Roscommon 2-12) and while that suggested that the defensive alignments needed to be improved on both sides, it also captured the imagination of the public, certainly in Armagh. For reasons that weren't clear then or now, the GAA decided not to allow the replay to be shown live on TV, which may have accounted for the increase in attendance from 32,600 at the first game to 43,400 on replay day. Compared to today's attendances, that might seem like a small crowd for a semi-final but it was big for the time. Five years later, when we played Kerry in the All-Ireland semi-final, there were less than 19,000 people in Croke Park.

Back in '77, there was a different feel to things, especially after we'd drawn the first game. Once again, there were far more Armagh supporters in Croke Park for the replay and, boy, did they make a racket! It turned out to be a completely different type of game. Neither side conceded a goal this time so it became a shoot-out for points and, in the end, we nudged home by the very minimum, 0-15 to 0-14.

Armagh, perennial losers and a team for whom few people had held out any hope fifteen months earlier, were in the All-Ireland final. What followed over the next few weeks was pure bedlam, but then it was never going to be any different.

To be honest, we hadn't a clue how to handle the build up to such a momentous game. How would we? This was brand-new territory and we had to negotiate it as best we could. Suddenly, the county football team was fashionable. We became public property and while many people did things with the best of intentions, others jumped on the bandwagon for their own ends.

Meanwhile, Dublin were preparing quietly for their fourth successive All-Ireland final. They were the reigning champions and had also won the title in 1974, so we were up against one mighty powerful force. That was always going to leave us as distant outsiders but, to complicate things further, we did stupid things which made life harder for us.

Not being used to All-Ireland final day, we did everything and anything we were told once we reached Croke Park. So, when the knock came on the dressing room door to tell us it was time to go out, we dutifully galloped out. It was an amazing experience because, however or wherever they got the tickets, Armagh people were everywhere, except Hill 16 – that was Dublin territory – everywhere else was a sea of orange. At least, that's how it looked to us. Running onto the Croke Park pitch for an All-Ireland final is the most amazing experience for any player, and we were so caught up in the moment that it took us a minute or two to realise that it was lashing from the heavens.

A great, big, black cloud was unloading its contents over north Dublin and here we were, the rookie Armagh boys, caught in the middle of it. Dublin were supposed to come out a minute or two after us but, having been told of the conditions, they wisely stayed where they were.

The stewards could knock on the door all they liked, but boys like Tony Hanahoe, Jimmy Keaveney, Brian Mullins and Co. weren't going to be forced out into the lashing rain, especially when there was every chance it would stop in a few minutes.

And so, while we kicked around in the torrents, trying to let on we weren't noticing the drenching we were getting, Dublin were back in the dressing room waiting for the shower to pass. And, when it did, they toddled out and down to the Hill 16 end, feeling fresh and dry while the drowned rats from Armagh were miserable down at the other end.

Okay, so it didn't decide the game or anything like that, but it was a classic example of how naïve we were compared to Dublin. By the time the introductions and the parade were over, we had been out on the pitch for a long time, still wearing our soaked gear while Dublin were all dry and comfortable.

It wasn't the only advantage they had. Apart from being an exceptionally good team, they were also in a different league in terms of big-game experience. They had beaten Kerry in the semi-final in a game which is still regarded as one of the best of all time, so it would have taken an incredible performance by us to upset the odds.

We knew that, but we certainly didn't know that we were in for such a trimming. One possible plus we saw for ourselves was that, having come from nowhere in a short space of time, Dublin might not know as much about us as individuals or as a team as they would with the likes of Kerry.

Crucially, though, they had gleaned some small insight into us two months earlier when we had played them in a challenge game. I missed it, but most of the All-Ireland final team played that day, so Dublin were able to refresh their memories when we appeared in the final. Sean 'Dingle' Daly went to town against Dublin in the challenge game, but they were lying in wait for him when he came on as a sub in the final.

One of the aspects of the 1977 final that annoys me is the way everybody remembers Tom McCreesh's slip for Dublin's first goal, early on. You'd think it was the main difference between the teams which, of course, it wasn't. Yes, Tom slipped on the treacherous surface, but where was everybody else?

Had it happened at the other end, I'm sure Dublin would have had cover in place, but then they had an experience and a resilience that we lacked. Wherever you looked, there was class in that team; from Paddy Cullen in goal through Kevin Moran in defence, Brian Mullins at midfield, Tony Hanahoe at centre-forward to Jimmy Keaveney at full-forward. In a sense, we were lambs to the slaughter.

Keaveney availed of that early opportunity to cut in along the endline before looping the ball into the net. I have always been convinced that he actually went for a point and, in fairness to him, he admitted to me that that was indeed the case. Admittedly, it took him twenty-five years to own up but better late than never.

He ended the game with 2-6 that day, and won the Texaco award for a second year in a row, which was some achievement, but then he was a massive talent who did so much to change Dublin's fortunes in the 1970s. Still, that doesn't alter the fact that his first goal against us in the 1977 final was a complete fluke!

Conceding an early goal was the last thing we needed but we did come back fairly quickly and, when Peter Loughran was impeded on his way towards goal, referee, John Moloney, pointed to the penalty spot. Paddy Moriarty trotted up from centre-back and, cool as you like, drilled the ball past Cullen.

Maybe the dream was on after all. Sadly, it only brought a brief respite and, by half time, we were trailing by 3-6 to 1-3. It was all over, really, but we still felt that if we could get a good start to the second half, we'd at least do ourselves justice, but it just wasn't our day.

That was typified by what happened on the re-start when Sean Devlin cut through and let fly, only to see his shot cannon off the upright. Dublin broke upfield and Keaveney scored his second goal. Dublin were on their way to glory.

I suppose the only satisfaction we can take from that final was that we didn't completely cave in once we were facing a comprehensive defeat.

I managed to score two goals, both of which involved Jimmy Smyth who continued to play his intelligent game right to the end. As I said earlier, if I timed my run to arrive at pace alongside Jimmy, there was always a good chance I'd get scores, and so it proved that day. Sean O'Neill claimed afterwards that I took fourteen steps without soloing the ball before scoring one of the goals, which is a complete lie. I've looked back on it and it was actually fifteen steps... I'm still waiting for Sean's apology.

My two goals and a point by Loughran cut the deficit to eight points around the three-quarters mark, but it was to be the closest we got. It was as if Dublin were idling in front and, once they heard the Armagh crowd in full voice after the two goals, they put the foot to the floor.

Bobby Doyle got in for his second goal and it was all over. I was marking Brian Mullins that day, which was quite a task as he was the dominant midfielder of the time. I always liked playing against Mullins who was a fantastic competitor. Big, strong and aggressive, but also as fair an opponent as I ever came across. True, you'd know you were hit when he powered in but it was always done openly and fairly. He gave it, he took it and he got on with the game.

We ended up losing by 5-12 to 3-6, a remarkable score for an All-Ireland final. It was fiercely disappointing to be beaten by twelve points – the biggest winning margin in an All-Ireland final since 1936 – because we knew it didn't reflect our true value. Dublin were definitely a better team but we made it a whole lot easier for them than it we ought to have.

The big difference was that they had a sense of ruthlessness about them that we knew nothing about. They made things happen, whereas we *hoped* they'd happen. There was purpose in everything they did and the longer the game went on, the more it became apparent that however hard we tried, we just weren't good enough on the day. Still, things can change very quickly. A year later, Dublin were hit for 5-11 by Kerry in the All-Ireland final and ended up losing by seventeen points. I'm sure if someone had told them that, after scoring 5-12 against us, they would concede almost as much and score considerably less a year later, they would have thought it was some sort of wind-up.

I had been Armagh's top scorer on 2-1 in the final and had played quite well, overall, but that brought very little satisfaction. It did, however, bring me a IR£100 Omega watch, presented by Jack Murphy jewellers in Newry who put up the prize for whoever was chosen as Armagh's 'Man of the Match'.

It's pretty rare for any player, let alone a midfielder, to score two goals in an All-Ireland final and still end up on the losing side but such was my fate. Later in the year, I was chosen alongside Mullins on the All Stars team with Paddy Moriarty at centre-back and Jimmy Smyth at centre-forward.

Paddy was Armagh's first and only All Star up to then, having been chosen at left corner-forward in 1972, so it was nice for the county to get such wide recognition five years later. I would win a second All Star in 1982, a year in which much of the credit for the award should have gone to Brian McAlinden.

Brian was a fantastic kicker of a ball and, providing a midfielder timed his run properly, it was quite easy to catch his kick-outs or clearances. He definitely played a big part in helping me win the All Star in 1982 but, unfortunately, he went through his entire career without winning one himself which was all wrong because he was as good a goalkeeper as ever played the game.

When the initial disappointment of losing the 1977 All-Ireland final subsided, we genuinely felt we could press on and become an even better team. With the exception of Tom McCreesh and Kevin Rafferty, who were in their thirties, the oldest player on the team was Colm McKinstry at twenty-eight. Jimmy Smyth was twenty-seven but a lot of us, myself included, were twenty-five or under: Jim McKerr, he of the long, flowing locks, and Joey Donnelly were only twenty-year-olds.

Jim was one of the great characters and, because he wore his hair so long, he was instantly recognisable on and off the pitch. He knew no fear and didn't give a damn who or what he had to take on.

Despite being several inches smaller, he used to give 'Bomber' Liston a run for his money. He also loved taking penalties and, even if he missed, he wouldn't think twice about putting his hand up for the next one. I remember one League game against Dublin where he missed two penalties and I said to him afterwards, "Jim, what if we had got another one?" I was suggesting that it might be a good idea to let someone else have a go but Jim looked at me as if I was losing it completely.

"What would I have done? Scored it, of course," he said. Confident to the last, that was our Jim.

Although there seemed no obvious reason why we couldn't develop as a squad after 1977, it didn't turn out like that. Well, not for a few years, anyway. We drew Cavan in the first round of the 1978 Ulster Championship and, after what had happened to them a year earlier, they were lying in wait for us. Expectations were high in Armagh and that probably had an impact on the team. Players weren't conditioned to deal with that sort of pressure back then. You trained, you played, but you didn't think too much about the mental side of the game.

For some reason, we didn't play Tom McCreesh against Cavan, which was a big mistake. His presence and experience were badly missed and we never really got going. If memory serves me correctly, Brian Canavan made his Championship debut that day, but it wasn't to be a happy one as we ended up losing by seven points – I think Brian got a bloody nose even before the ball was thrown in.

Welcome to the fast lane, Brian.

A year later we beat Fermanagh in the first round by 5-3 to 1-7 but lost the semi-final against Monaghan by two points. That was the year that Sean McCague masterminded Monaghan's return to the top table after decades in the doldrums.

It meant that six different counties, Derry, Down, Donegal, Tyrone, Armagh and Monaghan had shared the Ulster titles throughout the decade, something that hadn't happened for a long time. And, even though we felt we should have won more than one Ulster title, it was still a massive step up from where Armagh had been in the 1960s.

Reaching the 1977 final was a huge achievement, especially considering where we'd come from in the early part of the decade. Having done that, we were unlucky to come up against one of the truly great teams in Dublin. Had it been a different era, who knows what might have happened?

That also applied to Roscommon who won four successive Connacht titles in the period from 1977 to '80 but never won an All-Ireland. They, too, were unfortunate to have peaked at a time when those Kerry and Dublin teams were dominating the scene, but that's fate and, when it goes against you, there's nothing you can do only grin and bear it.

I watched the 1980 All-Ireland final in a state of total numbness. Kerry were like a heavyweight boxer who had just taken a ferocious uppercut followed by a few powerful hooks and were on the ropes, clinging on desperately.

Roscommon were sizing them up, trying to figure out how to deliver what would have surely been the knock-out punch. The outcome was very much in Roscommon's hands, even if they were up against the most successful football team of all time. The difference was that, on this particular day, Kerry weren't just vulnerable, they were there for the taking.

One more push and they would be gone. I watched it all unfold with a sense of pure envy. Roscommon had beaten us in the semi-final in a game we should never have lost and they were now poised to break Kerry's monopoly on Sam Maguire: that should have been Armagh.

We had blown our best-ever chance of winning a first All-Ireland title. And then a strange thing happened. For reasons that continue to haunt Roscommon to this very day, they failed to deliver the knock-out punch. Kerry were allowed to hang on, pumped a second wind into their lungs and gradually brought their vast experience to bear on the game, before eventually running out three point winners.

It was definitely a final that Roscommon should have won and, if you won't take my word for it, try Mick O'Dwyer's view: "Roscommon handed us that All-Ireland," he wrote in his autobiography. Micko, and the rest of the Kerry boys, had every reason to be relieved.

What made it absolutely galling for Armagh was that we should have beaten Roscommon in the semi-final. Losing that game still ranks as possibly the biggest disappointment of my playing career. Looking back to 1997, we could have no major regrets about losing the All-Ireland final to Dublin. Okay, so it was crushing to lose so heavily, but Dublin were simply the better team at the time and we had to accept that.

It was different three years later. I am totally convinced that if we had beaten Roscommon we would have won the All-Ireland. Kerry were without my good friend 'Bomber' Liston in the final which was a massive loss to them. You can't rely on the opposition being weakened to win All-Irelands but, I'll tell you this, Kerry were a different team without the Bomber.

Roscommon proved it in 1980 but still couldn't finish the job.

We would have.

Trouble was, we didn't finish the job against Roscommon in the semi-final having given ourselves every chance not just to win but to win quite easily.

That was the first year since 1977 that we really clicked back into gear. We beat Fermanagh and Monaghan to reach the Ulster final against Tyrone which turned out to be one of the highest scoring for years, producing no fewer than eight goals.

Now, it wasn't often that Brian McAlinden – one of the best 'keepers ever to play the game – was beaten four times but, then, it was one of those crazy games that happen from time to time. In fairness to Brian, he would have had every right to take his defenders and midfielders (myself and Colm McKinstry) in for questioning afterwards as he was left horribly exposed at times.

The goal-fest started from the throw-in when a long ball into our square was caught by Eugene McKenna, who spotted Patsy Kerlin motoring in from midfield. A quick pass and Kerlin boxed the ball to the net leaving myself and McKinstry looking accusingly at each other. I thought Colm was supposed to take up Kerlin but, in any event, the result of the mix-up was a Tyrone goal.

It was the start of a remarkable game where goals flew in at an incredible rate. I even got in on the act myself in the first half and, when we led by five points early in the final quarter, it looked as if we were on our way to a comfortable win. Back came Tyrone to cut the margin to a point before we saw the game out with two late points to win by 4-10 to 4-7. Then, as now, and indeed all through Championship history, Armagh-Tyrone games had a magic all of their own, even if they haven't always been high-scoring.

It was worrying to concede so much but, on the other hand, we were scoring freely which was encouraging and although Roscommon had an excellent side – winning four successive Connacht titles – we felt that our win over them in 1977 gave us a psychological edge.

In the second quarter of the 1980 All-Ireland semi-final, we played some of the best football I ever saw in my long career with Armagh. Martin Murphy and Jimmy Smyth scored two great goals and, by half time, we were five points clear, an advantage we extended to six early in the second half.

Surely we were on our way to the final? Even when McKinstry went off injured, we still looked certain to retain control of the game against a Roscommon team that was becoming increasingly frustrated. This was their fifth successive semi-final (including the 1977 replay) and they were still looking for their first win so, mentally, they would have been right on the edge. However much talent they had, it would have been hard to pare back a six-point lead if we kept our shape.

And then it all changed.

Brian Hughes, who had been playing brilliantly at full-forward, was brought out to midfield to replace the injured McKinstry which, in hindsight, was a mistake: Pat Lindsay was having big problems with Hughes in front of goal but the pressure eased once Brian went to midfield. Lindsay and his corner-men, Harry Keegan and Gerry Connellan, tightened the defensive bolts while, further afield, Roscommon got more adventurous. They tacked on a few points and, as their confidence grew, they added two goals from Michael Finneran and Tony McManus to run out six point winners, 2-20 to 3-11.

What a bloody sickener!

A twelve-point turnaround in half an hour. People will argue that a team which conceded a total of 6-27 in a provincial final and an All-Ireland semi-final are deluding themselves thinking they could possibly have won the final. But, bear in mind that Kerry had been hit for 4-10 by Offaly in their semi-final so their defence wasn't all that clever either and with Bomber out for the final, Kerry were there for the taking.

We were convinced that, had we beaten Roscommon, we would have been ready to beat Kerry on one of their less expansive days – a belief that was seriously fortified seven weeks later when we crushed them in a League game in Lurgan.

They had almost all of their All-Ireland-winning side on duty and while

League games in November weren't a noted post-All-Ireland speciality for Kerry, they still won a lot more of them than they lost. The atmosphere in Davitt Park that day was amazing. Estimates of the attendance range between 12,000 and 16,000, a fantastic turnout for a winter League game.

But, then, so strong was the conviction in Armagh that we could have won the All-Ireland, that the public turned out in huge numbers just to see how we'd get on. I was at centre-back that day and can recall taking a bang from Bomber that nearly split me in two. (Nothing illegal or anything like that or, if it was, the bloody rogue made it look innocent.) I caught the ball, the Bomber caught me, and I was seeing so many stars that I thought I had been rocketed to the Milky Way. I was feeling terrible but couldn't let on. Back then, you couldn't possibly show that you were hurt because it was an insult to your manhood. Nowadays, some lads seem to think it's a badge of honour to appear as if they have been shot when, in fact, their real aim is to get the opponent into trouble.

I'd have eaten the grass in Lurgan before I'd ever have admitted to the Bomber that he had hurt me. As for trying to get him sent off? I'd have been in like a flash to intercede if referee Seamus Aldridge had even considered it.

We were 1-5 to 0-0 up after twelve minutes and, while Mikey Sheehy and Tommy Doyle hit us for two quick goals, we were six points clear at half time and powered on to the easiest of wins. It was the first time in decades that we had beaten Kerry and, while it might only have been a League game, we regarded it as something of a mini-All-Ireland.

Every county judged themselves against Kerry at that time, so any day you beat them was a good day. I had some great battles with Jack O'Shea, Seanie Walsh and the late Tim Kennelly, in particular: nicknamed, 'The Horse', he would let a roar out of him early on just to stamp his authority but his bark was very much worse than his bite. In fact, he was one hell of a skilful player but fierce strong with it. I loved playing against him, not because he was easy to get anything out of, but because he was so honest. He'd give and take a bang like a real man and certainly wouldn't be involved in any sneaky stuff.

We thought our win over Kerry in that particular League game would set us up in a big way but we didn't even reach the League semi-finals the following spring and were later heavily beaten by Down in the Ulster final.

Retaining Ulster titles was a pretty rare occurrence back then but we were back on top in 1982 after beating Donegal, Antrim and Fermanagh.

I was carrying an injury that year and spent much of the campaign as a sub, although I did start the All-Ireland semi-final against Kerry. I even managed to score 1-3 but it didn't count for much as Kerry were at their awesome best and thumped us by ten points. It was a depressing day all round.

It was also a depressing time for Ulster football.

Apart from our win in 1977, none of the Ulster champions had won an All-Ireland semi-final since Down in 1968. It was a run that would extend until Tyrone reached the final in 1986. There was a tendency for the rest of the country to look at the Ulster Championship as a grim refuge for ugly football which left the champions hopelessly unprepared for what lay ahead in Croke Park.

And, since results are the only true guide of standards, it was difficult to argue against that view, even if people didn't always look at the reasons for the decline. After all, our Southern friends didn't have to contend with the awfulness of The Troubles which made life so difficult in the Six Counties.

It must also be remembered that the Dublin and Kerry teams of the 1974 to '86 era were two of the best of all time, so it was always going to be difficult to compete. Everybody looked at Ulster as a barren wasteland in All-Ireland terms, but Connacht champions weren't doing any better.

The National League was offering Ulster a little more hope. Armagh reached two finals in 1983 and '85, only to lose both. The 1983 final was an all-Ulster affair between Down and ourselves. We were appearing in the final for the first time and, once again, we experienced misery in Croke Park, losing by a goal. We could have no complaints either for, while we did well in the first half, we didn't convert enough of our chances and paid the penalty as Down upped their game in the second half.

However, it was different two years later when we lost the final to Monaghan. I have no doubt that a dodgy refereeing decision cost us that day. We were motoring along nicely on a horribly wet day and while our scoring rate wasn't as high as it should have been we still looked the more likely winners through most of the first half. However, just before half time we had a penalty awarded against us in highly controversial circumstances after our full-back, Thomas Cassidy, made a splendid catch in front of the Railway End goal.

He burst clear but was adjudged, by referee, John Gough, to have over-carried. He pointed to the penalty spot, which was a harsh call on two fronts: First, there was a big doubt over whether Thomas had over-carried and, even if he had, he was outside the square by the time he fouled so the very least he should have conceded was a free in.

Instead, Monaghan had a penalty which Eamonn McEneaney drilled to the net. It set them up for a five-point win. I came on as a sub that day in what was my last chance to win a major title in Croke Park as a player.

In fairness to Monaghan, they had a very good team and beat us again in a replayed Ulster semi-final a few months later. There was only a point in it at the end, but it was their day and they went on to beat Derry in the final before losing to Kerry in the All-Ireland semi-final replay.

I was to get one more shot at an Ulster final, albeit as a sub, against Derry in 1987. I had been injured some time earlier but reckoned I was fit enough to start. However, the selectors didn't agree. They brought me on as a sub – too late, in my view – and we ended up losing by two points.

It was another lost opportunity for Armagh. Had we won, we would have played Meath in the All-Ireland semi-final and, since Armagh had never played them before in the Championship, there would have been no baggage for either side.

Granted, Meath had taken over from Dublin as the new powerhouse in Leinster, but we wouldn't have feared them in any way. Many of our squad had All-Ireland semi-final experience too, while there was some fine young talent, led by Ger Houlahan, coming through. I reckon we would have been better able for Meath than Derry – who were well beaten in the end. Once again, all we could do was look on from afar.

By then, I was thirty-three years old and was finding it increasingly hard to shake off injuries. I had been on the Armagh panel since 1971 and, while the All-Ireland dream hadn't been realised, I had extracted just about everything else, and more, from my career.

I had won All Star awards at midfield (1977) and centre-forward (1982) which were not only great honours in their own right but also gave me a chance to get to know players from other counties on tour.

And then there were my most enjoyable days with Ulster in the Railway Cup, occasions I always treasured, too.

I enjoyed every moment of my playing career whether with club, county or province. And while I don't have an All-Ireland medal to show for my efforts, I have so many wonderful memories which I will always treasure. Besides, the All-Ireland successes would come in another guise in a later phase of my enduring love affair with Crossmaglen Rangers, Armagh and Gaelic football.

CHAPTER 20

Listen to nobody and you'll never be challenged. You can convince yourself that strength lies in total self-reliance and an unshakable belief that you know best but, in the long run, it's a bad policy.

Of course, you have to trust your own judgement and instinct as a manager, but nobody is a font of all wisdom and if you can pick up hints from outside you will become better. My theory is that the more you learn, the more you have to work from and, consequently, the more ideas you have to put before those around you.

I brought in lots of outsiders to talk to Cross and Armagh over the years and, I have to say, we benefited enormously. Martin McHugh is a man whose opinion I would always trust. I used him quite a lot with Cross over the years because, apart from his knowledge and experience, he was also a winner.

You must remember that, pre-1997, nobody in Armagh had any experience of winning anything at senior All-Ireland level. An All-Ireland junior title in 1926 and a minor title in 1949 were just about all we had to show for over one hundred years of trying, so it wasn't as if the county was populated by proven experts.

Apart from a few Under-21 successes, Donegal would have been largely the same, until 1992 when they finally made the All-Ireland breakthrough at senior level. McHugh, who had always remained optimistic and driven even during the worst of times, was central to the 1992 success and later showed his managerial strengths when steering Cavan to the Ulster title in 1997.

He's a very engaging man and people respond well to him. I was always delighted to have him in to talk to the players or, indeed, just to have a chat with him myself because I always came away with something new to think about.

There were lots of others I brought in over the years. There were three boys from Meath: Colm O'Rourke, Sean Boylan and Tommy Dowd; and from Down, that great man, Sean O'Neill.

I got Colm to come and talk to the Cross boys before the 1997 All-Ireland club final. We were planning a trip to Dublin for the weekend so I decided it would be a good idea for them to hear an outside voice. He took a training session in Thomas Davis's grounds in Tallaght and we were delighted with how it went.

I certainly felt we got a lot out of it at what was a crucial time for our club and, because Colm went down so well, it seemed like a good idea to bring in the old maestro, Sean Boylan. He spoke with both Cross and Armagh on a few occasions. What Boylan achieved with Meath was quite remarkable. First, they came from a long way back in the early-1980s to become the dominant force in football for a few years and, in the next decade, he did it all over again, building a new squad which won two more All-Irelands in 1996 and 1999. It was some achievement.

On one occasion, when I invited Sean to take a session with Cross, he asked me what I wanted from it.

I responded, "Sean, it's your session. Do it your way. I'll just watch and see is there anything I can pick up."

"Right, so... Sure we'll play a bit of football for a while and see how it goes," he said.

Now, because Sean Boylan was on the premises, lads were out to impress and, even though it was only a training game, the tackles began to fly hard and often. It was a wet, wintry night with dirt flying everywhere. You couldn't even see from one end of the pitch to the other.

Then, all of a sudden, I heard this unmerciful roar.

Holy shit, what's happening? I thought.

I galloped off in the direction of the roar to find Cathal Short lying in a heap, clearly in agony. We all gathered around, examining the situation for a minute or so, and then Sean says: "He'll be okay, lads. We'll carry on."

We lifted Cathal behind the goal and then followed Sean as he walked down the field, I thought it was a bit cruel and felt guilty leaving Cathal behind but Sean was about to make a crucial point.

He got the lads around him, and spoke.

"See, boys, Cathal will be okay. The medics will look after him so there's no need to worry. In fact, forget about him for now. What if he got injured in the All-Ireland final? What if any of ye got injured? Once you're injured, there's no more you can do, but there's something everyone else can.

"Ye can still win the game and isn't that what everyone wants? I've seen lads get distracted if one of their colleagues went off injured. Don't ever let that happen.

"Ye can't help an injured player but ye can decide whether ye win without him!"

And, what happened in the 2000 All-Ireland final against Na Fianna? Jim McConville, who would have been regarded as central to everything we did in attack, went off in the first half with a broken ankle, but there was no panic. We sent in Michael Moley, who did very well, and maintained business as usual. In fact, we scored a few crucial points between Jim's injury and half time.

Sean Boylan was right. When a player goes off injured, it's vital not to allow it to become a bigger issue than it should be.

One other piece of advice which Sean gave always stuck with me. He talked about the 1991 All-Ireland semi-final where Meath were trailing Roscommon by four or five points when the "All stewards to end of match positions" call went out over the public address in Croke Park.

It left Roscommon feeling that the job was done but galvanised Meath into a big push and the impact was dramatic. Meath clawed their way back and won by a point. Indeed, Sean said he was convinced that the PA announcement had changed the course of the game. It was something both Crossmaglen and Armagh were conscious of afterwards and probably explains why we won so many games late on.

Boylan's first Meath team were the masters of the dramatic comeback. To hear him talking about how they eventually reached a stage where they believed they could always recover, irrespective of how far behind they were, was inspiring. I certainly picked up some tips from Sean and I now copy what he did with us whenever I visit a club – I start by asking them what message they want to get across to the players and then try to put my own stamp on imparting it.

Boylan always intrigued me because he's such a pleasant, mild-mannered man, yet he managed to send out some of the hardest teams ever to play Gaelic football. Sean is such a charmer that you'd wonder how he was able to inject such a tough streak into his teams. Appearances can be deceptive so I can only assume that he had an equally tough streak himself. He certainly had a winning streak.

Brian Cody was another I brought in to have a chat with the lads. He's very passionate about everything he does and commands so much respect that you just know players will benefit from listening to him. His heart and soul is in hurling and when you see him spit on his hand as he walks along the sideline you know he means business. What's more, his players know he means business and that it's time to step things up.

Sean and Brian are the two managers I would listen to most. Both are great men who have done so much for football and hurling.

Kilkenny hurlers have always been very good at winning games late on, which is a reflection on their confidence and maturity.

It's the same with Manchester United. How many times have they scored late goals to win games? It's as if they believe they can do it and the opposition expects the worst to happen on the home stretch. A belief, held with conviction right to the finish, is a great trait in any group of players, in any sport.

Others who were extremely helpful to the Armagh cause were Billy Dixon and Phil Glasgow. Billy is an image consultant and Phil is an expert in sports medicine. Now, nobody would be surprised that an authority in sports medicine would be a welcome addition to any camp, but an image consultant?

I didn't know anything about Billy until 2005 when he addressed various groups at a meeting in Crossmaglen. Aaron went along and after listening to Billy for a while he ran back to the house and said, "You've got to hear this guy. He's great."

I couldn't go to the hall at the time but, afterwards, Billy dropped in on me at home and we chatted. After about twenty minutes, I felt he could do something for us so I asked him if he would come aboard.

Some players are sceptical when a new person arrives, but the first night

Billy talked to the squad they were won over. He dealt with little things, like how to shake hands with an opponent in a manner which shows you're in control and how to carry yourself in the parade to display confidence. Billy also came up with a plan to re-design the Armagh jersey. It involved the subtle blending of orange and white so that players' shoulders and chests seemed broader. Everyone was talking about how much bigger and more conditioned the Armagh players looked that year when, in reality, it was down to the jersey design.

One other idea he came up with was to bring the squad to Mullyash Mountain in east Monaghan. It's a famous historical landmark and a reputed burial spot of all sorts of high kings, dating way back. More importantly from our viewpoint, you can see all nine Ulster counties from the summit, which was why Billy suggested we go there the Sunday after winning the 2005 Ulster final replay against Tyrone.

It was a lovely day, so we could see the whole of Ulster stretched out below us. We were champions again; more than that we had retained the provincial title. It was all quite emotional in its own way but it was also important and had a special meaning. Everyone clicked into the symbolism of it all because, when we looked north, we could see into the counties we had beaten but when we looked south all we could see was forest.

We still didn't know who we would be playing in the All-Ireland quarter-final (it turned out to be Laois) but, whoever it was, we knew we were headed south to Croke Park and into the unknown, which made it all even more exciting.

It was a day that worked really well, as did so many of Billy's other ideas. He was one of the nicest men I ever worked with and I really was delighted to have him with us for a time.

Phil Glasgow's contribution lay in his remarkable ability as a physio and rehab man. He came to us in 2007 with a great reputation and lived up to all the wonderful reports we had heard about him. He was an absolute genius when it came to getting injured players ready to play as quickly as possible.

And then there was my old pal, Paddy McNamee, affectionately known as 'Paddy the Bishop'. Paddy was a lifelong friend and, when I took over as Cross manager, I brought him in as bag man. He did a great job so when I moved on to Armagh I brought him aboard, too. He had this routine with me where he'd take my wallet before every game and, very often on a big match day, he would have tears in his eyes. He was that emotional about Cross and Armagh.

He'd take his time returning the wallet after a game and, again, he'd often have tears in his eyes whether we won or lost. The whole thing meant so much to him. A great character and a man I'd trust with my life.

It's that kind of strength of character that can make a difference at any time of year, as we discovered in 2006 when we went to Barcelona for a short break early in the season. It was all very informal, players, management, wives and girlfriends having a few days away.

We headed down to a bar on the beach the night we arrived and, as often happens, various groups kept to themselves. Then, in walked a certain Francie Bellew and his girlfriend Grace. There was a fella belting out some music in the corner and, after a while, Francie went over and started talking to him. Surely Francie wasn't going to sing!

Absolutely not, but what he did was ask the musician to play one of Francie's favourite U2 songs. Within a few minutes Francie has grabbed a few couples, jumped up on the table and began the dancing. Suddenly, the place was hopping and it continued to rock until closing time. The whole group had been brought together by one simple gesture from Francie and it turned into a fantastic bonding session which set the tone nicely for the season ahead.

I always like to keep abreast of what's happening in other sports so, as part of the policy of listening to as many people as possible, I decided to invite Paul O'Connell to talk to Armagh in 2006. I love the way Munster play their rugby and have a special admiration for Paul, who is a giant of a man in so many ways. I met him a few times at various functions so I decided I'd like to have him come along and talk to the Armagh squad.

We were going to Dunboyne Castle Hotel for a weekend, so I rang up Paul and asked him if he would be able to come up and give a talk. It's a long way from Limerick to Dunboyne so, if he had driven to Dunboyne and back, it would have taken up his entire day. Over to 'Mr Fixit', Eamonn Mackle, who organised a helicopter to fly Paul to Dunboyne.

I didn't tell the lads he was coming but I was always going on at them about the Munster spirit and how impressed I was at the way they went about their business. Aidan O'Rourke had all sorts of sports pictures in his shop in Newry so I asked him to get one of the Munster team. For some reason, Paul O'Connell wasn't in the picture that Aidan brought, but I couldn't say anything.

Anyway, we had this big picture of the Munster team in the room and I was banging on about how these boys knew how to play when the door opened and in walked Paul. The lads were totally surprised, but not as surprised as Paul when he saw that picture of the Munster team without him!

He was a big hit with the lads.

He talked about how one of the main differences between rugby and GAA was in terms of who took responsibility for what. Once a rugby game starts, the players, led by the captain, are in charge until half time, when the coach can have his say. The coach can make substitutions any time he wishes but the actual on-field decisions are down to the players. It helps to generate real leadership skills in players all over the field.

It's an aspect of the game we could develop more in football and hurling. It's always better if the players work things out for themselves rather than playing to a rigid system which can only be changed by instruction from the sideline. Paul O'Connell left us with plenty to think about in that area and it certainly was well worth bringing him in.

His talk wasn't without its funny moments. In the course of various stories, he mentioned many of his Munster colleagues by their nicknames including Axel (Anthony Foley), ROG (Ronan O'Gara) and Strings (Peter Stringer).

At one point, while in full flow, he was interrupted by Paddy McKeever who piped up: "Hey Paul, who's ROG?" Typical Paddy. O'Gara might have played for Munster, Ireland and the Lions but Paddy hadn't heard the ROG tag. Either that or he was pretending not to know it which, I suspect, was the case.

Paul O'Connell wasn't the first rugby person I turned to for help. I invited specialist kicking coach, David Alred, to our training ground in La Manga in 2002 to work on our technique. David has vast experience with rugby and soccer teams and I felt that it was worth hiring him if it would bring about even a tiny improvement.

He worked on all aspects of kicking and there's no doubt that some players found it very helpful. Obviously, I was keen to have him go through things with Oisin McConville whose kicking was so vital to us, but it didn't work out at all. The more Oisin tried the Alred way, the worse he got so, in the end, we just told Oisin to go back to what he had been doing before. Oisin had enough confidence is his own kicking so there was no point in trying to change him.

The following year we went to Bath for a few days before the Championship and I invited along another famous rugby man, Shaun Edwards. Shaun was a proven winner both in rugby league and rugby union and one of the areas I asked him to deal with was how to maintain performance at a high level once you'd made the breakthrough, as we had in 2002.

Taking the next step can be very difficult but it was something Edwards had done quite often as a player and then as a coach. Bringing him in was a worthwhile exercise even though we didn't win any more All-Irelands – that was down to factors other than attitude and maintaining motivation at the obsessive levels required to stay at the top. We managed that alright, it was other little things that didn't go our way.

As I've said, you can never listen to too much good advice. Bringing in outsiders was something I always felt had been beneficial but, then, I had practical experience of the closed-mind syndrome from my playing days.

When we reached the 1982 All-Ireland semi-final against Kerry, a few of us thought it would be a good idea to bring in an outsider to give a talk. We wanted someone who had won an All-Ireland and who understood what it took to be successful at the very highest level. We had failed in the All-Ireland final in 1977 and in the 1980 semi-final so, clearly, our way wasn't working.

The response from County Board officials and team management to the 'outsider' suggestion wasn't quite what we had expected. In fact, it was met first with silence and then with the baffling comment to the effect that we didn't want anybody stealing our thunder. I couldn't understand where they were coming from and let them know, in no uncertain terms.

"That's all very well, but what if there is no thunder?" I asked.

There was no answer, nor was there any thunder after the semi-final where we lost to Roscommon. I felt the players had been let down, and all because some people were afraid that, if we were successful, an outsider might have got some of the credit. I'd had someone like Peter McDermott from Meath in mind, a man with vast experience of success as a player and coach.

It would have been helpful just to listen to someone explain how they had come through various challenges and moved on to the next level. It might have made something click with a player who was having doubts about himself or his game. Sometimes you can have a player who'll say everything is fine if you ask him but they are a bit like a child in school who pretends he understands what he's told, then goes home and can't make head nor tail of the subject but won't admit it.

I was convinced that an outside voice might have brought things along in 1982 but the Board didn't agree. At that stage, I had no idea that I would be managing Armagh twenty years later but, once I was, I made up my mind to use as much outside brainpower as I could find.

One of my great heroes has always been that outstanding Down man, Sean O'Neill. As a young fella growing up in the '60s and early-'70s, Sean was the icon, the man every kid wanted to imitate.

I got to know him when he was managing Ulster and always had the utmost respect for him so, when I took over in Cross, he was one of the first people I invited to talk to the squad. We were honoured to have him. After all, he was a legend of Gaelic football and here he was coming down to 'bandit country' in Cross to talk to a group who, apparently, had this daft dream about winning an All-Ireland title.

He's the most positive man you will ever come across and if you didn't feel better after listening to him, then you had a problem. We had some great times when he was Ulster manager. Sean and Brian McEniff were men who always believed passionately in the Railway Cup and, even when others began to lose interest in it, they remained committed.

Sean was in charge when I first came on the Ulster scene and I was impressed straightaway by the way he did business. A man of great detail, he would cover every angle over and over again. So much so that he could go on forever. Once I got to know him well, I used to sit near the front and he'd tell me to time the team meetings.

"Right, Joe... Time this for one hour exactly."

"Okay, Sean!"

The hour would pass and I'd start tapping my watch but Sean would be in such full flow that I'd be banging the face off the watch for ages trying to grab his attention. At last, he'd get the hint and prepare to wind down, or so we thought.

"Okay lads, we'll finish for now."

Just as we'd begin to shuffle to our feet, Sean would call us back.

"Sorry, lads, just one more point." And off he'd go again.

The thing was, though, that it didn't matter how long he talked, it was always interesting and insightful. He had a wonderful understanding of the game and of players and got huge satisfaction from managing Ulster. But then he had enjoyed an incredible playing career with Ulster, winning no fewer than eight Railway Cup titles.

My first Railway Cup win was in 1979. We beat Leinster on the rather unusual scoreline of 5-8 to 1-13 in the semi-final in Croke Park, to set up a final against Munster who were going for a fifth successive title. They were powered by the great Kerry team of that era, backed up by some excellent players from Cork like Jimmy Barry-Murphy, Billy Morgan and Kevin Kehilly. All in all, it was a very powerful combination but we had drawn with them in the final a year earlier, before losing the replay in extra time so we felt we were ready for them.

The All-Ireland club finals were played in Croke Park on St Patrick's Day, which fell on a Sunday, followed by the Railway Cup finals on the Monday. We stayed in the Skylon Hotel in Drumcondra on the Sunday night and, of course, we had one of Sean's famous team meetings.

It went on for a long time and, when it was over, we ran down the stairs to see what the rest of the world was up to on St Patrick's night. The Munster team were staying at the same hotel and, as Jimmy Smyth and I reached the foyer, we spotted Pat Spillane sitting in a corner reading a newspaper.

We sauntered over to him and Jimmy said, "Hey, Spillane! What's that you're reading?"

Spillane slowly lifted his head and, in a deadly serious voice, said, "D'you know what, boys? It says here that Munster are certain to win the five-in-a-row. I'd have to agree."

As it happened, Sean O'Neill was right behind us and heard Spillane's comment, which was designed to wind us up.

"Right, boys, back upstairs, there are a few more points I want to go through," said Sean.

He marched the squad back up to the meeting room for a second session leaving us cursing a chuckling Spillane and vowing vengeance on him the following day. As it happened, he didn't start the game but came on as a sub and was treated to a very special Ulster welcome every time he went near the ball.

We won by 1-7 to 0-6 and felt really great about it. Not only had we won the Railway Cup for Ulster for the first time since 1971 but we stopped Spillane and the Munster boys doing the five-in-a-row. There was added satisfaction for Armagh as there were no fewer than seven of us involved – Brian McAlinden, Denis Stevenson, Paddy Moriarty, Peter Loughran, Sean Daly, Jimmy Smyth and me. I played at centre-forward where I had another great battle with Tim Kennelly.

I loved the whole Railway Cup scene. It was a chance to get to know players from other Ulster counties and to see them as friends and colleagues rather than enemies who kicked lumps off each other for the rest of the year.

The GAA ran the Railway Cups over a weekend on a few occasions, which was an excellent idea because it gave players from all over the country an opportunity to meet and get to know each other. We had a particularly good weekend down in Ennis in 1984 when it was played over two days. That was the GAA's Centenary Year so a bigger effort than usual went into everything, from a playing and an organisational viewpoint. We beat Munster in the semi-final and Connacht in the final. It's an occasion which still stands out in my memory. I'm disgusted that the Interprovincials aren't given the respect they deserve any more. I think it's a big mistake and an indictment of the GAA if they can't maintain and promote a competition that was an integral part of the scene for so long.

I still remain convinced that the competition has a viable future. I was lucky enough to play for Ulster for years and to manage them much later, and every player I came across in both roles really wanted to play for their province. The loss of public interest in the Interprovincials did have a negative impact, but is that a reason to scrap them altogether? Not in my book, it isn't.

Ulster always put in a big effort but, unfortunately, the other provinces didn't reciprocate, especially in recent times. Brian McEniff did a mighty job as Ulster manager for years and I was chuffed to be invited to take the position after him. Tom Daly and Danny Murphy (Ulster council Chairman and Secretary) made it clear to me that they were very committed to the Interprovincials and did everything they could to ensure we were well prepared.

I brought in my good friend 'Banty' McEnaney, Tony Scullion, John McCloskey and Eamonn Mackle to work with me and, I have to say, the whole thing gelled very well.

I found the players to be just as interested in playing for their province as they were in my day. We played three or four trial games against club teams and, because lads were getting an actual game rather than training, they really enjoyed it. We hear lots of talk about too many games and burnout, but it's also the case than many inter-county players get very little action once they're out of the All-Ireland race. Not all of them are playing on club teams that win county titles so they can, in effect, be left largely inactive for a long time. That's why they like the idea of playing for their province if the chance comes along. Certainly, that's how Ulster players saw it.

Even lads who enjoy long inter-county seasons enjoy the Interprovincials. I recall how, after Ulster had lost a semi-final to Munster in Fermoy in October 2008, Davy Harte came to me in the Carrickdale Hotel as the squad were about to go their separate ways and said how disappointed he was to have lost.

"I would have loved one of those medals," he said. Now, here was a man who had won an All-Ireland with Tyrone a month earlier, yet he was disappointed not to have finished the year with an Interprovincial title.

Club, county, Interprovincial, All Star, Ireland … those are the jerseys every player wants but, now, one of them is missing. My view is that if the players want the Interprovincials to continue, as they most definitely do, then their view should be respected.

Find a slot for the competitions, preferably at the same time every year, market them extensively and see how they develop. Look at what proper marketing did for the International Rules games. I'm not saying we'll fill Croke Park for the Interprovincial finals, but I do believe that good crowds would return if all the provinces – and Croke Park – got behind the competitions.

There are few enough opportunities for players from different counties to meet each other without cutting off an avenue which was opened as far back as the 1920s. The argument that the International Rules games have taken over from the Interprovincials in terms of bringing players together doesn't hold because that competition involves much smaller numbers of players.

Besides, we have no idea how long the International Rules series will last. It came very close to being abandoned altogether a few years ago and, to be honest, it would have been no loss at the time because of the way the Australians were playing the game. In fairness, things have got back on track so I'd like to see it continue. It gives players a chance to play for their country, which is a huge honour. I know Aaron has really enjoyed his International experiences and I'm sure it's the same for all the others who have been lucky enough to be selected over the years.

Players also valued the Interprovincials, and they still do! I still believe that if the Interprovincials were linked with the All-Ireland club Championship, they could deliver two great occasions on St Patrick's Day. If the club and Interprovincial football finals were played in Croke Park and the hurling finals in Thurles, I have no doubt that they could be promoted and marketed as two attractive packages that would have the turnstiles clicking at two venues. Sadly, though, it's unlikely to happen and, in my view, the GAA will be all the poorer for that.

1971: A senior county man at the age of seventeen. Can't be long until the All-Ireland follows! I was picked to play at corner-forward against Donegal in a Dr McKenna Cup game in the Athletic Grounds. It was a pretty grim time for Armagh football around then and, unsurprisingly, Donegal beat us. Still, I had broken into the county scene and would remain there until 1987.

1972: School days are happy days, aren't they? Not when you lose a MacRory Cup final. It was my first, really big frustration in football and one that I still recall clearly to this day. I was on the Abbey CBS, Newry team that reached the final only to lose by two points to St Patrick's, Cavan. I'd still regard that defeat as one of the biggest disappointments in my entire career. In case anyone thinks the teams are two players short from the team list that follows, college games were thirteen-a-side between 1970 and 1976.
Abbey CBS: Gerard McCarthy, John Campbell, Peter Doran; Marty Slevin, Tony McLoughlin, Hugh Markey, John Crummie, Joe Kernan; Peter Treanor, John McPartland, Anthony Quinn, Eamonn Treanor, Dermot McGovern.
St Patrick's: Aidan Elliot; Paddy McGill, Eamon Gillic, John Sweeney, Ollie Brady, Gerry Smith, Ciaran O'Keeffe, Sean Leddy, Charlie O'Donoghue, Niall Brennan, Brian Brady, Hugh Reynolds, Michael English.

1973-74-75: Grim years for Armagh football. I was part of a team that, at one stage, had only Kilkenny below it on the national ratings. I was commuting from London for a year or two but eventually gave it up and stayed at home. It seemed, at times, as if we were going nowhere as a county, a view backed up by three early-round exits in the Ulster Championship.

1976: Small green shoots in the Orchard. After years of failure, we finally put a run together and won the Division 3 NFL title, beating Clare in a replayed final (1-7 to 1-6) – in Croke Park, no less. It gave us a feel for the great old stadium and a dream to aim for which, we hoped, would involve us getting back there. A few months later, Derry reunited us with reality, winning by 1-19 to 2-1 in the Ulster quarter-final. Imagine scoring just one point in seventy minutes. Still, we had a Cup to show for our League efforts which was something we could take from the year.

Armagh: (Division 3 final): Peter Keegan; Jim Finnegan, Tom McCreesh, Raymond Kelly; Noel Marley, Jimmy Smyth, Kevin Rafferty; Joe Kernan, Larry Kearns; Paddy Moriarty, Denis McCoy, Denis Stevenson; Peter Loughran, Colm McKinstry, Eamonn O'Neill.

Sub: Jimmy Christie for Stevenson.

1977: A first Ulster title for Armagh since 1953 and a first All-Ireland final appearance since the same year. A truly magical experience but, unfortunately, we were far too inexperienced and naïve to have a decent chance of unseating Dublin in the final. They exploited their experience in every way possible. Of course, we were up against an exceptionally good Dublin team. Had it been six or seven years earlier we would probably have taken an All-Ireland because they were easier to win back then.

The 1977 season ended well for me as I was chosen with Brian Mullins at midfield on the All Star team. Colleagues, Paddy Moriarty and Jimmy Smyth were also selected which was a huge honour for the county as Paddy 'Mo' had been Armagh's only All Star up to then. Now we had three in one year.

Armagh: (All-Ireland final): Brian McAlinden; Denis Stevenson, Tom McCreesh, Jim McKerr; Kevin Rafferty, Paddy Moriarty, Joey Donnelly; Joe Kernan, Colm McKinstry; Larry Kearns, Jimmy Smyth, Noel Marley; Sean Devlin, Peter Trainor, Peter Loughran.

Subs: Jim Loughran for Donnelly, Sean Daly for Marley, Frank Toman for McKerr.

Panel members: Eamonn O'Neill, Malachy Heeney, Noel O'Hagan, Fran McMahon, Thomas Cassidy, Raymond Kelly, Jim Finnegan, Redmond Scullion.

All Stars: Paddy Cullen (Dublin); Gay O'Driscoll (Dublin), Pat Lindsay (Roscommon), Robbie Kelleher (Dublin); Tommy Drumm (Dublin), Paddy Moriarty (Armagh), Pat O'Neill (Dublin); Brian Mullins (Dublin), Joe Kernan (Armagh); Anton O'Toole (Dublin), Jimmy Smyth (Armagh), Pat Spillane (Kerry); Bobby Doyle (Dublin), Jimmy Keaveney (Dublin), John Egan (Kerry).

1978: The year after the optimism. Cavan, whom we had beaten in dramatic circumstances to launch the big adventure a year earlier, were lying in wait for us. We weren't ready for them and they beat us easily (0-16 to 0-9) in the Ulster quarter-final. What we'd have given for the All-Ireland qualifiers back then. I often wonder how the history books would read if the qualifiers had operated throughout GAA history. I had my doubts about their introduction in 2001 on the basis that they removed the real tension and drama from the provincial Championships but there's no doubt they have livened up the summer. It's like this: you don't even think about them if you win a provincial title but they provide a strong safety net if you lose, especially when it's a close call.

1979: How often do teams score five goals in a Championship game? We leaked five in the 1977 All-Ireland final and hit five two years later in the Ulster quarter-final, beating Fermanagh 5-3 to 1-7 in Lurgan. I even scored one myself. We scored just three points, which isn't exactly textbook Championship form, and our season ended next time out when we lost the semi-final to Monaghan by two points.

Earlier in the year, I won my first Railway Cup medal when Ulster ended Munster's five-in-a-row bid with a four-point win in the final. I treasured every opportunity to play for Ulster.

Railway Cup final (Ulster): Brian McAlinden (Armagh); Denis Stevenson (Armagh), Tommy McGovern (Down), Finian Ward (Donegal); Kevin McCabe (Tyrone), Paddy Moriarty (Armagh), Mickey Moran (Derry); Peter McGinnity (Fermanagh), Liam Austin (Down); Colm McAlarney (Down), Joe Kernan (Armagh), Brendan Donnelly (Tyrone); Peter Loughran (Armagh), Peter Rooney (Down), Sean Devlin (Armagh).

Subs: Cathal Digney (Down) for Moran; Paddy McNamee (Cavan) for Loughran; Jimmy Smyth (Armagh) for Donnelly.

1980: Now here's a season where we threw away a glorious chance to do something special. We reached the League semi-final before losing to Kerry but it set us up nicely for the Ulster Championship where we beat Fermanagh, Monaghan, the defending champions, and Tyrone.

We blew a glorious chance against Roscommon in the All-Ireland semi-final and while they lost the final to Kerry, it was by no means a vintage Kingdom performance. By Kerry's own admission, they were there for the taking. 'Bomber' Liston was missing so the attack wasn't as potent as in other years. Would we have done it if we had beaten Roscommon? Yes. It was one of the few finals in which Kerry looked really vulnerable.

Ulster retained the Railway Cup final, beating Munster by four points on St Patrick's Day. I was at centre-forward, flanked by Peter McGinnity and Eugene Young.

Ulster final (Armagh): Brian McAlinden; Brian Canavan, Jim McKerr, Kevin Rafferty; Paddy Moriarty, Jim McCorry, Joey Donnelly; Colm McKinstry, Joe Kernan; Noel Marley, Jimmy Smyth, Fran McMahon; Sean Devlin, Brian Hughes, Peter Loughran. Subs: Hank Kernan for Devlin; Denis McCoy for Marley.

Railway Cup final (Ulster): Brian McAlinden (Armagh); 'Nudie' Hughes (Monaghan), Tommy McGovern (Down); Finian Ward (Donegal); Kevin McCabe (Tyrone), Paddy Moriarty (Armagh), Sean McCarville (Monaghan); Peter McGinnity (Fermanagh), Liam Austin (Down); Colm McAlarney (Down), Joe Kernan (Armagh), Eugene Young (Derry); Paddy McNamee (Cavan), Peter Rooney (Down), Peter Loughran (Armagh). Sub: Mickey Moran (Derry) for Loughran.

1981: Retaining the Ulster title has always been difficult and, while we reached the final against Down that year, they beat us by eight points. I couldn't start the final because of injury. I came on as a sub but it was one of those days when Down weren't going to be denied. Colm McAlarney was outstanding for Down while John McCartan scored two excellent goals.

1982: We landed our third Ulster title in six seasons which, in fairness, was quite an achievement even if we didn't make the All-Ireland breakthrough. We were unlucky that our good run coincided with the era of the great Kerry and Dublin teams. We were no match for Kerry in the All-Ireland semi-final, losing by 3-15 to 1-11. Not even our supporters thought we had a chance. Many of them didn't even bother to travel to Croke Park (the attendance was a little over 18,000) but then that was pretty much the norm in semi-finals involving Kerry at that time. Their supporters didn't travel because they expected to be in the final while the opposition fans stayed at home because they had no confidence in their own team.

Earlier that summer we'd beaten Fermanagh by 0-10 to 1-4 in a rather low-key Ulster final. I was carrying a niggling injury but managed to come on as a sub. It would be seventeen years before Armagh won another Ulster title. I had a good season overall and was delighted to win a second All-Star award, this time at centre-forward with the great Peter McGinnity at No. 10. He became Fermanagh's first All Star and it was the least he deserved. It would be a further eleven years before Armagh won another All Star award when Ger Houlahan was chosen at full-forward in 1993.

Ulster final (Armagh): Brian McAlinden; Denis Stevenson, Jim McKerr, Joe Murphy; Noel Marley, Paddy Moriarty, Peter Rafferty; Colm McKinstry, Fran McMahon; Dermot Dowling, Brian Hughes, Aidan Short; Sean Devlin, John Corvan, Mickey McDonald.

Subs: Joey Donnelly for Murphy; Joe Kernan for McDonald; Peter Loughran for Short.

All Stars: Martin Furlong (Offaly); Mick Fitzgerald (Offaly), Liam Connor (Offaly), Kevin Kehilly (Cork); Paidi O Se (Kerry), Sean Lowry (Offaly), Liam Currams (Offaly); Jack O'Shea (Kerry), Padraig Dunne (Offaly); Peter McGinnity (Fermanagh), Joe Kernan (Armagh), Matt Connor (Offaly); Mikey Sheehy (Kerry), Eoin Liston (Kerry), John Egan (Kerry).

1983: Beaten by Donegal in the first round of the Ulster Championship, but the big disappointment that year was in the National League final where we lost to Down by 1-8 to 0-8. We defeated Meath in the semi-final to reach the final for the first time and there was a great atmosphere in the run-up to the final, but the game didn't live up to expectations. A goal by Ambrose Rodgers was the decisive score.

NFL final (Armagh): Brian McAlinden; Denis Stevenson, Jim McKerr, Kieran McNally; Brian Canavan, Paddy Moriarty, Joey Donnelly; Noel Marley, Fran McMahon; Joe Murphy, Joe Kernan, Sean Devlin; John Corvan, Brian McGeown, Mickey McDonald.

Subs: Denis McCoy for Kernan; Kieran McGurk for Stevenson; Kieran Harney for McGeown.

1984: Remember the Centenary Cup? Played in 1984 to celebrate the GAA's 100th birthday, it was an open draw knock-out competition involving all thirty-two counties. It generated big interest as there was a real freshness to the pairings but, unfortunately, Armagh didn't make it very far. We drew Wexford at home but turned in a dreadful performance in Lurgan, losing by 3-3 to 0-6. There was an extra edge to the Championship that year, too, and we played well to reach the Ulster final against Tyrone, where we lost to Frank McGuigan! He kicked 0-11 from play in one of the best ever performances in an Ulster final and while his colleagues only managed 0-4 between them, it was still more than enough as we managed just 1-7.

My only consolation that year came in the form of a third Railway Cup medal when Ulster beat Connacht in the final in Ennis. We had a great team then. Check out the forward line... it had some scoring power.

Ulster final (Armagh): Brian McAlinden; Joey Donnelly, Thomas Cassidy, Jim McCorry; Kieran McNally, Colin Harney, Brian Canavan; Colm McKinstry, Fran McMahon; Tommy Coleman, Joe Kernan, Ger Houlahan; John Corvan, Paddy Moriarty, Peter Rafferty.

Subs: Jim McKerr for McKinstry; Denis Stevenson for Cassidy; Brian Hughes for Rafferty.

Railway Cup final (Ulster): Brian McAlinden (Armagh); Paddy Kennedy (Down), Gerry McCarville (Armagh), Joe Irwin (Derry); Michael Carr (Donegal), Martin Lafferty (Donegal), Jim Reilly (Cavan); Liam Austin (Down), Eugene McKenna (Tyrone); Peter McGinnity (Fermanagh), Joe Kernan (Armagh), Greg Blaney (Down); Martin McHugh (Donegal), Frank McGuigan (Tyrone), 'Nudie' Hughes (Monaghan).

Subs: Tommy McDermott (Donegal) for Irwin; Frank McMahon (Armagh) for Austin; Paddy O'Rourke (Down) for Carr.

1985: We got back to the National League final but, once again, we couldn't finish the job, losing to Monaghan by 1-11 to 0-9 on a wet, miserable day in Croke Park. We were raging with referee, John Gough of Antrim, who awarded one of the most dubious penalties I have ever seen given. I was carrying an injury and couldn't start but I came on as a sub. Eamonn McEneaney's goal from the dodgy penalty proved the difference. We later drew with Monaghan in the Ulster semi-final but lost the replay by a point. In fairness, that was a very good Monaghan side. Managed by Sean McCague, they went on to take Kerry to a replay in the All-Ireland semi-final. They would have won an All-Ireland title in another era but, like so many of us at that time, they came up against a Kerry team that broke all sorts of records.

NFL final (Armagh): Brian McAlinden; Denis Stevenson, Thomas Cassidy, Joe Murphy; Brian Canavan, Kieran McNally, Joey Donnelly; Jim McCorry, Fran McMahon; Aidan Short, Colin Harney, Kieran McGurk; John Corvan, Denis Seeley, Joe Cunningham.

Subs: Joe Kernan for Cunningham; Peter Rafferty for McGurk; Jim McKerr for Canavan.

1986: The hour-glass was moving quicker for me. I was finding it harder to shake off knocks and was also picking them up more easily. We reached the Ulster semi-final but were hit by a Down goal blitz as they beat us 3-7 to 0-12. Would I ever get a chance to play in another Ulster final? This was the year I won the last of my five county Championship medals with Crossmaglen, though we never made much of an impression on the provincial scene.

1987: Yes, I got another Ulster final chance, albeit as a sub. We lost to Derry by two points on a day when I wasn't best pleased with the team management. I had been injured some months earlier and was fully fit by mid-summer but I wasn't on the starting fifteen for the Ulster final. I was brought on – too late, in my view – so I don't have very pleasant memories of my last day in an Armagh jersey.

Ulster final (Armagh): Brian McAlinden; Vinny Loughran, Thomas Cassidy, Jim McCorry; Brian Canavan, Kieran McNally, Aidan Short; Kieran McGurk, Martin McQuillan; Neil Smyth, Paul Grimley, Ger Houlahan; Shane Skelton, Denis Seeley, Jim McConville.

Subs: Jim McKerr for Grimley; Denis McCoy for Smyth; Joe Kernan for Seeley.

1988: My friend and former colleague, Paddy Moriarty, took over as manager in late-1987 and asked me to join him, which I was happy to do. Paddy was an excellent manager and we worked very well together. Armagh lost the 1988 Ulster semi-final to Tyrone by four points but we felt the squad had made good progress.

1989: So much for progress! We lost the Ulster first round to Tyrone in Omagh. We were well ahead after thirty-five minutes but a bust-up near the dressing room door as the teams made their way in for half time seemed to inspire Tyrone, who came back to win by a point 1-11 to 2-7. It was in the days before qualifiers, so we were left with another long summer stretching ahead of us. If only there was a back door somewhere…

1990: Heartbreak. We reached the Ulster final after beating Tyrone and Down (replay) but came up a point short against Donegal. It was now eight years since Armagh had won an Ulster title but we would never have thought the wait would extend for another nine years.

Armagh (Ulster final): Brian McAlinden; Padraig O'Neill, Gareth O'Neill, Brian Canavan; Leo McGeary, John Grimley, Aidan Short; Mark Grimley, Neil Smyth; Ollie Reel, John Toner, Martin Toye; Jim McConville, Kieran McGurk, Ger Houlahan.

Sub: Shane Skelton for Toye.

1991: The last year in charge for Paddy 'Mo' and me. It ended in Newry when Down beat us by 1-7 to 0-8 in a dour, dogged game that certainly didn't look as if it would produce All-Ireland champions. But that's exactly what it did as Down improved with each game to end up with Sam Maguire. Paddy stepped down as manager afterwards and I went, too. In hindsight, we probably should have stayed on and kept building but, after four seasons, we felt we'd had enough.

1992: A breather after twenty years as a senior player and selector with Armagh.

1993/94: A new phase of my sporting life as Crossmaglen senior manager. Things hadn't been going well at senior level but some great young talent was coming through. Cross won four U-21 county titles in a row and five in six years and, while it took a few years for them to mature into what would become a hugely successful outfit, there was a sense that we were on the edge of something special. We lost to Maghery and Pearse Og in the 1993 and 1994 Armagh senior Championships but felt we were getting closer to the big breakthrough.

1995: Crossmaglen's defeat by Mullaghbawn was a shattering experience. We thought we had the measure of them but they were more experienced than us, which probably made the difference in the end. I came under pressure after that defeat as there were some in the club who believed I was using a style of football which went against Crossmaglen's traditional values. The truth was that we needed to change and, once we got it right, the club would go on to enjoy its best-ever run.

1996: Redemption at last. Crossmaglen won the Armagh title for the first time since 1986, beating Sarsfields, Mullaghbawn, Maghery and Clan na nGael. We immediately set our sights on bigger prizes and went on to win the Ulster title, along the way beating Burren, Castleblayney and Bellaghy.

1997: History makers. Crossmaglen Rangers are All-Ireland Club Champions – that has a lovely ring to it. St Patrick's Day 1997 is still recalled as one of the most special days in the club's history. We pipped reigning champs Laune Rangers by a point in the semi-final in Portlaoise and then defeated Knockmore of Mayo by 2-13 to 0-11 in the final. A truly magical day when the whole of Crossmaglen decamped to Croke Park to share in the splendid occasion.

Later in the year, we retained the Armagh title but lost to Errigal Ciarain in the Ulster semi-final. It was a painful lesson but it doubled our resolve to come back stronger.

All-Ireland final (Crossmaglen): Jarlath McConville; Martin Califf, Donal Murtagh, Paddy McKeown; Joe Fitzpatrick, Francie Bellew, Gary McShane; John McEntee, Anthony Cunningham; Cathal Short, Tony McEntee, Oisin McConville; Jim McConville, Gavin Cumiskey, Colm O'Neill.

Subs: Michael Moley for John McEntee. Other panel members: Paul Hearty, Paddy Moley, Frank Shields, Kieran Donnelly, Michael McShane, Colm Dooley, Paul Donnelly, Paul Larkin.

1998: Another Armagh county title and a return to the heights of Ulster champions, after beating Mullahoran (Cavan) in a replay, St John's (Antrim) and Bellaghy (Derry). Croke Park was beckoning again.

1999: We were full value for our five-point win over Eire Og of Carlow in the All-Ireland semi-final but we had the luck of seven devils in the final against Ballina Stephenites. We won by a point (0-9 to 0-8), despite having far less possession than Ballina who kicked away so many chances that it must still rankle with them to this day.

All-Ireland final (Crossmaglen): Paul Hearty; Martin Califf, Donal Murtagh, Colm Dooley; Frank Shields, Francie Bellew, Joe Fitzpatrick; John McEntee, Anthony Cunningham; Cathal Short, Tony McEntee, Oisin McConville; Jim McConville, Gavin Cumiskey, Colm O'Neill.

Subs: Gary McShane for Califf; Michael Moley for O'Neill.

Panel members: Jarlath McConville, Paddy Moley, Stephen Clarke, Oliver McEntee, Kieran Donnelly, Michael McShane, Paul Donnelly.

2000: An All-Ireland double and a third title in four seasons! Who would have thought it possible five years earlier when we couldn't even win a county title? We beat UCC in the All-Ireland semi-final and then turned in what I would regard as one of the best ever performances in a club final. It proved far too much for the highly rated Dublin champions, Na Fianna, who featured Armagh pair, Kieran McGeeney and Des Mackin.

All-Ireland final (Crossmaglen): Paul Hearty; Martin Califf, Donal Murtagh, Gary McShane; Joe Fitzpatrick, Francie Bellew, John Donaldson; John McEntee, Anthony Cunningham; Cathal Short, Tony McEntee, Oisin McConville; Jim McConville, Gavin Cumiskey, Colm O'Neill.

Subs: Michael Moley for Jim McConville.

Panel members: Kevin McKeown, Kieran Donnelly, Frank Shields, Oliver McEntee, Colm Dooley, James Hughes, Kevin Daly, Francis Fitzpatrick.

2001: A year to recharge the batteries after I stepped down as Cross manager early in the year. When the call came to manage Armagh in late-2001, there could only be one answer – go for it!

2002: The greatest year in Armagh history as we lifted our first-ever All Ireland title. What's more, everybody shared in it. It was thrilling to be closely involved with the exciting project but, in reality, it was a triumph for every Armagh person, at home and abroad. Indeed, one of the great satisfactions I took from it was to hear from people who were thousands of miles away from Croke Park on All-Ireland final day, yet they felt as if they were there. The idea that Armagh people woke up the following morning in Australia, America, or wherever, and felt that bit better about themselves was fantastic. The fact that, en route to the ultimate title, we beat Kerry and Dublin – the big two of Gaelic football in terms of All-Ireland wins – made it all the more special.

All-Ireland final (Armagh): Benny Tierney; Enda McNulty, Justin McNulty, Francie Bellew; Aidan O'Rourke, Kieran McGeeney, Andrew McCann; John Toal, Paul McGrane; Paddy McKeever, John McEntee, Oisin McConville; Steven McDonnell, Ronan Clarke, Diarmaid Marsden.

Subs: Barry O'Hagan for John McEntee; Tony McEntee for McKeever.

Panel members: Paul Hearty, Kieran Hughes, Cathal O'Rourke, Philip Loughran, John Donaldson, Barry Duffy, Ger Reid, Paul McCormack,

Simon Maxwell, Padraig Duffy, Colm O'Neill, Kevin McElvanna, Shane Smith.

2003: Under the pre-2001 system we would have been out of the Championship by May 11, when Monaghan beat us but, instead, we were still there on All-Ireland final day more than four months later thanks to winning four qualifier ties, plus a quarter- and semi-final. What's more, we were still very much in the game until Diarmaid Marsden's dismissal, which was totally undeserved. That remains one of the biggest disappointments in my long involvement in Gaelic football. Marsden's departure tipped the balance Tyrone's way and while he was later exonerated by Central Council, it was no consolation.

All-Ireland final (Armagh): Paul Hearty; Francie Bellew, Enda McNulty, Andy Mallon; Aidan O'Rourke, Kieran McGeeney, Andrew McCann; Tony McEntee, Paul McGrane; Philip Loughran, John McEntee, Oisin McConville; Ronan Clarke, Steven McDonnell, Diarmaid Marsden. **Subs:** Paddy McKeever for Marsden; Kieran Hughes for Mallon; Marsden for Clarke; Barry O'Hagan for John McEntee.

2004: Over-confidence may well have cost us the All-Ireland title. We had regained the Ulster title by beating Donegal in the final on a historic day in Croke Park but got it wrong against Fermanagh in the All-Ireland quarter-final. We should have been warned: Fermanagh had beaten Meath, Cork and Donegal and were clearly improving. For whatever reason, we didn't tune in properly to the challenge and while we started well, we lost our way and, ultimately, the game. Another great chance blown.

Still, there was good news for Armagh who won the All-Ireland U-21 title for the first time. Stephen (centre-forward) and Aaron (right half-back) were both on the team and Stephen also made his inter-county senior championship debut that year, coming on as a sub against Monaghan in the Ulster quarter-final.

Ulster final (Armagh): Paul Hearty; Enda McNulty, Francie Bellew, Andy Mallon; Kieran Hughes, Kieran McGeeney, Aidan O'Rourke; Philip Loughran, Paul McGrane; Paddy McKeever, Tony McEntee, Oisin

McConville; Steven McDonnell, Ronan Clarke, Diarmaid Marsden.
Subs: Brian Mallon for Clarke; John Toal for Loughran; Andy McCann for McGeeney; Justin McNulty for Bellew; John McEntee for Marsden.

2005: If there were ever more intense and more absorbing games than our three clashes with Tyrone in the Ulster final – draw and replay – and the All-Ireland semi-final any time over the last forty years, I haven't seen them. These were two serious heavyweights battering each other for all they were worth in three Croke Park showdowns, which drew total attendances of almost 160,000. In the end, there was only one point between us on aggregate scores. We held that advantage but, unfortunately, Tyrone were in the All-Ireland final having won the All-Ireland semi-final by a point after we won the Ulster final replay by two. It came down to a late point from a Peter Canavan free in the semi-final in one of those games where you felt that if it went on until midnight there would never be more than a point or two in it, either way.

That defeat overshadowed our earlier achievements, which made Armagh history, as we won the National League title (Division 1) for the first time and also lifted the Ulster title for the third time in four seasons. There was an added extra for me as it was also the year that Aaron forced his way onto the team at right half-back.
Ulster final replay (Armagh): Paul Hearty; Enda McNulty, Andy Mallon, Francie Bellew; Aaron Kernan, Kieran McGeeney, Aidan O'Rourke; Philip Loughran, Paul McGrane; Ciaran McKeever, John McEntee, Oisin McConville; Steven McDonnell, Ronan Clarke, Brian Mallon.
Subs: Paddy McKeever for Mallon; Andrew McCann for O'Rourke; Tony McEntee for Loughran.

2006: Another chunk of Armagh history as we won the Ulster title for the third successive year, again beating Donegal in the final. They must have been sick of the sight of us. It was the first time since Down's run in 1959-60-61 that the Ulster treble had been recorded. It underlined how consistent we had become but, unfortunately, we lost the All-Ireland quarter-final to

Kerry by 3-15 to 1-13. There was no way they were eight points a better side, but they pulled away in the closing minutes. We made one or two mistakes and were severely punished.

Ulster final (Armagh): Paul Hearty; Andy Mallon, Francie Hearty, Enda McNulty; Aaron Kernan, Ciaran McKeever, Paul Duffy; Kieran McGeeney, Paul McGrane; Martin O'Rourke, John McEntee, Malachy Mackin; Steven McDonnell, Ronan Clarke, Oisin McConville.

Subs: Paddy McKeever for Mackin, Aidan O'Rourke for Duffy.

2007: The end of the line. Things were beginning to unravel and, to some degree, we were running on empty. It was ironic that when we suffered our first Ulster Championship defeat for four years it came against Donegal, whom we had beaten five times (and drawn once) since 2002. We lost to a late goal in Ballybofey, scored by Brendan Devenney as Kevin Cassidy challenged Paul Hearty and, some weeks later, we lost on another one-point margin to Derry in Clones. The era was over – it was time for me step down.

It had been a remarkable six seasons, during which Armagh had won one All-Ireland title, reached two finals, three semi-finals and five quarter-finals. We had also won four Ulster titles, plus a National League title. We played thirty-six Championship games in 2002-2007, winning twenty-three, drawing six and losing seven. Naturally, we were disappointed not to win at least one more All-Ireland title but when you look at those figures they show that it really was a great era for Armagh football. Thanks to all who made it possible – it was quite an adventure.

All Ireland qualifier v Derry and my last game as manager (Armagh): Paul Hearty; Andy Mallon, Enda McNulty, Brendan Donaghy; Aaron Kernan, Kieran McGeeney, Ciaran McKeever; Kieran Toner, Paul McGrane; Paddy McKeever, Stephen Kernan, Martin O'Rourke; Steven McDonnell, Diarmaid Marsden, Oisin McConville.

Subs: Kevin Dyas for Ciaran McKeever; James Lavery for Toner; Paul Keenan for Paddy McKeever.

2008-2009: Hurler on the ditch! Not easy but I got used to it.

2010: Should I have responded when Galway called in late-2009? I have absolutely no regrets that I did, but I do have regrets about how it all finished. I would have liked to continue for another year but obstacles were put in my way which made it impossible.

Still, I walked away with my integrity intact which was vital to me. As for the year itself, I keep wondering how things might have turned out if Michael Meehan hadn't picked up a bad knee injury during the League. It ruined his Championship preparations but he returned as a sub in the drawn game against Sligo, only to get injured again in the replay. What a difference a fully fit Michael Meehan would have made to us in both games.

2011: Another great day out in Croke Park on St Patrick's Day, as Crossmaglen win the All-Ireland club day for the fifth time with no fewer than four Kernans aboard, one each in the full-back (Paul), half-back (Aaron), half-forward (Stephen) and full-forward (Tony) lines. In the end, it all goes back to the club – in my case, Crossmaglen Rangers – whom I'm proud to say have established themselves as the most successful football unit in the country over the past fourteen years. Long may it continue.

I'm heavily involved, nowadays, in the GAA Legends All-Ireland Golf Classic which I helped found four years ago with Bernard Flynn, Tommy Carr, Ollie Brady and Mick McGinley. It's a fund-raising venture for various charities and has already raised €250,000.

It includes four former players from all thirty-two counties (only those who have played senior football or hurling for their counties are eligible). We have some great fun – at home and abroad – while also raising money for charity. The GAA have come onboard in an official capacity, granting us official recognition, so this is a chance to say a big 'thank you' to President, Christy Cooney for his support. We're delighted with the response from players, public and sponsors for what is a very worthwhile project, which combines fun with the serious business of raising money for those who are less fortunate.